# Public
# Administration

# Public Administration

**Robert S. Lorch**

University of Colorado
Colorado Springs

**WEST PUBLISHING CO.**
St. Paul • New York • Los Angeles • San Francisco

COPYRIGHT © 1978 by WEST PUBLISHING CO.
    50 West Kellogg Boulevard
    P.O. Box 3526
    St. Paul, Minnesota 55165
All rights reserved
Printed in the United States of America

**Library of Congress Cataloging in Publication Data**

Lorch, Robert Stuart, 1925-
    Public administration.
    Includes bibliographies and index.
    1.  Public administration.  I.  Title.
JF1351.L67          350          77-11168
**ISBN** 0-8299-0144-2 Co.

For John D. Lorch

*

# Preface

This book is deliberately informal and argumentative in style—written that way in hope students will find it a readable and exciting approach to the study of public administration. Opinions of hostile camps are mobilized and sent impartially to their doom against one another. I as author have generally (perhaps too often) let the combatants exhaust themselves without taking sides or interfering with the outcome. In the discussion of ethics, for example, I have not offered any final answers of my own, only questions and points of view. In this, as in so many other areas, I feel a sense of regret that I could not sound a bugle and point the way. But perhaps professors in their classrooms, or readers themselves, can find their own way to truth, assisted one might hope by the conflicting ideas presented herein. There is no overarching philosophy or theme in this book that I myself can detect, nor is it consciously slanted, except insofar as I have consciously tried to employ techniques that might save students from the usual boredom of textbooks. Special attention is given to controversial areas of public administration, although, of course, the boundaries of that field are too vast and ill-defined to cover all disputed provinces. This book is perhaps best recommended for use as a text in issue-oriented introductory public administration courses, or as supplementary reading which nips at the heels of more formal and traditional works.

Certainly I would not want to lay responsibility on anyone but myself for these pages, but I must acknowledge with gratitude the numerous helpful criticisms made by Professor Aaron Wildavsky, University of California at Berkeley, Professor Robert Friedman, Penn State, and Professor Charles Walcott, University of Minnesota.

\*

RSL

# Contents

# The Managerial Revolution 1

# The Managerial Revolution 1

Our time has been called the "era of bureaucracy." We are said to be in the midst of a "managerial revolution," to live in an "administrative state," to be ruled by a "dictatorship of the bureaucracy." Cynical reference is made to "our ruling servants."

Growth of bureaucracy and public employment is worldwide. How does one account for it? Much has been attributed to the rise of technology and the explosion of knowledge—to govern a complex society requires a complex government. Also, economic interdependence (a by-product of technology) has put most people at the mercy of economic forces beyond their control. Millions look to government for help. Furthermore, the decreasing ability of legislatures to cope with complex and rapidly changing situations has resulted in transfer of much legislative power to executive agencies. A similarly decreasing ability of courts to adjudicate cases involving highly technical matters has resulted in a transfer of much judicial power to executive agencies. At the same time a remarkable combination of strengths in the executive branch has made it an ideal depository of legislative and judical powers. Also, popularity of the idea that government should provide an ever widening array of services results by necessity in an ever increasing public bureaucracy to deliver those services. And finally, bureaucrats are alleged by some unfriendly critics to be empire builders always eager to expand their corner of the bureaucracy and their power within it.

## DECLINE OF SEPARATION OF POWERS

Perhaps it would come as a surprise to most United States citizens, even to many who consider themselves well grounded in the workings of American government, to learn that the executive branch of the federal government makes more laws than Congress and decides more cases than the

3

courts. The United States Constitution, of course, tells us in the first sentence of Article I that, "All legislative powers herein granted shall be vested in a Congress. . . ." This is pure fiction characteristic of the poetic license taken by the authors of our Constitution. Congress never has had *all* legislative power, and it certainly does not have it all today—one need only glance at the massive *Code of Federal Regulations* containing the innumerable laws (politely called "regulations" or "rules") enacted by a battalion of federal executive agencies. The *Code of Federal Regulations* sags many feet of library shelving and is much larger, lengthier, heavier than its counterpart, the *United States Code*, which contains the laws enacted by Congress. So many new federal regulations are made that the federal government publishes a daily (except Sundays and Mondays) newspaper called the *Federal Register* to announce and publicize them.

Sometimes federal regulations are dismissed as simply details of secondary importance fleshing out important laws passed by Congress—while the executive may make supplementary regulations, it is really Congress that passes the important laws. At first, this allegation has the ring of truth because, technically, almost all federal regulations do supplement acts of Congress, are made under Congressional authority, and do fill in the details of laws passed by Congress. But, in truth, Congress very often abdicates its policy-making responsibility to the President or to this or that excecutive agency. Very often an act of Congress is like an empty bottle handed over to the bureaucracy with instructions to fill as they see fit. A classic example of this is the Federal Communication Commission's power to regulate the air waves in the public interest.

Another piece of fiction in the United States Constitution is the first sentence of Article III (dealing with courts) which says, "The judicial power of the United States, shall be vested in one supreme court, and in such inferior courts as the Congress may from time to time ordain and establish." But federal administrative agencies decide more cases and controversies than the courts. Nor are those cases of minor importance.

Courts themselves have encouraged the growth of administrative adjudication, and regularly apply the "primary jurisdiction doctrine" and the "exhaustion of remedies doctrine" to insure that administrative agencies are given first crack at deciding controversies involving those agencies. Furthermore, courts treat the adjudicatory decisions of administrative agencies as though they were the decisions of courts of original jurisdiction. Appeals from agencies go directly to appellate courts where administrative findings of fact are not normally questioned if based on substantial evidence.

Thus, administrative agencies do far more than merely execute the law—they also make law and adjudicate controversies. Most executive agencies (federal, state, and local) have today become living refutations of the doctrine of separation of powers. In executive agencies we see a union of powers, not a separation of powers—legislative, judicial, and executive power united within the agency. The Civil Aeronautics Board not only makes laws (rules) which airlines and pilots must obey, but also enforces those rules through a system of inspectors, and when an airline or a pilot is caught violating a rule he or it may be "brought to trial" before the agency and punished if found guilty. In a country such as the United States, which at least in theory champions the idea that the best defense against tyranny is separation of powers, it seems strange, even eerie, to note the degree to which legislative, judicial, and executive power has been gathered into the same hands within executive agencies. Of course, Congress, the courts, and the executive branch of government remain theoretically separated, and continue to check each other, but in reality both Congress and the courts have ceded vast powers to the executive branch and to its multitudinous agencies. More than half of all legal fees earned by lawyers today are earned in cases involving some arm of government, and many lawyers find themselves pleading cases before administrative hearing officers rather than before judges. The average citizen is far more likely to have a controversy adjudicated by an administrative agency than by a court of law, and the issue is far more likely to directly concern an administrative regulation than an act of any legislative body. When one considers the countless millions of Americans whose lives are directly affected by a deluge of regulations made by such agencies as the Veterans Administration, the Social Security Administration, or the Internal Revenue Service, one well understands how many legal disputes there can be over the meaning of those regulations. Persons entering careers in public administration today are embarking on an activity that often includes much, much more than narrow execution of law—it can also be a legislative career and a judicial career.

## THE GROWTH OF LEGISLATIVE POWER
## IN THE EXECUTIVE BRANCH

### Weakness of Legislative Bodies

How and why have bureaucrats acquired so much legislative and judical power? One must consider the weaknesses of legislative bodies such as Congress at the same time one considers the strengths of modern administrative agencies, for each affects the other. What then is alleged to be "wrong" with Congress. In considering its deficiencies, keep in mind that much of what afflicts Congress also tends to harass state and local legislative bodies as well.

First we must note that the fathers of the United States Constitution assumed Congress would be the central policy-making branch of government, and that the President's job, and that of the executive branch, would be to execute the policies (laws) set forth by Congress. Meanwhile, the fathers apparently did not expect the Supreme Court to become the "judicial legislature" it has become today. Our twentieth-century Congress makes very little policy without presidential initiative and support, and much policy-making power has been directly ceded to the executive branch in the form of rule-making power.

The President makes policy directly by use of his many powers, and/or indirectly by giving policy leadership to Congress. Congress seems to have reached an almost submissive state in which its first thought at the beginning of every session is, "What will the President propose?" Most important pieces of legislation enacted by Congress since the time of Franklin D. Roosevelt have been initiated by and/or supported by the President. In recent years, especially since Watergate, Congress has felt overshadowed and menaced by the imperial presidency. Congress has tried to assert itself and flex its muscles. How much of this assertion is play acting and how much is genuine muscle flexing remains to be seen. However, many observers point to some fundamental weaknesses of Congress for which there is perhaps no likely cure.

One alleged weakness is the size of Congress and the complexity of its procedure. Today there are 535 members of Congress, 100 in the Senate, and 435 in the House of Representatives. This large body of people cannot do business except through heavy reliance on committees. Legislative work is divided among subject matter committees which are centers of expert knowledge and have acquired life and death power over bills. As bills travel through Congress they fall into the potentially lethal hands of these committees. There are more than half a dozen occasions in the procedure of each house in which a bill can be killed or mutilated, more than a dozen dangerous stops through two houses. Furthermore, unless a bill passes both houses in exactly identical form (an unlikely event) it must go to a conference committee and then back to the two houses again. And still there is no law, for it must go to the President, and if vetoed, back to Congress for a possible override. A bill which is in any way controversial will have a congressional knife at its throat perhaps twenty or more places in its passage through legislative procedure. And even after a bill has become law, it may be meaningless until Congress votes money for executing it. If, for example, a law establishes some new agency, then that agency will require staffing, housing, supply, and so on for which an appropriations bill is necessary. Therefore, two bills must be passed, one authorizing the agency, another financing it. The second must go through the same tortuous process as the first, giving opponents another couple dozen opportunities to kill or cripple.

In short, there are so many opportunities to butcher legislation, so many places where enemies may lie in wait, that it is next to impossible to get controversial legislation through Congress. A legislative body that cannot deal with controversial and important problems in effect abdicates—leaving the vacuum to be filled by bureaucrats and judges. Congress with its jungle-like procedure cannot do what its neighbor the United States Supreme Court does. The Court is slender and tough, it does not have two houses or a battalion of committees, subcommittees, and jealous czars and potentates. Its nine members seated around a conference table decide more questions of important social policy each year in their unornamented way than Congress has decided in the past half-century. This, of course, is a matter of opinion as to what is important and unimportant. Congress does, in truth, pass hundreds of bills every year, but half are private laws not generally involving great social issues, and the other half chiefly concern small noncontroversial matters such as whether to add ten new barracks at a military base. Only a few bills during the average session of Congress come to grips with great public problems. And commonly when such a policy matter has been successfully addressed by Congress in recent generations, it has been done only after the President, using his remarkable powers, has applied pressure at every danger point in the legislative obstacle course to secure safe passage of an important bill. The faltering approach of Congress to racial discrimination in the United States is a typical example. Practically everything done by the federal government in this field has until recently been done by courts and by executive agencies. For almost a century after passing its Civil Rights Act of 1875 Congress paid scant attention to race problems, while the Supreme Court has been locked in unremitting struggle on that front since "separate but equal" first came under attack. The greatest power of Congress today is the power to do nothing; its complex procedures put odds heavily on the side of inactivity.

Besides its great size and its exceedingly complicated procedure, another alleged weakness of Congress is its lack of firm leadership—its lack, that is, of disciplined political parties of the English model in which every member of Congress could be made to toe the party line. However, the claim that party discipline would increase the power of Congress is of questionable validity. The reverse is very likely true—disciplined parties could lead to a further decline of Congress by putting power into the hands of party leaders who may also dominate the executive branch. If leaders of a disciplined majority party in Congress took charge of the executive branch, this would result in a marriage of the executive and legislative branches. In such a marriage Congress (like the British Parliament) could be reduced to a marionette-like role, with all strings leading to the chief executive. The absence of disciplined parties is what makes congressional procedure so lethal to all important legislation. While party discipline might make Congress less lethal, so also might it make Congress less alive.

Congress, and all levels of legislative bodies around the world, seem to be retreating to the status from which legislative bodies emerged centuries ago; moving back to the status of kings' advisors and kings' critics. Sweeping abdications of legislative and judicial power to the executive branch suggest that legislators know in their hearts they cannot legislate, that they are best at checking, overseeing, and influencing executives, and that they really have little choice but to leave the real responsibility for jousting with social problems to executives and judges.

## BUREAUCRATIC AND/OR PRESIDENTIAL POWER

A major cause of congressional weakness is the power of the President and of the bureaucracy, a power sensed, no doubt, by every member of the House and Senate. What are the sources and causes of that strength? Several critical changes have occurred in this century. To the legislative process it has been the onset of a paralyzing age. But to the executive process, to administrators and bureaucrats, it has been a time of powerful growth and expansion. Let us briefly examine the factors that have contributed to this imbalance of power.

### Knowledge Is Power

An enormous aggregation of technical and scientific knowledge exists among the five million federal employees. A fourth of all scientists work in the executive branch of the federal government, and many others work under federal contract. Much of the knowledge needed to legislate intelligently is available nowhere else. The more technological and scientific the nation becomes, the more technological and scientific knowledge is required to govern it; the more such knowledge is required to govern, the more the governors are dependent on those who possess such knowledge. Executive agencies are not only in possession of textbook knowledge; they are also experienced combatants on the front line of social problems and are often uniquely qualified to send word what armaments are needed for the combat. Executive agencies working with social problems become almost indispensable sources of intelligence for Congress, intelligence not only pointing to the solution of problems, but also pointing to the existence of problems, and to the size, seriousness, and dimensions of those problems. Many, perhaps most, proposals for legislation come straight out of the bureaucracy. Somewhere in the bowels of the department of agriculture there is, for example, an office or outpost waging war against the Indian fire ant. Hardly a better source of information concerning the resources and weapons needed to fight the Indian fire ant could be found than in that agency. Congress is guided by experts in countless other departments of knowledge across the whole face of the bureaucracy. Over the course of time Congress, as well as state legislatures and local councils, have come to rely heavily on the bureaucracy to identify problems, offer solutions, and suggest needed legislation in matters of immense scientific and technical complexity and importance. Legislators have found it easy to put more and more responsibility into the hands of experts, that is, into the hands of informed bureaucrats, not only listening to their recommendations but also giving them wide discretion and great financial resources to attack those problems in whatever way their professional judgment dictates. Congress itself is not and cannot be staffed to duplicate the bureaucracy's technical expertise. Congress is, of course, subdivided into several dozen subject matter committees which, assisted by staff, attempt to keep abreast developing problems. But the Senate Committee on Agriculture cannot begin to match the warehouse of science lodged in the Department of Agriculture. On the contrary, it depends and relies upon the department. Nor can the armed services committees begin to match the incredible depth and breadth of knowledge lodged in the Defense Department for waging pushbutton war. Congress is simply overwhelmed by the explosion of knowledge. It will fall even deeper under the avalanch of knowledge and even more dependent upon experts in years to come. Explosions of knowledge do not expire; on the contrary, they (like explosions of atoms) cause chain reactions. This process tells us that bureaucracy will become more, not less, abundant, that in generations to come legislative bodies will be more, not less, at the mercy of bureaucrats. Ultimately legislators may be confined to the role of errand running for constituents and to checking into miscarriages of justice within the bureaucracy—an ombudsman-like role.

## Discretionary Powers—Rulemaking, Spending, and Selective Enforcement

Since 1789, and even during colonial rule, legislative bodies at all levels of government have regularly allowed administrators at least some latitude to determine what the law means—to interpret it as they enforce it. After all, how can administrators enforce any law until they have read it and decided what it means? When "reckless driving" is outlawed, police obviously have to define "reckless driving" before they arrest anyone for it. Every law unavoidably invites some latitude of interpretation. It is not these unavoidable interpretations of law that have increased in recent generations. What has increased are laws that deliberately invite interpretation by executives, that deliberately call for exercise of executive discretion, and that plainly instruct administrators to fill in the details with rules and regulations. Even that has existed since 1789 and before, but it has become much more common in the past half-century. Much more discretionary power is lodged in the hands of executives today than in a former era. Reasons for this have been partly explained—as society grows more complex, Congress is forced to loosen its grip on lawmaking and yield much of it to specialists in the bureaucracy who have time and knowledge to make good laws (that is, good rules and regulations). Congress has empowered executive agencies to grant subsidies, approve contracts, condemn land, regulate credit, and use discretion in countless matters. Sometimes Congress phrases legislation in such broad generalities that those laws can hardly be said to be law at all, and become a license for administrators to do almost anything they can get away with politically and legally. Power granted the Federal Communications Commission to regulate use of air waves in the "public interest" is, to repeat, a case in point.

The vast discretionary power held by the President and by agencies within every department of the federal government is power that can be used to punish enemies and reward friends. Its potential for use in that way makes members of Congress wary of clashing with a president, and often wary of clashing with individual agencies of the executive branch. Administrative agencies armed with discretionary power to make rules, regulations, and "judicial" decisions can grievously harm or bountifully help commercial or other interests within congressional or senatorial districts. The smallest tariff adjustment, for example, may fatally injure a certain commercial enterprise and deeply embarrass members of Congress where that enterprise is located.

Executive agencies not only make rules, they enforce them. Many more rules stand in the *Code of Federal Regulations*, and many more laws in the *United States Code* than can possibly be enforced. Executive agencies have no choice but to select what to spend their limited time and resources enforcing. Clearly these choices can be made to favor the friends of the President and/or to injure his enemies. One can imagine officers of the Internal Revenue Service going out of their way to enforce certain tax rules against some individuals or corporations, while neglecting those rules in other cases. Hardly a regulation exists that doesn't benefit some more than others; a politicized agency can play these rules to the benefit or detriment of selected targets. We should not convey the impression that rule-making and rule enforcement is nothing but a cynical game of political back stabbing or back patting, but likewise it would be erroneous to leave the impression that these things are unheard of. Even if rare, mere suspicion of it can make many members of Congress think twice before crossing a president. Hatchet work against the President's enemies can be done by his subordinates throughout the bureaucracy without his ever being aware of it.

The federal government spends billions annually. Much, of course, is earmarked for specified purposes such as payment of the national debt. Much, however, is not specifically appropriated and, although this is supposedly spent for the purposes described by Congress in its various appropriation bills, it is still possible for agencies to exercise discretion within the confines of those purposes, and to elect when, where, what, and from whom to buy. For example, a decision by the Argiculture Department to establish a regional headquarters in, say, Omaha rather than Kansas City can bring millions of dollars to the former and deny those millions to the latter. Conceivably such a decision could rest on whether the members of Congress from Omaha are more friendly to the President than members from Kansas City—one never quite knows what goes into a decision of that sort. Power to spend appropriated money gives agencies of the executive branch (particularly the President himself) a mighty tool of influence. The President or his subordinates can from time to time direct the flow of money toward those places that will give him leverage with members of Congress and others. While there are legal limitations on a bureaucrat's freedom to spend appropriated money (such as laws providing for bids and purchasing from the lowest bidder), still, agencies find it possible to exercise great influence over spending.

## Ability to Influence Public Opinion

A third salient development in this century that has increased presidential power is radio and television. Through these communication miracles a president is now able to make himself personally known to nearly all Americans, and to win the good will and support of millions. Possibly no other development has so greatly magnified presidential influence over the public and its representatives. Anyone who can sway and shape public opinion can certainly influence Congress. Their instinct for political survival tells members of Congress to pay close attention to public opinion. Naturally, the President isn't the only one capable of using modern media to shape public opinion—members of Congress have access to the same media, as do numerous political figures. But none use it as effectively as a president—the media pays more attention to the President, everything he says and does is news. More than a hundred reporters cover the White House; every presidential utterance receives immediate attention and is instantly conveyed to the nation. A president may if he wishes ask for network time, and, depending on the issue at hand, is likely to have an attentive audience of millions. No other politician can equal the President's power to command national attention. A senator from Alabama, Nebraska, or Oregon might occasionally be covered by the media, especially in his own state, but only the most prominent senators receive national coverage, and then only occasionally. Likwise members of the House of Representatives are for the most part a mass of unknowns outside their own districts, and even in their own districts they find it difficult to reach constituents. The President of the United States, a thousand miles away in Washington, has a better chance of reaching and influencing the public in Iowa than any Iowan. This is translated into influence over Iowa's representatives in Congress.

We must take care not to overestimate this source of presidential power. It is certainly not absolute, for the President is by no means the only opinion leader in the nation. But it is, nevertheless, a very substantial source of presidential power that we experience. It is also a new, twentieth-century form of power that the authors of the United States Constitution could never have imagined possible. These late eighteenth-century authors probably assumed no president could ever have closer ties to the general public than Congress, especially not closer than members of the lower house. The Constitution presumes Congress is the chief link between the people and their government. That concept is now obsolete and the President has become by far the best known public official to the average voter. Perhaps no modern creation has more powerfully magnified the President, nor more forcefully suppressed Congress, nor more greatly changed the American system of government than radio and television.

## Predominance in Foreign Affairs

Another cardinal development that has greatly strengthened modern presidents is the rise of foreign affairs and national defense to preeminence among the concerns of the federal government. Perhaps this has not given the President leverage with Congress so much as it has simply deprived Congress of a chance to play a leading role in the most expensive and expansive undertaking of the government. In a sense, it has reduced Congress to a habitually secondary, almost juvenile-like role in its relationship with the President. Since the Second World War, presidents have managed foreign affairs almost as though Congress were a very junior arm of government not mature enough, wise enough, or responsible enough to be fully involved in something so critical as national survival. And, unfortunately, it may be that a body of 535 people cannot hope to play a key role in those aspects of foreign affairs which must be conducted speedily and secretly, and which are exceedingly complicated, requiring access to classified intelligence.

Congess does, of course, have its foreign relations committees and other mechanisms for oversight of matters pertaining to the nation's survival in a dangerous world. But as Senator J. William Fullbright, former chairman of the Senate Foreign Relations Committee, has so vehemently complained, it is simply not possible for Congress to keep a tight reign on the course of international affairs, though he and others have tried. Attempts have recently been made by Congress to intensify its role in diplomatic and military affairs, but it remains to be seen whether any substantial change will result. Congress, of course, has power to refuse to ratify treaties, but very little is done any more by treaty. Most international agreements are by executive agreement not requiring any specific approval by Congress. The Senate also has the power to confirm or refuse to confirm all ambassadorial appointments proposed by the President. But this is not a significant power; nominees are almost never refused, and if one should be refused the President has endless alternate methods for communicating with foreign governments, ambassador, or no ambassador. Congress also has the power of the purse, power, that is, to refuse money for purposes relating to foreign affairs such as money for the military, for the intelligence arms, for the United Nations, and so forth. But until recently Congress hardly ever chose to economize in these areas, trusting the judgment of the State Department, the Defense Department, the President and other authorities. Most Americans (and members of Congress) seem determined to go absolutely first class in national defense, and Congress has not until recently found it politic to pinch pennies or even to pinch billions in this area. Furthermore, once a president has committed the nation to a foreign venture, there is (rightly or wrongly) a natural tendency for the nation to unite behind the President at the outset, whatever misgivings may exist in Congress.

Congress is also placed at a disadvantage in foreign affairs by the Constitution itself which seems to put the main responsibility for conducting foreign affairs into the President's hands. The President is made commander-in-chief of the armed forces, can move air, land, and naval forces wherever he wishes, even ordering them into combat without benefit of a declaration of war by Congress. The Korean War was prosecuted from beginning to end without a declaration, and so was the Vietnam War. The power of Congress to declare war has been rendered almost meaningless by the necessities of pushbutton war, and by the complexities of international politics. In Vietnam as well as Korea there were powerful enemies behind the enemy. It made little sense to declare war on Vietnam, nor would it have been wise to declare war on the real more powerful enemies. That is always the problem with limited wars. A declaration seems to imply commitment to total war, not limited war. Our entry into the Second World War did not begin with a declaration of war, but with a steadily more hostile stance toward the Axis powers: lend lease, arms shipments, and the like. The nation entered the Second World War long before Congress made its declaration on December 8th.

No doubt responsibility for conduct of foreign relations has always been more or less, for obvious reasons, concentrated in the executive rather than the legislative branch. The most significant change has not been in the degree of presidential authority over foreign affairs but in the size of the foreign affairs and defense functions relative to the rest of the federal government's activities. About 80 percent of all federal expenditures are related to the cost of past wars and the threat of future wars—a multitude of defense, intelligence, and diplomatic activities. Probably three-fourths of all civilian federal employees work either directly or indirectly in some function connected with defense and foreign relations. If three-fourths of the federal government's activities are connected with defense and foreign relations, then that means a lion's share of federal activity is concentrated in activities in which Congress experiences great difficulty assert-ing itself—an area in which the President is preeminent. This, to repeat, has put Congress in a subordinate role with regard to 75 to 80 percent of what the federal government does. Before the Second World War no such condition prevailed. The federal government was almost exclusively con-cerned with domestic affairs; military and foreign affairs were a tiny frac-tion of the total.

## Welfare State

Still another development during the past half-century that has increased the size of the bureaucracy and also has increased presidential influence over Congress is the rise to popularity of a belief that government should take more responsibility for the welfare of people, cradle to the grave. Previously the role of government was commonly believed to be much more limited, to be comparable to "the cop on the corner" confining itself mainly to problems of law and order while leaving people the responsibil-ity of seeking their own welfare as individuals. Since the late 1920s a sharp change of philosophy has occurred in the United States and much of the industrialized world, chiefly brought about by changes in the economic system which rendered people more interdependent and less able as individuals to control their own fate. That change of philosophy put heavi-er responsibility on government to ensure that all citizens have a job or some form of income in lieu of a job, and government was also expected to make itself responsible for improving quality of life in many realms such as health, education, housing, and environment.

Each new venture has resulted in new additions to the bureaucracy, and we now find many people asking for more services while at the same time decrying bureaucracy.

Welfare state programs add in some curious ways to presidential power over Congress. Rarely does Congress get credit for inaugurating such a program. Often the President gets credit. He may even claim to have proposed the plan. When a bill embodying the plan is finally passed, he signs it in his office with great fanfare and television cameras whirring. Congress may only be remembered as the place where this laudable pro-gram was debated and criticized; the President on the other hand may be popularly regarded as its creator. President Franklin D. Roosevelt, not Congress, is associated with the New Deal. Furthermore, if money is to be mailed to millions, it does not come from Congress, but from the Secretary of the Treasury in the executive branch. And again, if there should arise an outcry against "bureaucracy and red tape," the President can lead the nation in sanctimonious condemnation of it. His unique ability to reach millions across the nation by radio and television gives him golden oppor-tunities to take credit for new programs, and at the same time to earn credit as a fighter against bureaucracy. Congress is lost in the dust; its 535 members chiefly remembered as a confusing cacophony of conflicting voices. The public gives Congress little credit for new programs, yet is tempted to blame it for a ballooning public service that threatens to turn every program into a bureaucratic nightmare.

## Prestige of the President

A modern president quickly becomes the greatest celebrity in the land, if not in the world. As head of the strongest and richest superpower his words and deeds are attentively covered by the media, here and abroad. Much of the time he acts in largely nonpartisan roles as representative of the whole nation, presiding over ceremonial events and appearing as a national leader in foreign affairs. Presidents have every opportunity to shed their partisan role and wrap themselves in the flag. It becomes difficult for ordinary people to detect when a president is being partisan. Even in presidential elections, each candidate will try to avoid excessive partisanism, and works hard to cast himself as someone who should be elected for reasons higher than party. The President's great prestige, plus his above-all-party stance, adds still further to his influence with the public and, therefore, with Congress. Hardly a member of Congress exists who wouldn't jump at a chance to have his or her picture taken with the President at the White House, or anywhere for that matter. Hardly a member exists who could resist the temptation to go back to his constituents and say, "Last time I had breakfast with the President at the White House I advised him to . . . ." Most members seek opportunities to be associated with the President, who therefore has public relations rewards to scatter among his friends and withhold from his enemies. This, then, is another tool with which a president can smooth the way for (or hinder the way of) controversial bills in Congress.

## Appointments

In addition to the sources of presidential power described above which are largely a product of developments in this century, there remain several, more traditional, sources. One of these is the patronage power. Despite the rise to near total dominance of the merit system in the federal civil service, there are still around 2,500 purely patronage positions useful to the President for controlling the executive branch and for rewarding his friends (or the friends of his friends). The President's appointment power is augmented by his ability to influence some so-called merit appointments in the classified service as well as some appointments outside the government.

### Veto

To override a presidential veto requires a two thirds vote in each house of Congress. Because of the heavy presidential influence over Congress described above, it is ordinarily very difficult to get anything through Congress opposed by the President, and still more difficult to find votes to override a veto. Even when Congress is overwhelmingly dominated by a party different from the President's political party it has been difficult for Congress to override a veto, although this is done with greater ease in a presidential election year. Twentieth-century accumulations of presidential power have made the President's historic veto power more potent than before.

### Budget

Neither the President's power as a budget maker or as a party leader are mentioned in the Constitution. Nor are they of especially recent origin, although his budget-making power stems from the Budget and Accounting Act of 1921. In that Act Congress did what it has done countless times before and since, it turned to the President for help in a job Congress seemed incapable of doing for itself. Before 1921, congressional standing committees were like the members of a large family writing checks on the same account without consulting one another how much each was drawing. This was fine so long as the treasury's only problem was what to do with surplus money. But when, after the First World War, Congress fell into the habit of spending more than the government received, Congress asked the President to submit a plan of expenditure (a budget) every year suggesting how much money Congress should appropriate annually to various agencies. This became the only coherent budget available to Congress, and although Congress still sometimes behaves like that big family writing checks on the same account, it does now have a detailed presidential plan to follow. While the President's budget is only a suggestion, it has become a powerful one often closely adhered to by Congress. The fact that Congress until recently lacked its own budget making capability has made Congress habitually dependent on the President's direction and guidance in exercising the greatest of all congressional powers, the power of the purse. Congress is now attempting to develop its own mechanisms for budget formulation with an eye to keeping appropriations within its own budget limits.

### Party Leader

A president is, of course, the de facto head of his political party. This gives him a limited degree of leverage over members of his party in Congress, but nothing like the leverage party leaders have in most other countries. His fellow partisans in Congress certainly do not want to embarrass their president or their party beyond reason. As party leader, the President also has some influence over allocation of party funds in congressional and senatorial elections. He also has power to find suitably prestigious federal jobs for prominent members of his party. But these are rewards for loyalty, not disloyalty.

In sum, the sources of presidential power are: (1) the expertise of the executive branch; (2) the President's discretionary power in rule-making, spending, and law enforcement; (3) the President's ability to influence public opinion through modern media of communication; (4) the President's predominance in foreign affairs; (5) the credit he earns with public opinion as sponsor of popular welfare-state programs; (6) the President's prestige as head of the greatest nation on earth, and his constant representation of that nation in the cloak of nonpartisan head of state; (7) his powers of appointment and veto; (8) his role as budget maker and party leader—all of these make the President very influential with most members of Congress regardless of political party. This great array of powers and capabilities when balanced against the clumsiness and weakness of Congress as an institution explains why much legislative power has slipped and continues to slip from the hands of Congress to the President and executive branch. A modern president is undoubtedly the chief legislator. He and the executive branch legislate in two ways: indirectly, by influencing the output of Congress, and directly, by making rules that have the force of law. Much of that legislative power represents an abandonment of responsibility by Congress.

## RETREAT OF THE COURTS

### Reasons for Growth of Adminstrative Adjudication

Why has so much adjudicatory power been lodged in executive agencies? Forces that have driven legislative power into the arms of executive agencies have driven adjudicatory power there too—rise of technology, speed of social change, and the increasing complexity of social problems. A variety of specific causes for this rise of administrative adjudication should be mentioned.

First, courts are not technically competent in some areas of litigation. Judges are experts in law, but not always in the things to which law is applied. This undoubtedly is the main reason why judges want executive agencies involved in civil litigation to apply their expertise to the issues in controversy, and to actually decide the case before it is appealed to courts. Judges, recognizing their own inability to be experts in all things, usually accept as final the facts found by the agency, even in cases to which the agency is itself a party.

Second, judges as a class are thought, with some justification, to be hostile to the welfare-state philosophy. Most judges were successful lawyers before becoming judges; most of their clients were business people, and most of their social connections in the business community. Lawyers are, after all, themselves business men or women. Advocates of welfare-state programs have often preferred to see litigation over such programs heard and decided in the first instance by agencies in charge of those programs, on the theory that bureaucrats in such agencies are likely to be sympathetic to programs they administer. Under this theory, members of the National Labor Relations Board presumably would be sympathetic to the principle that employers should be bound by a code of fair labor practices, and would therefore be better judges for hearing complaints lodged against employers than judges in courts of law.

Third, "judicial lag" afflicts American common law. Common law rests on precedent, that is, on the judicial practice of deciding today's case the same way similar cases were decided yesterday. Courts therefore are always looking backwards; they behave as though they were driving a car by looking through the rear view mirror. Such a system is fine so long as the road is straight, but trouble can arise when the road curves. Ours is a rapidly changing era. The road we travel is a spiral of change, and the doctrine of stare decisis (let the decision stand) is too clumsy, inflexible, and conservative. Agencies are not bound by stare decisis and are free to decide cases strictly in accordance with the needs of the hour and without reference to any decisions they may have made yesterday on the same subject. Agencies do not drive by looking through the rear view mirror. Consequently, they can adapt more quickly to a changing world.

Fourth, courts of law by long tradition employ a great many rigid procedures so complicated and mysterious that parties to litigation must be led by the hand. This procedural labyrinth makes trials expensive, lengthy, and very confusing. Administrative agencies are not bound by many of these procedures (for example, they usually do not have to adhere to rules of evidence), and therefore administrative adjudication has been championed by those who feel the best way to beat the delay, expense, and confusion of court trials is to detach as much adjudication as possible from courts of law and put it into the hands of those not under the thrall of traditional judicial procedure.

Fifth, courts cannot initiate action; judges cannot get up from their benches, strap on revolvers, and roam the streets in search of illegality. Judges must remain in the courthouse waiting for parties to knock on the door asking for a judicial remedy. Administrative agencies, however, are free to look for trouble, and when found, impose a settlement. The Federal Trade Commission does not have to wait for someone to come with a complaint. It can keep its eyes open for unfair trade practices, (for example, deceptive advertising) can accuse a suspect, and can bring that suspect to "trial" before the agency. This can be a very effective combination of police and judicial functions, wholly foreign to regular courts of law.

Finally, courts are usually predisposed to fix their eyes on competing private interests involved in lawsuits, rather than upon the public interest. In this respect courts tend to behave like umpires in ball games: by calling a penalty the umpire attempts to remedy wrongs committed by one team against another. But if the whole game is a brutalizing display from which the public should be protected, does the umpire ever call off the game? Courts, like umpires, tend to focus on competing private rights, not on rights of the general public. This is not always so, but is often so, especially of lower courts. Administrative agencies find it easier to consider the public interest. The primary mission of most regulatory agencies is to look after the public interest, and they are much freer than courts of law to make decisions consciously favoring the public, whatever may be the private interests involved.

*Three Judicial Doctrines:*   American courts have invited executive agencies to become "quasi courts" and to engage in "quasi adjudication." This has been done chiefly through regular application by courts of several doctrines pertaining to civil disputes involving government: (1) the primary jurisdiction doctrine, which holds that such disputes will be decided in the first instance by administrative agencies before they may be brought to courts; when such cases are brought to courts they are brought on appeal from administrative decisions; (2) the exhaustion of remedies doctrine, which holds that anyone who has a dispute with a government agency must not only try to get the dispute settled through agency adjudicatory processes, but must exhaust all possible remedies within the agency before the case is considered ripe for review by an appellate court; and (3) the substantial evidence doctrine, which holds that when an agency makes a finding of fact in the process of deciding a case, that finding is considered to be final and cannot be appealed if it is based on substantial evidence.

Here is how those three doctrines might work in a state university. Keep in mind that technically the university is an executive agency, created, like most other agencies, to execute certain functions—in this case the function of public higher education. Now suppose we have a student who thinks his grade in a certain course was unfair. Under the primary jurisdiction doctrine our student should not run immediately to a court of law. That would be counter to the court's doctrine (practice) of not listening to cases until the agency itself (in this case, the university) has had a chance to hear the complaint and issue its own decision. Suppose our student goes to the professor and makes his complaint known, but the professor after thinking it over says he will stand by his original grade. Should the student then go to court? No. He has not yet exhausted his remedies in the university. He should go beyond the professor. If there is a student grievance committee he should appeal to it. And he should lay his case before the department chairman, the dean, or the chancellor, exhausting every recognized avenue for redress within the university. Only then is the case "ripe for review" by courts. If, however, exhausting all those remedies would result in irreparable harm to the student (perhaps by delaying his graduation) then the case might be considered ripe for judicial review at once.

Now, after exhausting his university remedies, let us say our student sues in court to have the allegedly unjust grade set aside. Here he finds himself in a very difficult position. He cannot expect the court to determine what his grade in the course should have been, for that would be asking the court to review a finding of fact arrived at by the university that the grade was justified. In all probability the court would consider that to be a fact that could not be appealed, if based on substantial evidence. What hope, then, does the student have in court? Not much. And this he has in common with all citizens in civil conflict with the state. Unless one can find some legal error in the agency's action, there is little to be reviewed by any court. But if the agency committed some legal error such as exceeding its authority or acting arbitrarily, then there is perhaps hope for judicial remedy if one has the money to pursue it. But our professor did not exceed his authority, nor was he arbitrary.

*Congress Enlarges Administrative Adjudication:* To repeat, much of the growth of administrative adjudication has been spurred by courts themselves, but Congress also, exercising its constitutionally granted power to establish courts and (by implication) to determine their subject matter jurisdiction, has given numerous agencies power to adjudicate certain disputes. For example, it established a National Labor Relations Board endowed with power not only to promulgate fair labor practice regulations governing employer employee relations in interstate commerce, but also to decide disputes between employers and employees arising when one side accuses the other of violating NLRB regulations. After the NLRB (or any other agency with adjudicatory power) has handed down its decision, that decision may, of course, be appealed to a court of appeals, providing the appellant can find legal (as opposed to fact) errors in the NLRB's action. At times Congress has tried to make the decisions of administrative agencies final and nonappealable to courts. It attempted to give that kind of finality to the findings of selective service boards in disputes involving the assignment of draft classifications to individuals. However, courts do not like the idea of agencies exercising power that cannot be appealed to a court. Courts, in the eyes of most judges, should always be open at some stage to anyone claiming illegality, at least to anyone claiming that an administrative act is a violation of due process of law or is in any other way unconstitutional or illegal.

*Formal and Informal Adjudication:* It is easy to imagine how vast is the number of controversies adjudicated by administrative agencies, for there are about as many "adjudications" as there are uncertainties about the meaning of any regulation. Not all these adjudications are formal. In fact, only a tiny percentage are formal in the sense of having all the trappings of a courtroom proceeding. By far most administrative adjudications are informal, which means they fall short of involving the full courtroom panoply. For example, when a taxpayer has a difference of opinion with the Internal Revenue Service over a tax question, the matter may possibly be settled by a brief exchange of letters or by a conversation between the taxpayer and a low level contact person in an IRS office. But no taxpayer is obliged to allow the matter to be settled so informally. Every taxpayer has a right to "appeal" his case within the IRS, and may move the dispute from one level to the next until at some stage in IRS appellate procedure there is a full formal hearing complete with lawyers, swearing of witnesses, cross-examinations, rebuttals, and so on. Obviously the overwhelming majority of adjudications are highly informal and may involve nothing but a phone call. The term "adjudication" itself is somewhat vague. Just as it may not be certain whether a particular microscopic organism constitutes animal life or plant life, so it is not always certain where the line between asking a simple question and asking for an adjudication lies.

On the other hand, formal adjudication has its dinosaurs, its tremendous disputes dragging on for years, involving millions of dollars and whole law firms. This may happen when, for instance, a giant tobacco company is accused of violating the Federal Trade Commission's rule against false and deceptive advertising.

## Great and Small Interests Adjudicated

It is sometimes claimed that administrative adjudication involves only small cases, while courts handle all the great cases. As mentioned above, this is not at all true. Each year cases adjudicated by administrative agencies involve more money than all the money involved in cases adjudicated that year by courts of law. The fate of multimillion dollar enterprises often rests in the hands of administrative agencies. It is true that most great cases are appealed to courts, but courts, in listening to such appeals often place great reliance on findings of administrative agencies, especially on findings of fact, insofar as fact can be distinguished from law.

Most formal adjudications quite naturally involve substantial interests; few people consider it worth the trouble to mount a formal legal battle unless substantial interests are involved. A physician threatened with loss of his medical license will probably want to carry things as far as necessary to avoid economic capital punishment. On the other hand, a taxpayer in a $73 dispute with the Internal Revenue Service may rather pay than spend time, money, and effort fighting it.

## SUMMARY

Let us again visualize the picture sought to be drawn here. It is a picture that would startle the fathers of the Republic who wrote separation of powers into the Constitution believing the best defense against tyranny is a system of government that puts legislative, judicial, and executive power into the hands of separate and competing branches of government. That pillar of the Constitution, the doctrine of separation of powers, is crumbling because the circumstances we find ourselves in today seem to demand not separation of powers, but union of powers.

And union of powers is what we have in modern public administration —legislative, executive and, judicial power unified within agencies, the three powers held simultaneously by the same bureaucrats. Congress, for years, has been delegating legislative and judicial power to executive agencies; meanwhile courts have acquiesced in this, and encouraged it. Modern administrators, therefore, are not simply paper shufflers mechanically carrying out the will of Congress. Modern administration can be the most exciting and demanding of all professions; to administer is at once to legislate, to judge, and to execute. The union of executive, legislative, and judicial power has crowned the profession of public administration, made it worthy of the best minds, and established it as a subject of study for those who wish to understand the managerial revolution of our era.

## SUGGESTED READING

Becker, Theodore, ed. *The Impact of Supreme Court Decisions.* New York: Oxford University Press, 1969.

Berkley, George E. *The Administrative Revolution.* Englewood Cliffs, N.J.: Prentice Hall, 1971.

Burns, James MacGregor. *Presidential Government.* Boston: Houghton Mifflin, 1973.

Green, Mark J. *Who Runs Congress?* New York: Grossman, 1975.

Jacoby, Henry. *The Bureaucratization of the World.* Berkeley: University of California Press, 1976.

Matthews, Donald R. *U.S. Senators and Their World.* Chapel Hill: The University of North Carolina Press, 1960.

Neustadt, Richard E. *Presidential Power.* New York: Wiley, 1962.

Polsby, Nelson W. *Congress and the Presidency.* Englewood Cliffs, N.J.: Prentice Hall, 1971.

Reedy, George E. *The Twilight of the Presidency.* New York: New American Library, 1970.

Ripley, Randall B. and Franklin, Grace A. *Congress, the Bureaucracy, and Public Policy.* Homewood, IL: The Dorsey Press, Inc., 1976.

Schlesinger, Arthur M., Jr. *The Imperial Presidency.* Boston: Houghton Mifflin, 1973.

*

# Education in the Mysterious Science 2

# Education in the
# Mysterious Science 2

## BOUNDARIES OF PUBLIC ADMINISTRATION

Can such an all-embracing subject as public administration be defined, have frontiers, be an academic discipline, be studied, or taught? The scope of public administration seems limitless. As we have seen, modern practitioners of the craft are legislators and judges as well as executives. But the scope of modern administration runs even beyond that.

Suppose you are trying to improve public administration in Peru and you conclude the most important thing needed is more stability in Peruvian government. Are you studying public administration when you study how best to stabilize the government? And if you investigate Peruvian history, religion, economics, politics, and the nation's general culture including its literature and art to get at the roots of instability, are you studying public administration when you study all these things?

Suppose you are hired as a university consultant to recommend improvements in administration of the school of nursing, and you discover a major snag in its administration is disharmony between the school of nursing and the school of medicine. The trouble seems to center on vague rivalries between the nursing and medical professions. Are you studying public administration when you attempt to inform yourself about the complex relations between doctors and nurses? If that is public administration, then what is not—what are the boundaries and subject matter of public administration?

The public administration curriculum (whatever it may be) is generally claimed to have beneficial effects on the subsequent administrative talent of students. But does that curriculum really have any such effect? Many universities apparently assume so, although it is rare to find a university administrator with so much as one single traditional public administration course under his belt. Nevertheless, the number of colleges that have

27

master of public administration programs in the United States is growing—
in 1952 there were thirteen, today there are over 70.

## THE UTILITY OF PUBLIC ADMINISTRATION EDUCATION

Recently George Grode and Marc Holzer contacted a sample of persons
who hold a master's degree in public administration (MPA) and asked
them to report on the usefulness of their MPA training and degree. Only
a slight majority of the respondents reported that attainment of the MPA
resulted in their feeling "significantly more" *knowledgeable and confi-
dent.* And respondents primarily rated their *skillfunless* as only "somewhat" enchanced by the MPA training.

Although Grode and Holzer conclude that "a sample of MPA degree
holders believe that the acquisition of the degree is of significant benefit
to them in their professional careers in terms of competence gained" (p.
411), their research also seems to suggest that an astonishing number of
degree holders are not greatly impressed by the usefulness of their degree
work.

### The Ecole Nationale d'Administration

Doubts about the value of public administration education have fueled
recent controversies in France over the proper role of that nation's cele-
brated national school of administration (the Ecole Nationale d'Administration, abbreviated ENA). Recruitment of higher civil servants in France
is largely through the ENA. France divides its civil service into four
classes: administrative, executive, clerical, and typist. Ordinarily a civil
servant enters one of these classes and makes his career within it, just as
in the United States Army a person may enter the commissioned officer
class and pursue a career from bottom toward the top of that class, or a
person may begin at the bottom of the enlisted class and make his way
upwards within the confines of that class. To repeat, almost all those who
enter the highest of the four French civil service classes, enter through the
Ecole Nationale d'Administration.

The ENA was founded in 1945, just as the smoke of World War II
cleared. The school was designed for several purposes. First, it was supposed to be a vehicle for democratizing the recruitment of higher civil
servants, especially those in the most august and important administrative
agencies such as the council of state, court of accounts, foreign service, and
finance inspectorate, which, taken together, are called the *grandes corps.*
Democratization has been only partially successful. Most recruits to the
school still come from the upper-middle class, with only a handful from the
lower-middle class, and almost none from the so-called working class and
farmers. A second purpose of the ENA was to give a sense of unity to the

higher civil service in its dealings with politicians. This goal has succeeded so well that there is talk of an "ENA Mafia" and it is sometimes said that ENArchy reigns in France. A third purpose of the school was to raise the standard of top civil servants. This goal has only partially been realized owing in part to the rather small number of graduates from the school. Only 100 are admitted to the ENA each year, and some who graduate are snapped up by private industry.

No end of controversy rages in France over the ENA. Some decry its teaching methods; some say the ENA is too Parisian and Jacobin and has too little regard for provincial virtues; some say there is no need for an ENA since other schools would do a better job; some say you cannot teach administration in a school, that it has to be learned by practicing it; some condemn competitive examinations which, after two years, determine the fate of graduates; some oppose the four class system, and favor promotion of lower civil servants into the higher ranks by a system comparable to the American.

One great criticism of the school is its ranking of graduates by means of one single competitive examination given at the end of two years. This exam is a decisive point in a student's future career in the civil service: the top 25 or 30 are assigned to the *grandes corps*. Critics argue that no competitive written examination can assess administrative talent, that the result of the written examination is to instantly promote into the highest positions people who may be least imaginative, who may be intellectual swots. Criticism of the exam has its roots in the conflict about whether administration is teachable. Critics argue that graduates of the ENA have little use in their subsequent careers for knowledge learned at the ENA, and that success in administration results not from knowledge gained in school, but from various personal characteristics of the administrator. Although the curriculum, which is largely composed of legal studies, has been criticized as irrelevant to an administrative career, and although as a result of these criticisms law has been somewhat deemphasized and such subjects as statistics and economics substituted, the basic charge remains that none of this knowledge is critical to success in high level administration. Therefore, the whole concept of a school for administrators is attacked, most particularly the written exam, because, if knowledge taught at the school is irrelevant, then so should be the results of any examination over that knowledge.

Defenders of the ENA and its procedures point to the school's process for selecting new students. Selection committees look for personal qualities that supposedly make successful administrators; they look for recruits who use the language well; who are good communicators; who have common sense, imagination, independence of mind, character; who are careful and sensitive, yet courageous; who can quickly react to circumstances. Thus, hopefully, no one gets into the school who lacks the personal qualities requisite in administration. Furthermore, the faculty attempts to develop those qualities in students, and to some extent the final examination is slanted to test for those qualities. The faculty apparently tries to avoid giving high rank to students who are immature, naive, rigid, vacillating, and too subservient and lacking in independence of mind. Unfortunately, however, there is great debate over which personal qualities are requisite for success in administration, if any.

## Public Administration Education in Britain

During the greatest days of the British Empire the highest levels of the British public service were occupied by generally educated persons, not by persons specially trained in management. This remains substantially true of the present day Bristish higher civil service. Only recently have exams which candidates must take to enter the higher civil service included questions about quantitative methods, economics, management, and other specialties. For many generations recruitment into the British higher civil service favored person with liberal arts education at the universities. Only university graduates with good academic records were eligible to take entrance exams for the higher civil service, and these exams favored applicants possessing a general education. Today, under impact of reform, the exams are less biased in favor of liberal arts and are designed to more freely admit persons with other academic backgrounds. The British, like the French, recruit only about 100 individuals into the higher-civil service annually, and competition is severe.

In the early 1800s government offices in Britian were the preserve of sons of noble families. It fell to Lord Thomas Babington Macaulay in the mid-1800s to reform the British public service, and he decided that henceforth recruitment should be on the basis of merit, both for the upper and lower positions of the service. For recruitment of top level civil servants he chose as his model the method then in use for selction of young men for important jobs in the Indian colonial service. That system was intended to maintain British prestige abroad by use of able and cultured products of the British universities of the day. Entrance examinations were geared to the kind of general and classical education prevalent in those universites. Persons for lower positions in the civil service, clerks and the like, were recruited by means of examinations geared to the kind of education offered in that day by secondary schools. In the First World War era a four class system was set up: an administrative class at the top for advising ministers on policy matters and directly managing departments; an executive class of specialists in fields like taxation and accountancy; below them were the clerical and subclerical service. Generalists in the administrative class were, of course, better paid and more likely to be promoted to positions of high responsibility.

Since the Second World War there has been a good deal of discussion in Britain about the upper civil service and its proper selection and education.

In 1966 the Committee on the Civil Service (chaired by Lord Fulton) recommended that the four class system be abandoned, and that all classes be merged into a single ladder of ranks. This was done in 1971. The academic threshhold was also lowered. Formerly only those with a university degree of at least the 2nd class could enter competition for appointment to the administrative class. One argument for abolishing the class system is that to do so increases competition for high level administrative jobs. Rather than preserving high ranking jobs for persons in the administrative class, such jobs can now be aspired to by anyone at any level of the civil service. Thus, promotion is now supposed to be based more on merit than before. The old administrative class was accused of being riddled with semiincompetents who, once they had made it into the administrative (or executive) class, had a tendency to relax in the knowledge that no matter how lazy they might be, they would always hold high rank and position.

Another argument for merging the classes was that the old administrative class was recruited too much from privileged social groups, that is, from those groups wealthy and talented enough to send their children to Oxford and Cambridge. Resentment against the privileged social classes in British society translated itself into resentment against the civil service class system, and against the customary liberal arts, classical, and generalist education of the upper classes.

It is now popular in Britain to believe administrators should be taught administration, not just liberal arts. No one is certain what "teaching administration" means, but it is commonly said to include quantitative methods, economics, personnel administration, financial administration, and the like. Whether any of these specialized subjects really help *high level* administrators do their job is worthy of question. The competence and ability of British top level administrators has long inspired awe across five continents, despite their lack of specialized training in "management science." The same can be said of French and German higher civil servants, whose genius has for generations been envied.

Those who defend general education as the best preparation for high level administration, insist that success in high level administration has a great deal to do with the intellectual and personal qualities of those who hold such positions. And what are those qualities? The question is highly debatable, but defenders of general education argue that a high level administrator is by definition a person who coordinates the activities of large numbers of people of diverse specialties, and therefore he should not be a specialist himself, but a generalist with broad knowledge of many things. The more a high level administrator buries himself in a specialty, the less he knows of the rest of the world. He is apt to be biased toward his own specialty—to see the world through the tinted glass of that one specialty. This makes him less qualified than a generalist to coordinate other specialties.

Secondly, defenders of general education argue that a high level administrator is by the nature of his job a communicator: he does his work through the medium of written and spoken language and therefore needs to be able to organize, package, and articulate ideas. Those are skills emphasized in good liberal arts programs.

Thirdly, it is said good administrators should have independence of mind and should be careful in thinking things through to their logical consequences. What better training for that than courses in philosophy, or any course where the socratic method is practiced, that is, where the professor by a system of leading questions brings students face to face with the consequences of their statements.

Fourthly, it is argued that administrators work incessantly through and with other people, and that there is no better academic preparation for this than study of literature and humanities.

While the British have not completely abandoned their faith in general education as a useful preparation for high level administrators, this faith has been modified. The written civil service entrance examinations are friendlier to specialists of various sorts, though not hostile to liberal arts. A British Civil Service College was established in 1970 to give training in management to persons after they have entered the civil service. One purpose of the school is to help specialists get the knowledge they are supposed to need to become general administrators, but there is some muttering among specialists that they are still not adequately valued for high administrative posts.

Although the teaching of public administration is a growth industry in Britain as it is in America, very little of this teaching is done in the leading universities. One reason for this is that it is still not altogether fashionable to teach public administration in British universities. They still cling to the traditional idea that it is their role to be concerned with the education of administrators and to let teaching about administration science continue to emerge as a by-product of broad undergraduate education in the social sciences, humanities, and in other subjects relevant to anyone in administration.

Another reason why British universities have not jumped on the bandwagon to offer degrees in administration is that it is still not clear in the minds of many British university professors just what public administration is. A good many are confused. On the one hand there are people who say public administration should be a separate discipline. But again there are those who deny the subject exists, and would be surprised to learn that what they have been teaching all along as sociology, or as psychology, or as political science, or as economics, or as literature, or as speech, is really public administration.

Furthermore, many British university professors have their doubts whether management or public administration training contributes much to administrators or to effective administration. These doubts are strengthened when the advocates of "administrative training" seldom respond clearly, convincingly, or with one voice when asked to explain the basis of their claim that public administration teaching contributes to administrators. To make things worse, numerous graduates of public administration courses and programs which flourish outside British universities openly confess that their course work and training were not appropriate to their present jobs.

## Why Public Administration Education?

Considering these serious doubts about the usefulness of public administration training, one wonders why public administration courses are suddenly so popular and well attended today in Britain and America. One theory, of course, is that these doubts about its usefulness are groundless. Another, more cynical theory, is that while public administration training contributes little to administrative talent, nevertheless it is extremely useful to have a record of such training on one's vita because in today's large scale bureaucracy it is hard to convince anybody you have a skill unless you can point to a diploma or transcript to prove it. Public administration courses are, therefore, sometimes sought purely for reasons of occupational protection and career advancement. Degrees constitute quasi certification. Generalists in administrative positions sometimes feel vulnerable unless they can point to a record which says they do in fact know what they are practicing.

Universities in the United States have not hesitated to embrace public administration, and are going full speed ahead teaching the subject although hardly any two people can agree what public administration is or ought to be as a practice or as an academic study. In deep despair someone once defined the practice of public administration as that which public administrators practice. Likewise perhaps the best definition of public administration as an academic discipline is that it is what teachers of public administration teach. But this leaves the mysterious science of public administration more inscrutable than before.

## Degrees and Courses

What, then, is taught under the label "public administration?" This varies widely among the 70 plus MPA programs now functioning in the United States. The ten courses most commonly included in general MPA programs are:

Introduction to Public Administration
Comparative Public Administration
Political Nature of Public Administration
Organizational Theory
Problems in Public Administration
Personnel Administration
Budgeting
Planning
Statistics
Research design

Frequently the larger MPA programs offer specialized degree options. For example, if a student is interested in urban administration, then, in addition to several so-called "core public administration courses" the student is channeled into courses supposedly of particular value to an administrator in local government. There may be options in such vague areas as environmental management, human resources management, policy analysis, criminal justice and, of course, general public administration. Core courses common to all such options often include an introductory survey course in the fundamentals of public administration, a quantitative analysis course, and an organization theory course. These options and core courses, to repeat, vary from institution to institution. Some MPA degree programs are offered by political science departments, others by separate schools of public administration/affairs.

Public administration courses are also regularly taught as part of the political science curriculum because the political science profession considers public administration to be one of the major subdivisions of political science. Also, many colleges offer continuing education courses in public administration for person who do not want to enroll or who are not qualified to enroll as regular degree students at a college, but who, nevertheless, want to take courses in public administration. Some colleges offer certificate programs in public administration for such people; a certificate appropriate for framing is given to those who complete a certain program of courses.

## PUBLIC ADMINISTRATION VERSUS BUSINESS ADMINISTRATION

Feuding between business administration and public administration on some college campuses has reached an epic scale comparable to the fight between the Capulets and Montagues. However, in some locations cordial relations have flowered, and one can only hope it will not end with stabbings and poisonings.

The development of separate schools of public administration and business administration headed by separate rival deans, staffed by sepa-

rate rival faculties, outfitted with separate rival curricula and degree programs, and backed by separate rival client groups in the community is a
perfect example of administrative pluralism in American bureaucracy—
the academic bureaucracy in this case. Without the existence of separate
constituencies beyond the university, the thrust for separate organization
of PA and BA within the university would be weaker. These separate
constituencies—business administrators and their professional organizations on the one hand and public administrators and their professional
organizations on the other—have a grossly exaggerated view of their own
uniqueness and distinction from one another. Public administration and
private administration in reality have much in common and are steadily
growing more similar. In any complex organization, whether private or
public, one finds the same basic processes of administration: defining
purposes, planning, organizing, recruiting, selecting, rewarding, communicating internally, communicating externally, budgeting, decision
making, managing, motivating, controlling, and measuring results. Most of
the curriculum of BA and PA revolves around those basic functions, but
courses and faculties are normally duplicated.

There are, of course, differences between the public sector and the
private sector. But there are also differences within each sector that may
have more impact on methods of administration than their publicness or
privateness—for example, size. In a sense, all large-scale organizations
today are public, are compelled to address public goals and use methods
prescribed by laws and rules. Airlines, for example, are not permitted to
serve a purely profit motive, or to set prices, run service, or keep their
books solely according to the dictates of profit. The American economy is
not as capitalistic as the world imagines. Nor is it socialist. Ours is a "mixed
economy" with mass infusions of public regulation of private enterprise
obscuring many of the differences between public and private administration.

Some of the alleged distinctions between the public and private sectors
have always been pure legend. It is an article of faith in the business
community that private business is more efficient than the public bureaucracy. But the exasperations most of us experience as we become victims
of bungling repairmen and mechanics does not inspire confidence in
business efficiency. Nor does the spectacle of great private firms begging
for government subsidies as the last hope for their survival. And, one might
ask, is business less corrupt than the public bureaucracy? If a bureaucrat
is caught taking a bribe it makes the front pages, and he may go to jail and
be fired. But bribes, kickbacks, and under-the-table payments are so frequent in business that disclosure of it is not considered news, except
perhaps where a multimillion dollar payment to a foreign head of state is
uncovered.

Is private business more moral and ethical than the public bureaucracy?
Is nepotism, the preferential treatment of relatives, greater in the public

bureaucracy? Do blood and friendship have more to do with hirings, promotions, and pay raises in the public sector than in the private? Are top positions filled on a who-you-know basis more in the public sector than in the private? In short, does merit play a greater role in business than in the public bureaucracy? (Dismissal rates are about the same in both.)

Is private business less wasteful? Is it wasteful when four service stations work the same intersection or when tremendous productive effort is mobilized for the manufacture of hula hoops? The belief that somehow private business is more moral, less corrupt, less wasteful, and more efficient than public administration fuels the separatist tendencies of these two academic "disciplines" which otherwise have so much in common.

Undoubtedly there are differences between PA and BA, undoubtedly the profit motive makes a difference, and undoubtedly American private business is admired the world over for its talent for getting things done, and done magnificently. However, some of these admirable successes of American business may have more to do with the influence of American culture than with the influence of managerial techniques, for example, it may have to do with the work ethic which plays a central role in American productivity. Hard work gives personal pride in our culture; joy through labor, salvation through work is in the air. Likewise our ideas about bureaucratic structure (to be discussed in the next chapter) foster productivity. But these American cultural characteristics benefit management in both the private and public bureaucracies. The virtues and successes of American public bureaucracy have not been glorified like the virtues and successes of American private management, but careful observation might reveal that both sectors are extremely productive not only because they employ similar managerial processes, but also because public and private managers are cut from the same cultural cloth and are alike in other ways. Keep in mind that the typical manager in modern large-scale American priviate enterprise is an employee, not an owner; he manages for a salary just like his brother in the public bureaucracy, and he works in a bureaucratic setting no less than his brother in public administration. The fact that quite a few business managers move back and forth between the private and public sectors, and that senior public administrators are also commonly hired for managerial positions in private enterprise, suggests that the same basic managerial skills and traits are applicable to both the private and public sectors, and that these skills are essentially the same whether taught by a school of public administration or by a school of business administration.

There are, to repeat, differences between public and private administration. Certainly public administrators work within a framework of law; they must hire, fire, and promote according to law and must pursue various goals set by law, and so forth. But business is also subject to an endless variety of governmental rules and regulations that concern nearly every aspect of their operation including hiring and firing (the National Labor

Relations Act, for example, and the affirmative action regulations). Private businesses are increasingly subject to laws concerning such things as safety and environmental protection that affect what they may produce and how. In these and many other ways private firms are forced to pursue public goals and are ever more encircled by law. Public administration exists in a political environment. But so increasingly does business administration. Success of a firm may depend on the political and legal skills of managers.

Sometimes it is said public administrators work in a fish bowl, that what they do is open to public scrutiny because it is public business. Sunshine laws, and freedom of information acts testify to this. But private business is also coming under closer scrutiny. Regulatory agencies and legislative committees freely exercise their power to lift the skirts of any private business that falls under their jurisdiction. No end of requests for information press upon business managers.

Basically, administration is administration no matter what is administered. Basically, the same curriculum is suitable (if any curriculum is really suitable) for both public and private administrators. Thus, some universities have unified all professional training in administration under one hat. In such programs all students take the same core curriculum, then branch out into specialized courses depending on what kind of organization they expect to work for.

Perhaps nothing is so confused, wasteful, and disjointed in the academic world as programs in administration. This is partly because no one knows for sure what administration is, or how to teach it; and partly because academic empire builders seek every argument and every ally to build separate schools; and partly because allies for separatism are to be found in separate community client groups with exaggerated views of their mutual uniqueness.

## TRAINING AT THE TOP

In-service training is not something reserved for people at the bottom of the organization. High ranking civil servants also need to keep up to date with their profession, and since they generally have two professions—their subject matter specialty and their administrative functions—they need help in both areas. As a matter of fact, the vast majority of high level administrators have never had a single course in administration, and learn their "second profession" (administration) through first-hand experiences. This is true of most college administrators who first become professors of, say, philosophy, then gradually or suddenly become administrators by being elected department chairman, or be being "discovered" by other administrators. These amateur administrators often stay full-time or part-time in administration the rest of their working lives. Most administrators in the public service reach managerial jobs by rising through the ranks within a specialized agency, and their vision of the public service is therefore somewhat limited to what they have seen within their agency. Thus a GS–16, 17, or 18 in the forest service may have started out with a degree in forestry, and over the years received a fair background in the study of trees and forests, and may be well indoctrinated in the lore and institutional goals of the forest service. By the time he reaches the peak of his career he may know a lot about the peculiarities of administration in the forest service, and may have picked up a little knowledge of automatic data processing, purchasing, personnel administration, and various other corners of knowledge useful to administrators. But to be a more effective administrator, he may need to go back to school and learn more about the mechanics of modern large scale administration. He may need to take courses in areas such as political science, sociology, and economics that deal with social forces and the general mechanisms of government through which those forces work, and courses that deal with the goals of the government at large and the nation at large. With the help of this broadening of vision, a high level administrator may be better equipped to understand the forces at work on (and within) his agency, and perhaps he will be better equipped to coordinate the policies of his agency with the larger policies of the nation as a whole. If a policy-making administrator in the forest service understands the political and social and economic forces that have led to enactment of "affirmative action" rules, to cite but one example, he may be better equipped to direct his agency along a path of intelligent cooperation with such rules and policies. The more an administrator understands about the political, social, and economic background of the great policies of government the better he can mesh his own policies (that is, the policies he makes for his particular agency) with the larger overarching policies of government.

To help high level administrators get this kind of education, and to help them acquire more knowledge of the technical side of modern large scale administration, the federal government has in recent decades embarked on several interesting programs of in-service training for mid-level, senior-grade, and supergrade administrators. Most of this training has consisted of short-term, in-service programs designed to improve the skills of scientific, professional, and technical employees.

However, some specialized courses have been sponsored by the United States Civil Service Commission's Career Education Awards Program to develop managerial skills of senior federal administrators. Some have been conducted at private institutions such as the Kennedy School of Government at Harvard University, the Woodrow Wilson School of Public and International Affairs at Princeton University and the Maxwell School of Citizenship and Public Affairs at Syracuse University. Also, about 2,000 senior federal executives each year attend two-week programs at the Executive Seminar Centers at King's Point, New York; Berkeley, California; and Oak Ridge, Tennessee. Most senior administrators selected to attend these high level management training programs are outstanding civil servants marked for eventual assignment to bigger jobs.

It is not always clear just what these encounters between mid-career administrators and long-haired academicians are supposed to accomplish, but the sessions are presumed to have a salutory effect on those destined for higher responsibility. In reality the most salutory (but least anticipated or intended) effect may accrue to the academicians, not the administrators. Furthermore, although the most promising senior administrators attend these programs, it is by no means certain that those who agree to attend are the type destined for highest responsibility. The ablest men may not want an academic interlude; they may be too shrewd to leave the ramparts to their competitors, even for two weeks.

## The Federal Executive Institute

At Charlottesville, Virginia, just a hundred miles southwest of Washington, D.C., the United States Civil Service Commission has established a Federal Executive Institute. The institute cannot be compared to West Point or Annapolis for it is not to educate young recruits. On the contrary the Federal Executive Institute is more comparable to the National War College for generals and admirals—the institute is for "generals and admirals" of the civil service. It is an interagency facility created to serve the development needs of high level federal executives, primarily at grade levels of GS–16 and above, or their equivalent in services not under the civil commission.

One approaches the white-columned entrance to the main building via a sweeping curved drive leading from a thickly wooded countryside. The structure looks like something that might have been designed by Thomas Jefferson, whose home is nearby. Executives are whisked from pressures of their everyday jobs and deposited in this lovely spot for weeks or months of residential study. There are the usual conveniences of a liberal arts college—dormitories, dining rooms, libraries, classrooms, even sport and recreation facilities where executives play together. It is official doctrine that executives who play together will learn together. Less than one percent of the federal civil service is eligible to attend this spa, only the top ranks. Nor do all of them attend. The institute has limited capacity, perhaps around 300 a year can be accommodated.

The institute offers a variety of programs: some three-week sessions designed to instruct new GS–16s in the arts of leadership and management as they embark on careers in the supergrades; some seven-week sessions for the education of senior executives already in the senior grades; some one-week courses focussing on single issues. Also, various conferences are held.

Among the most highly valued goals at the institute is education about the realities of American government, the realities of government in a democracy. These realities are compared with how the system is supposed to work in theory. Executives are given an appreciation that democracy in America is an essentially ambiguous process in which goals and values can be realized in a multitude of different ways. The diffusion of responsibility in American public administration is stressed, and executives are taught how to function more effectively in this fluid arrangement. Some study is devoted to the classic areas of administrative management: budget, personnel, property, information, and so forth. But the main emphasis is not on "narrow efficiencies" but on larger efficiencies; executive education at the institute is focussed on goals, objectives, and priorities, and on efficiency in the sense of doing the right things to achieve those larger goals.

It is perhaps worth noting here that national goals, objectives, and priorities are very hard to define in a democracy—debate over them is continuous. Therefore, when the institute teaches goals, one may fairly ask, "Whose goals?" One may inquire whether the teaching of goals, if such a thing goes on, might not constitute education in favor of a particular set of goals favored by managers of the institute, that is, by its ultimate manager in the White House. An administration straining for control of policy-making in the bureaucracy will obviously want to place sympathizers in senior positions, and will want to indoctrinate those already in senior policy-making positions. Therefore, anyone analyzing the program of the Federal Executive Institute would want to investigate whether its program could conceivably be affected by the President's desire to explain and teach his view of "national priorities and goals" to the generals and admirals of the civil service. If the institute's program is so effected, one might well argue that it would be legitimate: senior policy-makers holding employment under a president should at least hear and try to understand the goals and priorities of that president, though that may not be all they should hear.

The Federal Executive Institute is only part of the federal executive development program. Because the managerial knowledge possessed by many high level administrators is more or less limited to their experiences in only one agency, and because "broad based" managerial knowledge can, it is believed, best be acquired through on-the-job experiences in several managerial settings, the federal government has a one-year program to give selected GS–15s (few are selected) broader experiences. The GS–15s spend most of the year as temporary managers in an agency completely different from their own, and in so doing get a clearer picture of what the entire government looks like. Also a few weeks are spent at the Federal Executive Institute studying such subjects as the role of the federal executive, policy and budgetary processes, the federal political and administrative environment, and modern management systems and practices. While at the institute they have an opportunity to get acquainted with GS–16s, 17s, and 18s who happen also to be there, and to hear tales of managerial problems encountered at those levels of administration. The object of the program is to make generalists out of specialists.

## Management Training Below the Federal Level

Many state and local governments are at a competitive disadvantage in attracting and holding competent managers. People with managerial skills can often find better paying jobs in the private sector or in the federal government. Many states lack executive development programs, however, the picture is brighter in some other states. Since passage of the federal intergovernmental personnel act, state and local officials have been permitted to attend in-service-training programs offered by federal agencies.

States are delivering an ever increasing number of services to the public and are in need of ever more sophisticated delivery systems. This means ever more competent and knowledgeable managers are needed who understand large scale organizations.

## SUMMARY

As an academic study and as a practice, public administration is hard to define; its scope is vague. Battles rage in this country and abroad over the question whether public administration can be taught and, if so, what should be taught under that label, and how. Nevertheless, degree programs in public administration have rapidly increased.

Where schools of public administration and business administration exist on the same campus their relationship may be hostile and uncooperative. Yet public administration and private administration have much in common and are steadily growing more similar. In any complex organization (whether private or public) one finds the same basic processes of administration: defining purposes, planning, organizing, recruiting, selecting, communicating internally, communicating externally, budgeting, decision making, managing, motivating, controlling, and measuring results. Most of the curriculum of business administration and public administration revolves around such basic functions, but courses and faculties are sometimes duplicated.

Training for senior managers has been given increasing attention in recent years by the federal government. Most senior career officials have two professions: (1) their subject matter specialty and (2) their administrative functions. In most cases their second profession (administration) is learned on the job without any formal training, and their experience is usually confined to the specialized milieu of a single agency. In an attempt to give senior administrators broader understanding of federal administration and of federal policies, various programs of instruction have been set up, some of which take place at the Federal Executive Institute at Charlottesville, Virginia.

## SUGGESTED READING

Armstrong, John A. *The European Administrative Elite.* Princeton: Princeton University Press, 1973.

Brown, R. G. S., "Fulton and Morale." *Public Administration,* Summer 1971, pp. 185–195.

Byers, Kenneth T., ed. *Employee Training and Development in the Public Service.* Chicago: Public Personnel Association, 1970.

Chapman, Brian. *The Profession of Government.* London: Allen and Unwin, 1959.

Chapman, Richard A. *Teaching Public Administration.* London: Royal Institute of Public Administration. 1962.

Chapman, Richard A. "The Fulton Report: A Summary." *Public Administration,* Winter 1968, pp. 443–451.

Chapman, Richard L. and Cleaveland, Frederic N. *Meeting the Needs of Tomorrow's Public Service: Guidelines for Professional Education in Public Administration.* Washington D.C.: National Academy of Public Administration, 1973.

Cleveland, Harlan. *The Future Executive: A Guide for Tomorrow's Managers.* New York: Harper & Row, 1972.

Egger, Rowland. "Civil Servants at Mid-Career: Management Training in American Universities." *Public Administration,* Spring 1976, pp. 83–98.

Engelbert, Ernest A. *Guidelines and Standards for Professional Masters Degree Programs in Public Administration/Public Affairs.* Washington D.C.: The National Association of Schools of Public Affairs and Administration, 1974.

Ginzberg, Eli. *The Manpower Connection: Education and Work.* Cambridge, Mass.: Harvard University Press, 1975.

Grode, George and Holzer, Marc. "The Perceived Utility of MPA Degrees." *Public Administration Review,* July–August 1975, pp. 403–412.

Honey, John. "A Report: Higher Education for Public Service." *Public Administration Review,* November 1967, pp. 294–321.

Laski, Harold J. "The Limitations of the Expert." *Harper's Magazine,* December 1930, pp. 101–110.

McCurdy, Howard E. *Public Administration: A Bibliography.* Washington, D.C.: College of Public Affairs, American University, 1972.

Medeiros, James A. "The Professional Study of Public Administration." *Public Administration Review,* May–June 1974, pp. 254–260.

Metcalf, Henry C., and Urwick, L., eds. *Dynamic Administration.* New York: Harper & Brothers, 1941.

Mosher, Frederick C. *Democracy and the Public Service.* New York: Oxford University Press, 1968.

Ostrom, Vincent. *The Intellectual Crisis in American Public Administration.* University, Ala.: University of Alabama Press, 1973.

Presidential Task Force on Career Advancement. *Investment for Tomorrow.* Washington, D.C.: U.S. Civil Service Commission, 1967.

Sheriff, Peta. *Career Patterns in the Higher Civil Service.* London: Her Majesty's Stationery Office, 1976.

Society for Personnel Administration. *A Proposal for a Federal Administrative Staff College.* Washington D.C.: 1953.

Stanley, David T. *The Higher Civil Service: An Evaluation of Federal Personnel Practices.* Washington, D.C.: The Brookings Institution, 1964.

"Symposium on Continuing Education for Public Administration." *Public Administration Review,* November–December 1973, pp. 487–532.

United States Civil Service Commission. Personnel Bibliography Series No. 41. *Planning, Organizing and Evaluating Training Programs,* 1971.

Waldo, Dwight. "Developments in Public Administration." *The Annals of the American Academy of Political and Social Science,* November 1972, pp. 217–245

*

# Getting It All Together 3

# Getting It All Together 3

Public administration as a field of study is a blend of numerous other studies including sociology—the science of people interacting with one another. The literature of sociology has much to tell us about administration, for administration is above all a form of social behavior. Administration is also an attempt to control social behavior.

## WHAT IS AN ORGANIZATION?

As many sociologists see it, wherever two or more people regularly interact they become a social organization, and all social organizations exhibit the same general characteristics or patterns just as all cats have the same *general* characteristics (one tail, four feet, two eyes, etc.). Four general characteristics of human groups are: (1) they all have a system of norms; (2) they all have a system of roles; (3) they all have a system for social control; and (4) they all have a ranking system. These four qualities are said to characterize every human group whether it be a fraternity, a family, a football team, a nation, a legislative body, a university, or a bureaucratic agency or office. An administrator needs to know a good deal about the norms, roles, social control, and ranking systems of the environment in which he is functioning. Most administrators instinctively acquire such knowledge although they may not be aware they know, and may not recognize the sociological jargon.

### Norms

Norms are rules governing behavior of group members. Some of these rules are formal, some informal. Formal norms are made for the group by persons recognized by the group as having authority to make such rules, for example, a rule made by a barracks sergeant that the barracks floor will be scrubbed every Friday night. Other rules grow, sometimes unaccountably, from the group itself; for instance, a rule that the barracks sergeant is always to be referred to (out of his presence) as "prune head."

Almost all human behavior is governed by formal and/or informal norms. Each of us is subject to an incredible number of norms, partly because we belong to an incredible number of norm setting groups, and partly because common habits develop as to the manner of doing almost everything that is humanly done. We are drenched in norms. When, how, and what to eat; when, and what to wear and how to wear it; when to sleep and when to rise; how to greet each other; how to speak (rules of grammar are informal norms); all the rules of etiquette governing every conceivable human relationship; even our natural functions are governed by norms—the time, place, and manner of sex, the time, place and, manner of eliminating bodily wastes. It would be a challenge to think of any human activity not governed by norms.

Some norms are more rigidly enforced than others. The norm governing when to eat bacon and eggs is mildly enforced whenone is held "somewhat odd" for regularly eating bacon and eggs at the "wrong" time. However, the norm condemning desertion in wartime is severely enforced.

Some norms pertain only to some members of a group; others aply to everyone. Our society does not generally accept crying by boys: boys who cry may be called sissies. Girls, heretofore, have been free to cry almost any time. However, both boys and girls are expected to show some form of remorse at a funeral; laughing is generally not good form. Although norms may seem to make slaves of us, still, in another sense they liberate us from the tyranny of constant decision making.

The existence of formal and informal norms is one of the never-absent characteristics of every human group including every agency, subagency, office, and unit of government.

No would-be rule can be considered a norm unless it is accepted by the group; the less it is accepted the less it is a norm. The bullet-perforated "no shooting" signs one so often sees in the countryside are monuments to blasted and rebuffed norms. It makes no difference that some norms are accepted only because failure to accept results in punishment. Every norm carries with it the threat of punishment for violators, as well as promise of reward for all who comply. A bank robber holding employees at gun point sets norms for their behavior during his sojourn in the bank. His norms are rigidly obeyed; the threat of punishment for disobedience is clear and probable, the reward for cooperation is life itself.

## Role

A second characteristic found in every group and organization is role specialization. Members of each group become specialized in their duties and are expected by the group to behave in particular ways appropriate to those duties. In the family group, fathers are expected to do certain things and act in certain ways, mothers act out their role expectations, and children behave according to defined patterns. Each occupies a specialized role, although it is interesting to note how women and men are challenging these roles in an attempt to change norms. Every role is a collection of rights, duties and obligations generally recognized by group members as belonging to that role and to the person who occupies it.

Role expectations actually constitute norms. The role of father in a family, the bundle of expectations of him in that role, is a bundle of norms. So long as people conform to the the role-defining norms they agree upon, they get along fairly well; when their behavior deviates from those norms, trouble starts.

Some roles are formal and some informal, just as some norms are formal and some informal. Formal and informal exist simultaneously in the same organization. In formal organizations such as a government bureaucracy, persons in authority theoretically determine who is going to do what. Often this is done very carefully and scientifically—jobs designed, described, and related to one another. But all such designs become partial failures because every work group tends, informally, to readjust the formally determined roles (this is a great shortcoming of all formal personnel classification systems). In the course of time (often a very short time) the table of organization as it appears on the chart hanging in the manager's office may bear little relationship to the actual organization as it informally functions. The group informally, spontaneously, unwittingly develops roledefining norms which may be quite at variance with the formal role-defining norms handed down by management. In other words, one finds in every formal organization, two overlapping organizations: the "formal organization" as it appears on the chart, and the "informal organization" as it spontaneously develops. Some management experts argue that it is often desirable to adjust the formal organization to conform to the informal organization.

Groups without formal roles will informally and unwittingly generate roles. Every person in every group has a specialized group role somewhat different from the role of every other member. One such role is that of leader, a person who is expected to coordinate the roles of group members to accomplish group goals.

## Social Control

Another characteristic identifiable in all groups is a system of punishments and rewards, commonly referred to as social control. The stick (negative sanctions) and the carrot (positive sanctions) are used by the group to motivate members to comply with group norms.

Sanctions may be formal (manager states that anyone persistently late for work will receive a letter of reprimand). Or sanctions may be informal (the group ostracizes a squealer). Every norm, formal or informal, is backed up by threats against violators. Severity of the sanction, and tolerance for deviation, depends on how important the norm appears to the authority that established it. The power to make norms and the power to punish violations are held by the same authorities. Thus, one who holds a formal authority role in the formal organization and who hands down formal rules (norms), also has power to hand out formal punishments and formal rewards. Likewise the group stands ready to punish violators of its informal norms.

Just as formal and informal organizations often operate within the same group at the same time (sometimes cooperatively, sometimes uncooperatively), so do formal and informal sanctions operate simultaneously on the same terrain. Formal sanctions against theft may be backed up by, or shall we say, redoubled by informal sanctions. A soldier apprehended for petty theft in the barracks may be both officially and unofficially punished—officially court-martialed and unofficially ostracized. Formal and informal sanctions may conflict, just as formal and informal norms may conflict; officially a soldier may be punished for failure to salute a disliked officer, while behind the scenes he is patted on the back by fellow troopers.

## Social Ranking

A fourth characteristic evident in every group is social ranking—groups not only create roles but also rank those roles. Rank may be conferred by authorities in the formal organization, or informally by the group. Rank has to do with power; social ranking creates a pecking order—a power hierarchy. With rank goes prestige and status.

An individual may have high rank, prestige, and status in one group and low rank, low prestige, and low status in another. For example, a school custodian may be at the bottom of the school caste system, but at the top in his secret society where, as exalted grand potentate, he rules over his fellow members.

### FORMAL ORGANIZATIONS

In the forgoing discussion of norms, roles, social control, and ranking, a distinction was made between formal and informal norms, formal and informal roles, formal and informal social control, formal and informal ranking. A formal organization is the combined formal structure of norms, roles, social control, and ranking. However, it cannot be over-emphasized that the formal organization is only part of the group structure; the other part, equally important, is the phantom, informal structure. Any person who realizes there are informal norms, roles, social controls, and rankings that exist within every formal organization has made great progress toward possession of managerial skill. Managers within formal organizations must deal with these phantoms no less than with the visible formal organization.

## Formal Bureaucratic Structure

*Max Weber:* Sooner or later the name Max Weber (1864–1920) is invoked in nearly every conversation about bureaucracy, for he was one of the first to systematically study and describe it. Despite his cumbersome style (long sentences, qualifying phrases, dependent clauses, digressions from digressions) he was a giant in many areas of social theory, and one of the founders of modern sociology. In his written work he seemed to abhor straightforward declarative sentences, and buried every main point deep in irrelevant minutia, page after rambling page. Yet through it all comes the image of a careful scholar, painstaking and thorough. Strangely, Weber seems to have been almost obnoxiously blunt in face to face encounters. If it were not for that unfortunate quality, sociology might have lost Weber to politics.

Max Weber lived through what many modern Germans consider the finest hour of German history. If not the finest, surely the proudest, for in 1871, when Weber was seven, the German principalities, having united in victorious war against France, decided to make it a permanent union. The ceremony took place in Versailles Palace just outside Paris where on January 18, 1871, as German guns bombarded Paris (the city surrendered ten days later), William the First of Prussia was crowned Kaiser of the Reich.

Victory over Napoleon III at Sedan, defeat of France and creation of a new unified German nation, stupendous growth of German industry, outpourings of German culture (*Der Ring des Nibelungen* was played for the first time in 1876 at the Bayreuth Festspielhaus), all this produced in the hearts of millions of Germans an intense pride and served as confirmation in the minds of many that the German race and its culture were superior.

Son of a well-known German parliamentarian, Max Weber apparently wanted to be a politician—not a low level politician, but a statesman with impact on national affairs. Perhaps because of the rough edges of his personality, he never succeeded in that, but as a writer he dealt with numerous subjects of important national concern. He was a dedicated nationalist, proud of the Germany of his time which he considered to be not only powerful but also enlightened, protective of individual freedom, and tremendously productive and industrious. He also admired the military virtues and hierarchicalism of the Kaiser Reich. All this no doubt had something to do with his interest in bureaucracy, for he saw bureaucracy as a central characteristic not only of the German government but also of German industry and social institutions; he credited bureaucracy with much of the success of the German Reich.

Weber was not without criticism of bureaucracy. Bureaucracy is good, he said, when limited, but when unlimited and allowed to run rampant it can become a Frankenstein, thirsty to regulate everything, and hostile to individualism. Max Weber was a nationalist, but, like his father, also a liberal. He was, in other words, a national liberal, not a national socialist. Weber lived long enough to see, and to suffer the (to him) tragic defeat of Germany in 1918.

Among the strongest and most enduring institutions of Prussian government was its admired bureaucracy. Before the unification, Germany was a collection of numerous principalities, the strongest of which was Prussia in the Northeast of Germany whose capitol was Berlin. It is beyond the subject of this book to trace how and why the Kingdom of Prussia was first established—suffice it to say it was founded in 1701 and its first kaiser, Frederick the First, was crowned that year in Konigsberg. King Frederick wished his government to be staffed with competent people, not merely with the sons of noble families. He therefore established a civil service system that became an exemplary model for the rest of Europe and the world, and became a source of strength for the Prussian state, and continued to be a source of strength for generations, even up to the present time. This civil service became powerful, and won high respect from the general public because of its competence and priest-like dedication to duty. The Prussian civil service became a model imitated by other German states prior to unification in 1871, and was, of course, the model for the whole German nation after unification (accomplished by Prussia under leadership of Otto von Bismark). Despite Nazi attempts to politicize it, and more recent attempts to "democratize" it, the German civil service continues to enjoy very high status in West Germany today.

Many features of King Frederick's civil service remain benchmarks of today's West German civil service. He gave high status to officials; the duties of each official were spelled out, as were the relations of officials to one another in the hierarchy; some officials were appointed after competitive examinations; professorships corresponding to knowledge desirable in public administrators were set up in the universities; lower positions were filled by ex-soldiers. Although his system lacked a well defined statement concerning the salary, pension, and tenure rights of civil servants, these rights ultimately became ironclad features of the civil service, together with the right of immunity from suit for errors of duty.

Max Weber was among those who held the German civil service system in high regard and believed that it contributed greatly to Germany. He observed bureaucracies similar to the civil service bureaucracy functioning in other institutions of German life such as the army, the church, industry, and in fact wherever large scale operations were carried on. He turned his analytic attention to those bureaucracies and attempted to define how bureaucracy works and what it is. In his writings he describes a model (or ideal-type) bureaucracy. In so doing he did not intend to precisely describe every bureaucracy, any more than a sketch of a chair precisely mirrors every chair. His object was to define the term bureaucracy by conceiving a perfect, or ideal model of it, just as one might try to define a circle by fabricating in one's imagination a perfect circle to which all circles in nature are only an approximation.

Here, in broad strokes, is a quick sketch of Max Weber's ideal-type bureaucracy. To begin with, there is a hierarchy of positions and authority. Each position in that hierarchy is defined: boundary lines are established around its powers, duties, and area of action. An official with higher rank may supervise his subordinate, but it is not his duty to take over the work of his subordinate—their jobs are different. Subordinates render obedience not to the man but the office. Officials are subject to authority only with respect to their official duties, not their personal lives. Work is divided, and positions established and arranged in hierarchies, in such a way as to get the organization's work done as efficiently as possible. Each position is occupied by one who has specialized training in the work of that position. Written rules spell out the powers and duties of each position. For each level of position there is a fixed salary. Officials do not own their offices; their office is entirely separate from their private affairs; officials must account for their use of official property. Each position involves enough work to constitute the primary occupation of its holder. Merit and only merit governs appointment and promotion.

*Nonbureaucratic Organization:* Weber's ideal-type bureaucracy is easier to visualize when compared to its opposite. In nonbureaucratic administration people are generally appointed to positions because of pull or social rank, not merit. Officials are often unpaid; the office is used by its holder to extract graft or tribute. Decision making is highly personalized, case by case, not according to rules, and often amounts to bestowal of favors. In nonbureaucratic organizations it is hard to distinguish between the private affairs of the officeholder and his official affairs, the two are commingled—public and private money, public and private correspondence, public and private domicile, and so on.

*Advantages and Disadvantages of Bureaucratic Structure:* Nonbureaucratic organization may be sufficient for simple societies, but where large enterprises requiring coordination of many people exist, a bureaucratic form of organization may be indispensable. The advantages of bureaucratic organization are great. Bureaucracy can operate like a machine with great precision and speed in accordance with calculable rules, by experts without regard to persons, with a minimum of friction, and with continuity. Individuals may come and go, but the organization continues. However, these advantages are accompanied by some negative consequences. The extreme impersonality of Weber's ideal bureaucracy may come at the expense of morale and esprit de corps; emphasis on hierarchy may result in poor upward communications and therefore in the concealment of problems; the emphasis on rules (doing everything by the book) may lead to a suppression of creativity and to conformity and reluctance by officials to exercise judgment; emphasis on merit can have disruptive effects when management is unable to precisely explain the meaning of merit to those penalized for an alleged deficiency of it.

*Official Norms, Roles, Social Control, and Ranking:*  Returning to norms, roles, control, and ranking, let us glance at how they exhibit themselves in bureaucratic structures, disregarding temporarily from our view all unofficial and informal phenomena.

—OFFICIAL NORMS:  There are numerous official norms (commonly called standard operating procedures—SOPs) governing how organizational business is to be accomplished, and defining who does what. These SOPs enable the organization to carry on no matter who joins or leaves, and helps an organization deal rapidly with masses of people. Each problem is made to fall into a standard category to be dealt with routinely according to SOP.

—OFFICIAL ROLES:  Official roles in the form of detailed job descriptions are designed to subdivide the organization's work. These official roles, or job descriptions, are designed also to accomplish the organization's official goals by providing each official with a narrow but highly specialized job, avoiding friction by keeping each official to his well-defined sphere. Every member of the organization is replaceable by a new official who need only learn the specific skills of the specific job: the organization proceeds in an orderly fashion notwithstanding changes in personnel. Positions are arranged in a hierarchy, and all upward and downward communications theoretically flow along formal channels of authority.

—OFFICIAL CONTROL:  Official control is accomplished largely through the process of official employment contracts which are more or less assumed to exist when an official takes a job in the bureaucracy and agrees to do the work according to organizational SOP in exchange for a certain wage. The ultimate official control is the permanent threat to terminate the employment of those who fail to live up to the contract. Limited failures by an official to perform properly are generally met with limited official sanctions such as temporary suspension, letter of reprimand, or refusal to promote. Also, there are positive sanctions (rewards) for those who perform their contracted duties in an exemplary fashion—promotions, letters of commendation, and so forth.

—OFFICIAL RANKING:   All roles are staffed on the basis of merit, and for the sake of convenience these roles are divided into three broad categories: workers who do routine work; middle managers (functionaries) who apply policies from above to workers below; and policy makers who, as their label implies, make broad policies directing the organization toward its official goals.

*Theory versus Practice:*   It bears repeating that the preceding description of official norms, roles, control, and ranking in bureaucratic structures totally ignores unofficial and informal phenomena. In most real-world bureaucracies those informal aspects of organization have a direct modifying impact on the official (formal) structure, and have a lot to do with the deviations of every real-world bureaucracy from the ideal type.

## Riggs' Sala Model

Max Weber pictures for us a model or ideal-type bureaucratic organization. Fred W. Riggs in his fascinating book *Administration in Developing Countries,* picture for us a model of a different kind, the "sala model" as he calls it, which is a form of governmental organization commonly found in "transitional societies" midway in transition from primitive to advanced industrial. His model does not exactly correspond to any specific real-world society, but is a model roughly comparable to that which prevails in many transitional areas of the globe. People from the advanced industrial world who seek political or economic contacts in transitional societies, sometimes fail in their endeavor because they are baffled by the non-bureaucratic practices there. These practices are what Riggs summarizes with his sala model of organization.

Riggs takes *sala* from the Spanish language. In Latin America it means a government office. The word appears to be cognate to the French *salle,* used in Southeast Asia and numerous other parts of the French-influenced world with reference to government offices. Thus the word has wide currency in many transitional societies of Asia, Africa, and Latin America where administrative practices are followed roughly comparable to Riggs' model.

At first glance the sala model looks like Weber's ideal-type bureaucracy. But on deeper investigation it turns out to be only the facade of bureaucracy that covers the reality of nonbureaucratic organization. Riggs points out that transitional societies exhibit characteristics of both nonbureaucratic primitive ways (from whence they are emerging) and the bureaucratic ways (toward which they are moving). A transitional society may, for example, have a civil service law that provides, in the finest bureaucratic tradition, for appointments and promotions based on merit. But when one looks beneath the facade, beneath outward appearances, one finds the old primitive ways still practiced—positions given and promotions awarded as bestowals of favor to those who, because of social rank or wealth, are able to secure appointments and promotions largely without regard to other considerations.

One might object, "But our own civil service sometimes mocks the law." And, indeed, the differences between a transitional society and an advanced industrial society are only ones of degree. Neither has a perfect bureaucratic system, but advanced industrial societies come much nearer the bureaucratic ideal than transitional societies. In a transitional society one might expect to find officeholders treating the office they hold as if it were their personal property; they perform duties only for those who pay the established bribe. Well, we find payoffs in the United States, and we find some bureaus treated as the personal property of certain interests (the Civil Aeronautics Board is said to be suspiciously responsive to the ten or twelve leading airlines). But the difference is that in the United States and other Western advanced industrial bureaucratic societies, laws against bribery and use of public offices for private gain are not flouted to the same degree as such laws in transitional societies. Most public employees in advanced industrial bureaucratic societies are paid regular salaries and that is all they ordinarily get for their service. This is not at all the case in transitional societies, where practically no one takes a public job for its salary. It is widely accepted that public offices are taken primarily by people with little interest in serving the public, who expect to make a personal fortune (or at least a living) by giving public service to those who can pay the necessary bribe. In transitional societies going to work in the bureaucracy is like going into private business.

When one looks at the public bureaucracy of transitional societies one sees a wide gap between theory and practice. Many governments in such societies have all the outward trappings of a Weberian bureaucracy, yet almost everywhere the survivals of primitive practice are just beneath the surface. This can be very confusing to a Westerner trying to deal with bureaucrats in transitional societies as though they were dealing with bureaucrats of the Western type. It is a mistake to take at face value the government organization chart and civil service laws of a transitional society. A Westerner might walk into the central office of some government agency, look at its organization chart, and "see" that the agency is highly centralized. His response is to recommend decentralization—more field offices. But he has been misled; the chart bears small relation to reality— the agency is already highly decentralized. Official bureaucratic norms in the sala model are habitually disregarded; the official norm of obedience to superiors is especially ignored. Informal, unofficial norms allow everyone to engage individualistically in the practice of corruption, resulting in an extreme form of "decentralization." No matter how much the top officials may want centralization, it is almost futile for them to seek this by writing rules commanding obedience to superior authority, or by drawing organization charts showing centralization. None of this changes actual practice. Official bureaucratic norms are largely a facade in transitional societies; unofficial nonbureaucratic norms are often stronger. This extreme conflict of formal and informal is a central characteristic of the sala model.

## VARIOUS APPROACHES TO THE STUDY OF ORGANIZATION THEORY

Practically every public administration curriculum includes a course in what is called "organization theory." Organization theory is the study of theories about what an organization is; why organizations exist; their chief characteristics, especially as those characteristics are manifested in the public bureaucracy. For some, the study of organization theory is almost synonomous with the study of public administration, and unless kept under tight reign, an organization theory course can be as sweeping and all-encompassing as public administration itself.

In recent generations the study of public organizations (bureaucracy) in the United States has featured several basic approaches. These have more or less come upon the stage in chronological order, each having its moment of highest popularity, but none has displaced another, nor is any approach untainted by the others. Before about 1930 the "traditional," "scientific management," and "rational" approaches were dominant; since 1930 the "human relations," "behavioral," "decision-making," and "ecological" approaches have gained ascendancy.

### Traditional

The traditional (and earliest) emphasis in the modern study of organizations has been characterized by the study of separate organizations such as an army, a church, a school, or a hospital. Practitioners of this approach have typically paid little attention to the study of "organization" per se, or "administration," and have commonly viewed administration as something quite distinct from politics and policy-making (heresy today in most quarters) and tended to view administration as routine supervision, housekeeping functions, and record keeping.

## Scientific Management

Scientific management was a drive to make a science out of administration, to pinpoint the principles of scientific management, and apply those principles to both government and industry. This fascination with scientific management did not begin in political science departments or economics departments, nor anywhere in the social sciences. It sprang from the minds and hearts of civil engineers. As early as the 1880s and 1890s engineers attending annual meetings of the American Society of Mechanical Engineers heard papers contending that engineering principles could be applied to the working of human groups engaged in production. It was claimed that people working together are like the parts of a machine—in fact, they are a machine, and mechanical engineers should be interested in machines whether animate or inanimate.

Frederick Taylor became the symbol of scientific management. He was a member of the ASME and was chief engineer of the Midvale Iron Works where he had started as a simple worker. One cannot say Taylor discovered scientific management. Many besides Taylor were involved, but Taylor's fame lies in having been the first to gather up the many threads of thought on the subject and weave them into a single fabric in his book, *The Principles of Scientific Management*, first published in 1911.

Taylor's interest, and that of most early scientific management enthusiasts, was not public administration but rather industrial production, especially production at the workshop level. Their aim was to increase productivity, and their solution was to find the "one best way" of performing every task in the organization. Planning work in such a way as to employ that "one best way" is the manager's job; doing the work is the worker's job. The lessons in this for public administration were soon noted by others.

Time and motion studies were at the heart of Taylorism. Each task is divided into the motions necessary to complete it, these motions are then arranged in the most rational manner. The time required for each motion is carefully measured and totalled up to arrive at the time required for the whole job. Once time and motion studies had made production in the workshop efficient and economical, then the same principles should be applied to the relationships among workshops, and then among the next higher level, and so on up through the organization. But Taylorism focussed its main attention on the workshop; it was left to Henri Fayol to shift attention from the workshop; to the whole organization. In his major work, *Administration Industrielle et Generale*, presented in 1908 as a paper to the Congress of the Societe de l'Industrie Minerale, Fayol tells us that the first thing one does to rationalize an organization is establish the purpose of the organization; then you pinpoint the functions necessary to reach that goal; next, you subdivide those functions into certain subcategories; then further subdivide those subcategories into individual tasks; and finally, group these tasks in the one best way to get the job done economically and efficiently.

Through this tireless dividing, subdividing, and arranging the work of an organization, certain principles are said by Taylorites to emerge. One principle of organization, for example, is that hierarchical distinctions among members of an organization are the result of differences in their authority, while vertical distinctions result from differences of function. Unity of command, specialization of function, and span of control are other alleged principles of scientific management.

Taylorites were not wholly unaware of the human relations side of management, but they stressed physical structure and formal relationships. An organization is a machine they said, and a machine functions best when all parts are cooperating. Taylorites did not spend much time studying how to get psychological or spiritual cooperation among workers, they focussed on arranging for the best physical layout of workers and materials so that all could smoothly and efficiently cooperate. Motivation to cooperate was assumed; motivation was in their view bought with a pay check.

## Rational View

A third emphasis in the study of organizations is sometimes called the rational view (though, for obvious reasons, the advocates of other views would not want to be called "nonrational"). The term "rational" is apparently thought to be suitable for an approach emphasizing "principles" of public administration (assuming that administration were such a rational thing that it could be reduced to principles, and that all one has to do to be a good administrator is know and practice those principles). This approach also stresses the dichotomy of politics and administration, and assumes that "economy and efficiency" are the goals of all good administration. Subdivision of work, specialization of labor, hierarchical organization, and chain of command are thought by the rational school to be the keys to economy and efficiency. Had Max Weber's work been known in the United States during the heyday of this approach, he might have been one of its heros. Between the 1890s and the 1920s, when the rational view was ascendant, administration itself was viewed as consisting mainly of functions such as planning, organizing, staffing, directing, coordinating, reporting, and budgeting—all of which was summed up by the acronym POSDCORB.

Frank J. Goodnow, one of the first to teach political science courses comparable to modern courses in public administration, held that politics and administration are two distinct functions of government. This was the main principle of his book, aptly named *Politics and Administration*. To Goodnow administration is the execution of policies; politics, on the other hand, is the process of making those policies. Administrators should keep out of politics and policymaking, he said, and leave such things to the legislative branch.

Rationalism and Taylorism traveled on parallel tracks for about 50 years, from 1880 to 1930, and cross-fertilized each other. Soon political scientists were saying public administration should not only be separate from politics but should be scientific and governed by "principles" of good management. Thus in 1927 W. F. Willoughby published *Principles of Public Administration* which, as its title suggests, asserts that there are principles of administration. Furthermore, he insisted that the job of civil servants is analogous to that of professional managers in business, and the job of Congress is analogous to that of a board of directors—policymaking and administration are different activities carried on by different sets of people. He stressed the need for efficiency in administration which he said can be achieved by application of the "principles" of administration. Willoughby's book would have been the first college textbook in public administration if Leonard D. White had not beaten him there by publishing *Introduction to the Study of Public Administration* the year before. Both White and Willoughby accented the efficiency-principles theme, although White was mainly interested in personnel administration while Willoughby was mainly interested in budgetary reform.

The emphasis in all this was on correctness of organizational structure and on efficiencies to be gained therefrom, not on human relations, though it would be unjust to accuse the scientific management people and their counterparts in political science of being totally unaware of the need to treat people right if you want them to be efficient.

## Human Relations

The year 1932 might serve as a date to mark the dawn of human relations as an emphasis in modern formal study of organizations, for it was in that year that Elton Mayo and F. J. Roethlisberger reported the results of an experiment they had been conducting for the past five years at the Hawthorne plant of the Western Electric Company. The "discovery" resulting from this study is that people generally seem to work better and are more productive when their performance on the job is made the object of a great deal of flattering attention. The Hawthorne experiments were not originally designed with a human relations focus. On the contrary, they began with a Taylorite approach to find out what physiological conditions in the workshop affect production: heat, illumination, and so on. Mayo and Roethlisberger found, to their surprise, that production under conditions of this study often increased as the physical hardships of production worsened. The experimenters concluded that physical conditions in the workshop are sometimes less important than the attitudes people subjected to those conditions attach to them. In the case of workers who participated in the Hawthorne experiments, the fact that they were the object of attention apparently had an effect on their productivity exceeding the effect of physical variables in the workshop.

The human relations emphasis in administration has by now subdivided into numerous schools, each sounding a slightly different chord, but all sharing a common predilection for viewing organizations as social groups.

## Behavioral

The behavioral approach to the study of organizations was in some ways a rebellion against the traditional, rational, and scientific management approaches. The term "behavioralism" seems to have been introduced in 1925 by John B. Watson, a psychologist familiar with the thought of Sigmund Freud and perhaps weary of Freud's tendency to draw conclusions inadequately grounded on hard empirical evidence. Watson wanted a word to represent an empirical method in the study of human behavior.

Behavioralists see organizations as social systems, and are interested in both the formal and informal structure, and interactions between the two. By contrast, rationalists, and scientific management people are in the habit of confining their attention to the formal organization and physical layout of organizations. Behavioralists tend to be interested in organizations as living breathing collections of interacting people who are sometimes in conflict, sometimes in cooperation. Behavioralists are interested in the sociology and psychology of people in organizations, and do not want to be armchair philosophers about these things. They don't like to make any statements about how people behave in organizations unless they have watched that behavior and quantified their observations; they hate to rely on intuition for insights into how organizations actually work.

Behavioralists do not always completely disregard the contributions of "traditionalists," (as they like to call nearly everyone else) but have been known to dismiss much of it as unscientific philosophizing. Some of these traditionalists have been given inferiority complexes by the onslaught of behavioralism, but others will stand up and defend themselves, confess the use of intuition, admit to being armchair philosophers, confess to considerable ignorance of statistical and quantitative methods, confess to never mailing a questionnaire or holding a stop watch or counting anything, and will rashly say, "Look here, there are so many variables affecting how people in organizations behave, one can hardly begin to quantify them all." Some traditionalists insist that an informed and careful observer operating without great emphasis on statistical method may arrive at useful insights as valid and as important to research as any conclusions drawn by behavioralists who, while they are observing this or that detailed piece of human behavior seldom get around to drawing any conclusions about large matters because they never feel they have enough data about large matters to justify a "scientific" conclusion. Traditionalists insist they can spend a few months or years rummaging around an organization, say, an organization the size of the government of Brazil, and write a book of "impressions" which, while perhaps not absolutely leak proof, are better than the results one gets from a born-again behavioralist who, after he has brought his behavioralist sledge hammer down on a gnat, has little to show for the effort. So, at least, say some "traditionalists."

Behavioralists and traditionalists are sometimes prepared to see merit in each other's approaches, and it seems possible that the best approach to the study of organizations is one that includes both traditional and behavioral techniques.

### Decision-making

Another approach to the study of organizations is that which focusses on the "decision-making" process. This approach is a close cousin to the behavioral approach, for decision making is a species of the behavior in organizations, the species considered by those of this school to be the one most worthy of study by anyone wanting to get a clear understanding of an organization. Herbert A. Simon is one of the most notable advocates of the decision-making approach. His book, *Administrative Behavior*, sets forth the view that to understand an organization one has to look at who makes decisions in it, and what influences those decisions. Simon emphasizes that many forces enter into the decision-making process, some rational, many nonrational. If decision-making theory is correct, students of organizational behavior should be able to outline the true structure of an organization by tracing the flow of influences which result in major decisions.

### Ecological

Another approach to the study of organizations is sometimes called the ecological approach. An example of this may be found in the work of Fred W. Riggs, previously discussed. Ecology means the relationship of an organism to its environment. Thus, the ecological approach focusses on the effects of social, political, cultural, economic, and other environmental forces on organizations. Riggs' sala model shows how the administration of public agencies is affected by the social environment of transitional societies.

### ORGANIZING

Organizing as used here means the process of arranging and designing the formal structure of an organization: dividing work into individual positions, grouping positions, ranking positions and groups of positions, and establishing standard operating procedures. Of course, there are numerous ways to slice up work, and there is a wide choice of hierarchical arrangements and standard operating procedures. Just how all this is done in a particular organization depends on all sorts of things such as tradition, geography, and above all politics.

## Politics

Politics has a great deal to do with how an organization is formally structured. For example, in a university the question whether to combine sociologists and anthropologists into one academic department may depend on how well sociologists and anthropologists are getting along personally. Evidence of the importance of politics (using the term in its broadest sense) in determining the structure of organizations is everywhere.

Every piece of government structure in the United States, including every agency of the bureaucracy is the result of a political decision. National, state, and local legislative bodies, employing their rich political process, ordain and establish by law much of the bureaucratic structure, while at the same time leaving considerable authority to agencies themselves to structure things as they see fit. In their attempts to influence the organizing authority, agencies and subagencies within every bureaucracy are a seething mass of competitors for power, each wanting to expand its size, to develop new areas of responsibility, and to invade the territory of the other. Each jealously guards what it has like a dog with a bone, while at the same time snatching away as many other bones as its political teeth make possible. Warfare among agencies of the federal bureaucracy is energetic, colorful, and the subject of constant gossip in Washington. Presence of the United States Forest Service within the Department of Agriculture instead of the Department of the Interior can be traced largely to politics, as can the uniquely independent status of the United States Corps of Engineers within the Army and the Federal Bureau of Investigation within the Justice Department.

It could be argued that every organizational decision ever made by man on this planet is political, if by political one means influenced by the wishes of people. Formal organizational structure may represent nothing more than a temporary peace treaty among various centers of power contesting over who is going to control what. The highly political nature of the organizing process is illustrated by the proceedings of the American Constitutional Convention of 1787. One learns from the *Federalist Papers* and from other reports of those who attended the convention how it came to pass that the structure of the United States Government and the powers of its various branches and subdivisions were decided by compromise among powerful interests represented at the convention, the most famous example being the "Great Compromise" between the big states and the little states. Populous states wanted the representation of each state in Congress to mirror its population; little states, on the other hand, wanted each state's representation to be equal because each state was supposed to be the sovereign equal of every other state regardless of population. The convention nearly broke up over this volatile question until Benjamin Franklin proposed a congress comprised of two houses, one based on representation according to the formula demanded by big states (the House of Representatives) and the other based on the formula demanded by little states (the Senate).

Although duels between and among bureaucrats over organizational structure seldom make headlines like the great battles in Congress, still, these lesser bureaucratic battles in which nearly every civil servant sooner or later becomes a warrior, are identical in kind if not in magnitude to the greater struggles. Quite possibly politics is high (if not supreme) in the thinking of most administrators with a decision to make about organizational structure. Structure, after all, determines the chain of command, and the chain of command is the chain of power. A decision about structure is at bottom a decision about power, and all power decisions are political.

It bears repeating that many factors influence the wants, wishes, desires, and demands of people concerning organizational structure: geography, tradition, economics, and an endless variety of prejudices. While politics may be the hand that structures organizations, that hand is driven by many forces, some open and unvarnished, some veiled and enigmatic.

### Principles or Proverbs?

Until fairly recent times it was popular to believe that certain definite principles exist governing how organizations should be structured to achieve their goals economically and efficiently, and that these principles are no less valid for administration than the principle of gravitation for physics. But to Herbert A. Simon and others, these so-called principles did not appear very rational; they took delight in punching holes in them and calling them "proverbs."

One target was the so-called principle that an organization is more efficient when the number of people supervised by managers at each level is limited to a small number, say, seven or eight. Critics of this "span of control" principle argue that it contradicts another principle which says flat structures are generally more efficient than tall structures ("flat" meaning a small number of hierarchical levels, "tall" meaning numerous hierarchical levels). These principles often conflict because a flat structure in large organizations demands broad span of control, while narrow span of control often demands a tall structure. One cannot follow both principles in a large organization at the same time; they contradict.

Another so-called principle of organization is that no member of an organization should receive orders from more than one superior (the principle of "unity of command") and consequently organizations should be arranged hierarchically with a single top-to-bottom chain of command. Critics of this principle say it clashes with the so-called principle of "specialization of task" which says specialists such as lawyers or accountants should be assigned to separate task-specialized agencies: lawyers to a department of law under the attorney general, accountants in a finance office, and so on. If, for example, the legal counsel of a state university is going to take orders exclusively from the president of the university under the principle of unity of command, then obviously he cannot under the principle of specialization of task also be assigned to a department of law taking orders from the state attorney general. Yet the principle of specialization of task would seem to support the idea that all state legal services should be under the jurisdiction of the attorney general. The same problem affects other specialities: finance, planning, supply, and so on. Should a school accountant take orders as to technical accounting procedures from the principal of the school where he is an accountant, or from the school district's finance department? Either way is unsatisfactory, and a violation of one or another so-called principle.

Critics of these alleged principles also make light of the nebulous jargon with which they are stated. Take the term "specialization of task." What does it really mean? What, for example, does "specialization of task" say about organizing graduate education at a four-campus university? Does it say graduate education should be specialized geographically by campus, or specialized functionally on a university-wide basis? Geographic specialization gives you four graduate political science departments, one on each campus; functional specialization gives you one graduate political science department serving all campuses (political scientists on all campuses being members of one centralized department). But is there not specialization whichever way one goes? Some critics say the term "specialization of task" is absolutely meaningless, for no matter how an organization is structured, that structure constitutes some form or variety of specialization: if not by function, then by place, or by process, or by clientele, or by something.

One so-called principle of organization holds that an organization will be more efficient if it is structured by grouping workers according to either their (1) purpose; (2) process; (3) clientele; or (4) place. But critics of the principle point out that no matter how workers are grouped, the minute they are cast into one mold they lose the advantages of other molds. For instance, once grouped by place, they lose the advantage of being grouped by function. Furthermore, and perhaps more importantly, the words "purpose," "process," "clientele," and "place" are foggy. Is the United States Forest Service organized by purpose, process, clientele, or place? Actually it seems to be organized by all four: its purpose is to manage forests, its process is management of forests, its clientele are those who use the forests, and its place is the forest.

Critics of the so-called principles of organization, such as Herbert Simon, prefer to call those principles "proverbs." Like proverbs, they often come in contradictory pairs; the proverb "look before you leap" is contradicted by the proverb "he who hesitates is lost." However, it has been pointed out that proverbs can offer some degree of guidance so long as one is wary of their shortcomings. Proverbs, even when they come in contradictory pairs, serve to highlight some possible advantages or disadvantages of whatever course of action one might be contemplating: if one is contemplating a leap, then the proverb "look before you leap" is worthwhile, even if at the same time one remembers "he who hesitates is lost." And if one is contemplating a reduction in hierarchical levels in one's organization, it does no harm to think that "span of control" should be narrow, nor is there harm in remembering simultaneously the contrary principle that organizations work better when the number of hierarchical levels is few.

## SUMMARY

As many sociologists see it, wherever two or more people regularly interact they become a social organization. All social organizations, including, for example, public agencies, have four characteristics: a system of norms, a system of roles, a system for social control, and a ranking system. Informal norms, roles, social controls, and rankings are generated spontaneously and unwittingly by the members of every group. However, in formal organizations such as a bureaucracy, formal norms, roles, social controls, and ranking systems are established, but these do not obliterate the informal. Thus, every formal organization has within it or beside it informal structures which managers should not overlook, for the informal structures profoundly affect the formal.

Bureaucracy is one form of formal organization. Max Weber defined bureaucracy by describing how it functions when functioning perfectly. He gave us an ideal-type or perfect model bureaucracy. Many of his conceptions of bureaucracy were drawn from his observations of German public and private bureaucracy in the period between the unification of Germany in 1871 and the defeat of 1918. Weber's bureaucratic model does not correspond exactly to the way public business is executed anywhere in the real world, but does correspond more to practices in Western advanced industrial societies than to practices elsewhere.

Fred W. Riggs drew a model of how public business is transacted in transitional societies which are midway between primitive and advanced industrial societies. He called it the "sala model," sala meaning "government office" in numerous transitional societies with French or Spanish heritage. The sala model is characterized by an extreme contrast between a facade of bureaucratic practices that thinly masks the reality of still surviving primitive methods.

The study of organizations has been approached from various angles, some at sharp odds with others. Also the question about how to best "organize" an organization is the subject of hot debate. Just how the work of an organization is divided into positions, how positions are then grouped and ranked, and what standard operating procedures are established, depends on many forces such as tradition, geography, and above all politics. Whether there are any valid "principles" of organization is questionable.

## SUGGESTED READING

Bendix, Reinhard. *Max Weber: An Intellectual Portrait*, Garden City, New York: Doubleday, 1960.

Blau, Peter M., and Scott, Richard W. *Formal Organizations*. San Francisco: Chandler, 1962.

Blau, Peter. *The Dynamics of Bureaucracy*. Chicago: University of Chicago Press, 1955.

Etzioni, Amitai. *Modern Organizations*. Englewood Cliffs, New Jersey: Prentice-Hall, 1964.

*The Federalist*. New York: Putnam, 1888.

Fayol, Henri. *General and Industrial Management*. New York: Pitman Publishing Corporation, 1916.

Gerth, H. H., and Mills, C. Wright. *From Max Weber: Essays in Sociology*. New York: Oxford University Press, 1946.

Goodnow, Frank J. *Politics and Administration*. New York: Macmillan, 1914.

Heady, Ferrel. *Public Administration: A Comparative Perspective*. Englewood Cliffs, New Jersey: Prentice-Hall, 1966.

Katz, Daniel, and Kahn, Robert L. *The Social Psychology of Organizations*. New York: Wiley, 1966.

March, James G., ed. *Handbook of Organizations*. Chicago: Rand McNally, 1965.

March, James G., and Simon, Herbert A. *Organizations*. New York: John Wiley, 1958.

Mouzelis, Nicos P. *Organization and Bureaucracy: An Analysis of Modern Theories*. Chicago: Aldine, 1969.

Porter, Lyman; Lawler, Edward, and Hackman, J. Richard. *Behavior in Organizations.* New York: McGraw-Hill, 1975.

Presthus, Robert. *The Organizational Society.* New York: Alfred A. Knopf, 1962.

Riggs, Fred W. *Administration in Developing Countries.* Boston: Houghton Mifflin Co., 1964.

Roethlisberger, Fritz and Dickson, William. *Management and the Worker.* Cambridge: Harvard University Press, 1939.

Savage, Peter. "Optimism and Pessimism in Comparative Administration." *Public Administration Review,* July-August 1976, pp. 415–423.

Simon, Herbert A. *Administrative Behavior.* New York: Macmillan, 1947.

Taylor, Frederick W. *The Principles of Scientific Management.* New York: W. W. Norton & Co., Inc., 1967.

Weber, Max. *The Theory of Social and Economic Organization.* Edited by Talcott Parsons. New York: Free Press, 1964.

White, Leonard D. *Introduction to the Study of Public Administration.* New York: Macmillan Publishing Co., Inc., 1948.

Whyte, William H., Jr. *The Organization Man.* New York: Simon and Shuster, Inc., 1956.

Willoughby, W. F. *Principles of Public Administration.* Washington, D.C.: The Brookings Institution, 1927.

# Ebb and Flow of Central Power 4

# Ebb and Flow
# of Central Power    4

Centralization and decentralization are always rivals. Decentralization won a victory when English barons forced King John under threat of civil war to sign the Magna Charta in 1215. But in France, centralization triumphed under Louis XIV who during his reign kept rebellious French nobles dazzled and pacified with court ceremonies at Versailles. History is littered with giant conflicts between central and local power, not the least of which is the still-continuing American struggle over states' rights.

Battles over centralization are not restricted to kings and nations, but are a constant feature of the internal life of every organization, large and small. One finds it in the offices of public agencies and corporations where contests between big bosses and lesser bosses continue on a more or less permanent basis. Never does either centralization or decentralization win total victory. All organizations are partly centralized and partly decentralized—the question is never either-or.

Many, if not all, decisions with regard to structure are monuments to the victory of some people over others, or to the defeat of some by others. This seems emphatically true of decisions concerning centralization and decentralization where the question is, at core, whether power shall be held by persons nearer the center or by persons nearer the periphery. Power ebbs and flows between these poles. Arguments made in favor of decentralization or in favor of centralization tend, of course, to serve the self-interest of those who make the arguments; reason and logic are marshaled like platoons of infantry and thrown onto the battlefield to serve the ambitions of their masters. Perhaps there is no objective good or bad, no objective best or worst in organizational structure, for all questions concerning organizational structure are in a sense political. Every structural change in an organization benefits or injures some persons more than others, and it is this tangle of benefits and injuries that fuels controversies over how organizations should be structured. Nevertheless, it is worth reviewing some of the commonly heard arguments for or against centralization. Like

**71**

the so-called principles of public administration, they do offer guidance, though perhaps not absolutely reliable guidance.

## SOME ARGUMENTS FOR
## CENTRALIZATION AND CONSOLIDATION

For illustrative purposes let us talk for the moment about consolidation of local governments and centralization of their functions. We could use any number of other illustrations, say, consolidation of functions in a university or consolidation of functions in a hospital. But local government makes a fairly good illustrative vehicle because almost everybody is at least vaguely familiar with it.

### Economies of Size

Advocates of consolidation claim it often results in more efficient utilization of such things as equipment, physical plant, and personnel. A small town may buy a bulldozer and then discover the machine stands idle and rusting most of the time because there isn't enough bulldozer work to keep it or its operator fully utilized. Joint ownership of a bulldozer by ten villages, or consolidation of their bulldozing functions, or contracting with the county for bulldozer work would obviously be more sensible. The same would be true of countless other small scale functions all of which can be wasteful because they lack the critical size necessary to fully exploit equipment, buildings, and people.

Furthermore, small scale functions do not often reap the benefits of division of labor and specialization. A very small town may saddle its city manager (if it has one) with direct personal responsibility for everything in city hall—he may have to serve as his own city planner, city clerk, city budget officer, city engineer, and so on. Larger towns may have separate specialists in charge of those activities. A larger town reaps the benefits and therefore the economies of size—it is big enough to hire specialists and keep them busy and happy practicing their specialty and associating with others in the same specialty. The city manager himself can become a specialist in what he is supposed to be doing, and is not driven to being an amateur in all sorts of technical fields beyond his central expertise (which is to hire and coordinate other experts). The larger the city the more likely it can justify not only specialists but teams of specialists. Very large cities, for example, can afford a crime laboratory in the police department because there is enough call for its services to keep the team busy, thus improving the quality of police protection. Also, the larger the town the more easily it can launch systematic training programs for its employees. A two-officer police force is not likely to have a very sophisticated in-service training program for those two officers, but a fifty-person force may be able to schedule regular well-attended classes and hire professionals to teach them. By consolidating local governments or their functions, everything can be done on a larger scale, and with greater professional competence simply because size permits specialization and justifies acquisition of specialists.

The economies of scale extend, of course, to purchasing. Typewriters are cheaper by the dozen. Small purchasers reap none of the advantages of large scale buying. Furthermore, buying itself is a field of specialization —large scale purchasers can usually afford to hire purchasing experts who more than pay their own salary by shrewd buying.

Consolidation also has the alleged advantage of preventing duplication. Why heat twenty city halls, hire twenty mayors and twenty chiefs of police, and do everything by twenties when by consolidating twenty towns into one regional city (or some such thing) those twenty city governments with all their small-scale amateurism can be forged into one large enough to do things economically and expertly? But it is worth noting that beyond a certain size, economy and efficiency lose their positive correlation with scale and sometimes become negatively correlated with scale.

## Less Working at Cross Purposes

Because every human group tends to develop its own system of norms, roles, social control, and ranking it therefore by the same process develops a sense of self-identity which, with only the slightest encouragement, can become a sense of determined chauvanistic autonomy. While centralization tends to harness organizational subgroups to a common goal; decentralization on the contrary aids and abets the forces of subgroup chauvanism, gives subgroups maximum opportunity to assert their self-interest at the expense of the larger organizational interest, allows subgroups to work at cross purposes against one another, and makes coordination of effort all the more difficult. Those who would chart the organization's course and lay plans for the future often find those plans upset by unruly semiautonomous organizational subgroups. Centralization of authority in organizations minimizes the troublemaking potential of subgroups, decentralization maximizes it. These problems are all too evident in the relations of local governments with one another. Their separate wills-to-independence and wills-to-power complicate all attempts to bring order out of chaos in metropolitan areas. It is hard to get suburbs surrounding central cities to join with that central city and with one another in common goals, for example, a common metropolitan library system or a common sanitation system—each governmental entity clings to its life and its autonomy. Where centralization of urban services has occurred in metropolitan regions the results often richly justify the effort, but centralization is seldom achieved without bitter resistance from autonomy-loving locals. When achieved, conflict is often decreased and coordination made easier.

### Less At the Mercy of Pressure Groups

All agencies and all governments no matter how large are subject to the blandishments of pressure groups, but there is reason to believe that pressure groups find it more difficult to push around or capture a big unit of government than a small one. Pressure groups are therefore very often leagued with those fighting for decentralization. Local interest groups such as building contractors and neighborhood clubs seldom see any profit to themselves in proposals to consolidate local governments or local government functions. It is probably harder to push Los Angeles County around than to push, say, Beverly Hills around: thus, there would be many interests in Beverly Hills violently opposed to consolidation of that city or its functions with the county government.

### Less Confusing to the Public

American voters are saturated with decision making. They have more choices to make on election days than anyone could possibly handle intelligently without making a career of researching the merits of candidates and issues. Consolidation of local governments or local functions could drastically reduce the number of elected officials and economize demands on citizen attention.

The forgoing sample of alleged advantages to be gained by consolidating local governments or their functions are comparable to arguments favoring consolidation in other areas. Also, since consolidation means centralization, these same general arguments are commonly put forth in support of centralization of power within bureaucracies or within agencies such as universities. It is now frequently insisted that the most efficient and economical way to run a university is to centralize control of university "housekeeping functions" into the hands of computer-armed professionally trained administrators at the state capitol who (they claim) know how to run a tight ship.

## SOME ARGUMENTS AGAINST
## CENTRALIZATION AND CONSOLIDATION

### Democratic Virtues

The efficiency of a university may not mean the same thing to a professor as it does to a computer-armed economist at the state capitol, but efficiency is always measured according to the goals set by those who do the measuring. Efficiency in government need not necessarily be measured in terms of economical use of dollars, nor even in terms of how much professional expertise is possessed by employees. A two officer police force may have benefits for the community not measurable by their cost per unit, or by their expertise or lack of it. There is something, after all, to be said for the close, easy, and democratic relationship one so often finds between village officials and their fellow citizens. The ultimate efficiency of a "democratic" government is its democraticness, not its cost or technical skill. Of course, an intelligent and skillful public servant might serve the public better because of his or her talents, but this is not always true. There are intelligent scoundrels, and furthermore, intelligence itself and professional skill can create social distance between the public and its expert servants. Expertise leads to professionalism, professionalism can lead to elitism, and elitism by public servants can be hostile to government *of, by,* and *for* the people—it can become government of, by, and for the elite. No one is apt to be less democratic than an expert who thinks he knows best, and who resents intrusion by the public (or its representatives) into his area of expertness. Professionalization of the public service may make it more efficient in some ways, but in other ways may make it less efficient insofar as it sets the stage for (or practices) managerial fascism, democratic only in its pretensions.

Where democracy is a virtue, the possible democraticness of decentralized operations may be considered adequate compensation for the possible want of skill and economy of such operations. Defenders of local government are sometimes driven to despair by the undeniable charms of centralization—by the efficiencies to be gained, for example, through a metropolitan-wide government which suppresses preexisting local governments in the area; or by the efficiencies to be gained through transferring responsibility for school textbook selection and school curriculum determination to state boards of education; or by numerous other claimed advantages of centralization. Defenders of local government sometimes feel lost and beleaguered as they recite their claim that localism puts government closer to the people, makes government more democratic and more in line with what Abraham Lincoln had in mind when he spoke of government of, by, and for the people.

Defense of decentralization in the name of democracy is embarrassed by the fact that centralization and even dictatorship is also advanced in the name of democracy. The idea that government should be of, by, and for the people is not the exclusive property of pluralists or those who favor fragmentation of power as the best defense of freedom and popular rule. Both Adolf Hitler and Valdimir I. Lenin, for example, said they believed in government of, by, and for the people. Neither, however, had faith in the ability of the people to decide what is good for themselves without guidance from a political party composed of people who know best. The people, they said, need the same kind of direction children get from parents. This, by the way, is the attitude professionals and experts sometimes feel toward laymen, the attitude of professional public administrators, who, as a class, sometimes consider it a bad bargain to sacrifice efficiency for democracy. It was Mao Tse-tung's brooding suspicion of the uncommunist, elitist tendencies of professional bureaucrats that moved him to launch his cultural revolution of the 1960s and set millions of red guards rampaging against the establishment. Perhaps all struggles against elitism are futile; Robert Michels tells us there is an "iron law of oligarchy" and that it is as certain as the rising and setting sun that every organization will sooner or later be run by an oligarchy. Sociologists include, as we have been seen, social ranking as one of the characteristics of every social group, thus perhaps confirming Michels' iron law of oligarchy. Defenders of decentralization sometimes point to these hierarchical and centralizing tendencies in society and argue that affirmative action is needed to resist such tendencies if government is to be "of" the people and "by" the people as well as "for" the people.

In debates between supporters and opponents of federalism, one usually hears some mention of the utility of federalism as a preserver and stimulator of democratic virtues. One also generally hears some mention of the same thing when consolidations of cities, school districts, and other units of local government are under discussion. But one less often hears concern for the fate of democratic virtues when centralization versus decentralization of an administrative agency is debated. If a reduction in the number of Department of Agriculture field offices, for example, is proposed, or if consolidation of ten state colleges under one chancellor is suggested, one seldom hears a concern expressed whether to do such things constitutes a threat to civil liberty or a threat to the practice of democracy, although sometimes it is muttered that such consolidations make public access to the agency more difficult and formal, and in that sense less democratic.

However, there are a variety of complaints commonly voiced against administrative centralization. While some of these complaints can probably be classified as sour grapes from the mouths of middle managers who have seen power snatched away from them (or fear it) by the process of centralization, nevertheless, their unhappiness must itself be counted as a possible disadvantage of centralization.

## Too Much Staff Power

Middle level line managers commonly complain that centralization means putting power into the hands of staff people surrounding top managers. A top level manager, upon acquiring new responsibilities as a result of centralization, is forced to hand much of this new work load over to his staff because he himself has only limited time and knowledge. However, this process is said to be good for an organization because the specialized talents offered by staff experts surrounding the boss are profitable. Middle managers do not always see such great advantages in the centralization of staff functions; it leaves middle managers at the mercy of that centralized staff. A top manager might, for example, centralize purchasing under a purchasing officer on his personal staff, and prohibit subordinate line managers from making any purchase over $200 without permission of that purchasing officer. This, of course, would annoy subordinate line officers by taking a portion of their power, and this annoyance would flair every time the central purchasing officer turned down a line officer's request. Line officers may find their power chipped away by centralization of first one then another service, all done in the name of efficiency.

But logic seems to favor large scale purchasing by professional purchasing experts at the top of the agency rather than small scale purchasing by amateurs at the bottom. In fact, logic at first blush seems to favor centralization of most organizational housekeeping functions into the hands of professional staff people at the top: personnel, budgeting, accounting, payrolls, supply, stenographic services, reproduction, space control, mail, records, and so on. Often it is claimed that centralization of these staff services does not in any way diminish the power of line officers, but on the contrary, helps them do a better job by putting housekeeping functions into the hands of experts. Middle managers should, it is argued, favor centralizing staff functions if centralization makes the middle manager more efficient. But middle managers complain that when they lose control of staff services it does not make them more efficient—on the contrary it causes them to lose power over policymaking and policy execution when they lose power over staff services upon which those functions depend. Loss of staff means loss of power to do their essential function. Some of that power is lost to the top boss, but much of it is lost to staff officers who surround the top boss. Managers quickly learn how mythical is the myth that staff only advise. Staff people become the alto ego of the boss who usually lacks time and expertise to supervise his staff.

Line officers brood over the privileged position of top officers who constantly hover near the top boss—they are suspected of having Rasputin-like influence with him. Staff officers form a phalanx around the boss; line officers find that phalanx tough to crack. The fact that many of these top level staff officers are bright young people with high rank and high pay also contributes to the hositility middle managers feel toward central staff officers. When these young staff members come down from headquarters to inspect a line officer's operation, they are often received with mixed contempt and fear—fear because they are regarded as spies for the boss.

A line officer is at the mercy of those who control the staff services upon which he relies; staff officers can sabotage his operation if they see fit. Take something like office "space control." If a line officer doesn't have more or less final authority over, for example, the location and character of office space used by his organization, those who would injure him can do so by assigning him and his associates cramped and noisy offices below the dignity required by his operation. Or to use another example, if a line manager doesn't control the people who work in his mail room, then all sorts of shenanigans could be perpetrated against him. Mail clerks could serve as spies for his enemies, relaying intelligence about incoming and outgoing communications, and could deliberately mislay important mail. Or, to use still another example, a line officer who does not control his own stenographers and must rely on a centralized stenographic pool, could find himself unable to get reports out on time, or out neatly, or out correctly if the central stenographic pool is controlled by his enemies. Opportunities for central staff officers to wound uncooperative line officers are endless.

Thus, to repeat, centralization of staff services may result in centralization of policy—which could lead to what is known as "hidden management" (the use of power over staff services to affect policy). A fundamental question in every proposed centralization is whether the anticipated efficiencies are weightier than the resulting inefficiencies imposed on middle management. This question is being asked with increasing concern by university administrators as they watch the steady erosion of their powers through centralization of control over many important staff functions into the hands of agencies at the state capitol.

### Increased Job Satisfaction and Motivation

In the minds of many practitioners and professors of administration it has now become an established truth that people work more enthusiastically when they have something to say about what they are doing. Decentralization means putting decision-making authority lower in the organization; this is said to do a lot for morale of managers at those levels who receive new flexibility and semiautonomy. Furthermore, it is said to be easier for organizations to attract and retain energetic, initiative-taking middle managers if the job allows discretion and flexibility.

Furthermore, decentralization could enhance the job satisfaction of many nonmanagerial employees by curbing excessive job specialization. Curiously, while centralization is lauded for the specialization of labor it allows, decentralization is lauded for the specialization of labor it avoids. This oddity arises partly from the fact that while specialization makes jobs in mass production narrow and specialized and dreary beyond imagination, specialization makes certain other kinds of work more interesting. Many professional people such as doctors, lawyers, and teachers, do find joy in specialization. A political science professor seldom wants to be liable for teaching every course in the political science curriculum. He doesn't feel he can do a competent job trying to be an expert in everything. He wants to settle into one specialized area of political science such as public law, public administration, international relations, comparative government, American Government, or politics. He appreciates an opportunity to specialize, to feel he is truly on top his subject and in a position to advance the frontiers of knowledge in that sector, and to direct students and associate with other specialists. Specialization can be as satisfying to professionals as it is depressing to mass production workers. But even professionals can grow weary of their specialization and yearn to break away and explore new territory. Some professors of political science regret falling into specialization to the point where they find themselves teaching one specialized course over and over again. This is most likely to happen in large departments where narrow specialization is supportable.

Judges often like to specialize for the same reason as professors. But judges, like professors, grow weary of overspecialization, and, for example, after a decade of hearing nothing but juvenile cases or nothing but traffic cases, often desperately yearn for a change. Whether specialization is to be counted an advantage or a disadvantage depends very much on what kind of work is being subdivided into specialties, how specialized the work becomes, who is doing that work (some people don't want "job enlargement"), and how long and to what extent an individual is confined within his specialty.

Every advance toward centralization is generally paid for by some disadvantage, and likewise every move toward decentralization usually comes at a cost.

## ADMINISTRATIVE PLURALISM

Power in Western-style democracies is usually pluralistic, is shared, and exercised by numerous powerful semi-autonomous political, economic, and social groups elbowing each other for power. This "social pluralism" is reflected in the public bureaucracy; bureaucracy itself becomes pluralistic. Rather than being a neat hierarchy, it becomes under the influence of social pluralism a somewhat disintegrated collection of powerful semi-autonomous agencies. Social pluralism intensifies administrative pluralism. This is primarily because alliances are formed between individual agencies and the powerful clientele groups they serve—for example, the alliance between boards of medical examiners on the one hand and medical associations on the other. Sometimes it is hard to distinguish between the agency and the client: they look and act very much alike, they revolve around each other like the earth and the moon. Which is earth and which is moon sometimes evades detection.

All organization charts are deceiving. Certainly a glance at an organization chart of the federal bureaucracy can be deceiving. All lines of authority seem to converge on the President. Charts do not reveal the administrative pluralism beneath this orderly appearance. Charts do not show the hidden lines between, say, the Food and Drug Administration and drug industry executives. Casual observers might get a totally erroneous picture of presidential power over the federal bureaucracy by looking at an organization chart showing him at the top of a great heap of agencies. Many presidents have woefully lamented their inability to control the bureaucracy they are presumed to head.

Much administrative pluralism stems from the realities of American politics which demand that a president pay careful attention to the wishes of each agency's clientele when he appoints the chiefs of those agencies. An array of unacceptable appointments can arouse the anger of an array of well heeled, politically aggressive and alert pressure groups. Administrative pluralism stems, of course, from other causes as well, such as the inability of executives to control life-tenured subordinates in the classified civil service, but its most important cause is the adherence of policy level administrators to outside interests.

Pressure groups often agitate for administrative decentralization. When decision making is scattered among the various arms and legs of an organization, those extremities become inviting targets for pressure group assault. Client groups fight for as much autonomy in their favorite agencies as they can get. Many so-called "independent" agencies owe their independence in large part to the political efforts of interest groups: the Veterans Administration, for example, or the Civil Aeronautics Board.

American presidents often brood over how to control the wayward bureaucracy they are theoretically in charge of. Of course, a president can, when absolutely necessary, get his way with almost any piece of federal bureaucracy—he has various levers of power for dealing with them including the legal authority to fire any of several thousand senior policy making officials. But pushing those levers could be costly—the greater a subordinate's client group support, the more costly it is to touch him. It would be a mistake to overdraw presidential helplessness, but a more common error is to overestimate his ability to control the bureaucracy.

Administrative pluralism not only affects presidents. It also affects the ability of all administrators at whatever level to coordinate and control subordinates. The forces of social pluralism impose upon the bureaucracy a great deal of administrative decentralization. Whether this decentralization is good in any given situation, or whether it is bad, is debatable—the advantages and/or disadvantages are fundamentally the same whether decentralization is forced by pluralistic pressures, or whether deliberately and rationally devised.

## FEDERALISM

Federalism has been a great American experiment with decentralization, and for generations has spawned controversy between "federalists" and "antifederalists," which were the names of the first national political parties in the United States (federalists advocated strong central government; antifederalists favored emphasis on states' rights). Antifederalists were not really against federalism so much as against strong central power.

### Against Federalism

Although there are no significant moves afoot today to "abolish" states, it is discussed from time to time as an academic question. Modern pro- and antifederalist arguments are an interesting commentary on the competing virtues of centralized and decentralized power. Today the main argument against federalism by its critics is that decentralized authority isn't needed in the United States today as much as it was earlier. Circumstances which gave birth to federalism 200 years ago no longer prevail. Geography then almost demanded state sovereignty. Distances in the New World were awesome before the days of railroads, telephones, radio, television, automobiles, and airplanes. Most people, it is true, spoke the same language, had a roughly common culture and were bound together by the comradship of arms and the common struggle for independence. But distance and the complications of travel and communication made decentralized government the only sensible form of organization. The thirteen states spread along a thousand miles of coast line were separated by dense forests, rough country, and poor roads. Travel from, say, Georgia to the national capitol was an enormous journey to contemplate. Furthermore, the states had a long tradition of separateness and long experience as semiautonomous colonies under the British Crown. These freshly independent states naturally wanted to retain as much self-governing authority as possible, consistant with a national government endowed with sufficient powers to defend the union and look after various common concerns. It was wholly natural for the fathers to write a constitution which carefully and grudgingly listed the powers of the federal government while leaving everything else to the states. This scheme in effect conferred on states sovereign power to deal with most of the matters governments in those days had to deal with.

Critics of federalism tell us that most of these early justifications for federalism have now disappeared—once so far-flung, the nation is now tightly bound together by miracles of modern transportation and communication. Not only has state sovereignty lost its excuse for existence, but has become a downright annoyance, a barrier reef around which the federal ship of state must apprehensively navigate, and upon which more than one federal program has been dashed and wrecked. The great problems of America are no longer identifiable or solvable by individual states. Unemployment is not a Wyoming problem or a Kansas problem but is a national problem. It cannot be solved separately by New York or California; it must be attacked and solved nationally, even internationally. The same is true of problems pertaining to inflation, depression, poverty, juvenile delinquency, environment, and so on. Scarcely anything stops at a state line. Commerce, which the fathers so carefully classified as either interstate (under federal control) and intrastate (under state control), is now so completely national in character that the Supreme Court agonizes with every attempt to draw a line between intra and inter state commerce and is steadily finding it more thorny to exclude any kind of commerce from federal control. Even crime has become increasingly national in scope. It was once assumed that enactment of criminal law was the peculiar province of states, for it was within states that crimes were committed, and there that they were solved. A kidnapper in 1789 was not likely to run a thousand miles with a victim. Today criminal syndicates operating out of New York, Chicago, or Los Angeles conduct operations on a national scale rivaling General Motors in size, scale, and scope. What, ask the critics of federalism, is the sense of trying to draw lines between interstate and intrastate commerce—is it not hairsplitting forced upon us by the useless carcass of federalism? What, furthermore, is the sense of having 50 (sometimes 51) laws on every subject: fifty divorce laws, 50 marriage laws, 50 murder laws, and so on? Is there any jusitification for having a Pennsylvania, an Arizona, an Oregon? Why not let the national government in Washington, D.C. simply legislate for the nation in all matters except those the national government chooses to let the states handle? So runs the argument of many modern antifederalists.

### For Federalism

Profederalists say it's too soon for an autopsy on federalism. They admit that it might be more efficient to have one divorce law instead of 50, perhaps even more economical to dispense completely with the apparatus of 50 state governments. But federalism is, they contend, still alive and useful—old and crippled perhaps, feeble and bumbling perhaps, but still useful in some important ways too often forgotten by "efficiency-minded" managerial types. For example, consider the opportunities for self-government it affords; consider how important it is in a democracy for democratic procedures to be practiced and regularly exercised. Survival of democracy as a political system requires maximum opportunity for exercise of democratic procedures by ordinary citizens. Those opportunities not only educate citizens in the arts of self-government, but also encourage many people (including thousands who campaign for public office and other thousands who help them) to express themselves through the political structure. It is not possible for the computer boys to calculate the value of such opportunities when totaling up the efficiencies and inefficiencies of state government, or of the federal system.

Perhaps as important as this vast training school of self-government is the value of federalism as a bastion against tyrannical concentration of political power in the hands of czars in Washington, D.C. Friends of federalism cite this as another great immeasurable, incalculable plus of federalism beyond the ability of quantifiers to quantify. The fathers had this particular virtue of federalism very much in mind when they drafted the United States Constitution—the best defense against tyranny is division of power, setting power against power. The fathers fragmented power at numerous points in the structure of government—they divided it among three warring branches of government: executive, legislative, and judicial. The legislative branch was itself split into a house and a senate. Officers of each branch held terms of differing lengths and were chosen in different ways. The crown jewel of this system of fragmented power was federalism: the division of power by the constitution between the states and the central government. No one in the constitutional convention seemed greatly concerned about efficiency, except perhaps to see how little efficiency they could tolerate while at the same time having a central government able to coin money, field an army, and accomplish a few other necessary things. There was, on suspects, a deliberate effort to concoct a system of government whose powers were in such disarray that it would be next to impossible for anyone to gather enough of it together to become a tyrant. This plot against tyrannical plots has worked surprisingly well for nearly two hundred years, and it is only now, say the defenders of federalism, that we are on a toboggan slide toward the dictatorship of professional career administrators who in the name of efficiency inveigh against divided power, inveigh against decentralized power, and paint a picture of that shining tomorrow when clumsiness in government will be conquered and orderly instructions will flow uninterrupted from the center to the periphery.

In all fairness it must be pointed out that not all opponents of federalism can be classified as efficiency addicts with a pent-up longing for hierarchicalism. On the contrary, many antifederalists concede the value, and indeed champion the value of fragmented power as a defense against tyranny, but at the same time doubt whether federalism is as efficient for dividing power as social pluralism. Federalism and separation of powers can fail disasterously as dividers of power when the separate levels and/or branches of government are in the hands of the same political group.

Power which appears fragmented on an organization chart may in truth be a monolith of concentrated power—made so by the glue of political cohesion. Many antifederalists also insist that civil liberty and political freedom does not by any means depend solely on fragmentation of governmental power, it also depends on such things as a tradition of civil liberty and a high level of general education.

## Federalism Today

In the popular mind federalism is pictured as a kind of layer cake—central government on top, states on the bottom. Actually this is a grossly erroneous view. Not only does it fail to correspond with today's federalism, but it fails as a legal definition of federalism. Chief Justice Roger B. Taney liked the term "dual federalism;" to him (and to the court of his day) the federal system is a system of "dual sovereignty," the federal government being no more sovereign than any state. Both were sovereign, each within its own sphere of activity. The United States Constitution more or less draws a line between matters over which the central government is sovereign and the things over which the states are sovereign. The layer cake image, therefore, is perhaps legally false.

But it is also made false by the spread of federal power throughout the framework of supposed state authority. Through its financial power the central government has bought its way into the states. The picture now is more accurately that of a marble cake in which the stuff of federal power has seeped through and permeated the states. Money has become one of the most serpentine of all destroyers of American federalism. Federal grants to state and local governments have gone far toward addicting those governments to the federal money-drug. States now get about half their total revenue from federal sources. This leads to a kind of schizophrenia among recipients—on the one hand they want the "free" money, on the other hand they want autonomy and freedom from the moneylender. But this is contradictory, for moneylenders seldom give without some expectation of return. Federal grants-in-aid are given only to those governments which agree to follow a long list of federal regulations. Federal grants also usually require recipients to put up matching funds, thus paralyzing the freedom of those governments over a great swath of their budget.

The list of federal grant-in-aid programs is long. Many by-pass the states and go directly to local government, thus impairing the traditional parent-like role states have held in relation to their local governments. This has further weakened the rationale for having such a thing as state government. Federal grants going directly to local governments include money for such things as the Neighborhood Youth Corps, equal employment opportunity programs, community action programs, preschool education for deprived children, air pollution control, law enforcement assistance, water and sewer systems, and model cities.

With taxpayers near the point of rebellion, the temptation for states to take "free" federal money is great—especially great when that money is offered "no strings attached" and is called "general revenue sharing." The idea of giving money no strings attached was born (or at least earnestly discussed) during the John F. Kennedy administration, but did not become law until the Richard M. Nixon administration. Nixon, in signing his revenue-sharing bill, spoke glowingly of a "New Federalism" the plan would spawn. His phrase "New Federalism" was a modification of the term "Creative Federalism" Lyndon B. Johnson liked to use to describe the anticipated results of many new grant-in-aid programs enacted during his administration. Nixon, supposedly a conservative President, spoke of "power to the people" and the "new revolution" when describing how revenue sharing would revitalize and strengthen government at levels closest to the people.

Unfortunately, however, those levels closest to the people are not as close to the people as they sometimes seem, for they are not as closely covered by the press (especially not by the television press) as is the central government, and are therefore perhaps not really closer to the people than the federal government. Federal, general revenue-sharing funds have not always been disposed of by state and local governments with a great degree of ingenuity. Mississippi bought a $600,000 jet airplane for its governor; Burlington, Vermont spent $300,000 for uniforms for the city band. Lots of shiny, highly visible items of questionable necessity have been acquired with sharing funds (new police cars, new buildings), but it is uncertain whether revenue-sharing money has been used any more wisely by levels of government "closest to the people" than it would have been if spent by the national government.

Nor has general revenue sharing been completely without federal strings. Congress promptly attached the first string when it passed the bill: none of the money could be used for programs which discriminate by race or sex. No doubt the objective of such a proviso is laudable, but it suggests the possibility of future provisos—Congress is not likely to surrender power over the purse so lightly, and, of course, bureaucrats are always searching for new levers (money is a superb lever) with which to enforce their stream of regulations.

## SUMMARY

Every organization is partly centralized and partly decentralized—never totally one or the other. Centralizing forces are always in conflict with decentralizing forces. Advocates of centralization often argue that centralization is good when it consolidates inefficient small-scale operations into larger-scale operations able to reap the economies and efficiencies of size such as bulk purchasing and specialization of labor. Centralization is also said to aid coordination of organizational activity by curbing subgroup chauvanism, and by shielding those subgroups (or subagencies) from the blandishments of pressure groups. Consolidation and centralization of governments can reduce the number of elective officers and help focus public attention on the remaining officials.

Advocates of decentralization admit that many economies and efficiences can be gained through centralization but point out that those advantages are too often gained at the expense of other values. Efficiency in government is not necessarily measured in dollars; the ultimate efficiency of a democratic government is its democraticness. Decentralized government is, they say, closer to the people, and more democratic.

Middle managers often object to centralization within organizations when it deprives them of power to make and execute policy, and puts that power into the hands of staff officers surrounding top level managers. This loss of power and flexibility makes it difficult to attract energetic middle managers.

Social pluralism intensifies administrative pluralism—alliances are formed between individual agencies and the powerful clientele groups they serve.

Federalism has been a great American experiment with decentralization. However, today some of the early justifications for federalism have disappeared, and the critics of federalism say it is an archaic institution that serves only to complicate the solution of national problems. But defenders of federalism insist it affords opportunities for the practice of self-government, and continues to protect democratic institutions by fragmenting power. American federalism today is less than the federalism envisaged by the fathers of the United States Constitution. Federal power, including especially federal financial power, has intruded upon the autonomy of states. Whatever may be the value of federalism as a preserver of democratic virtues, its future seems cloudy in the age of central management.

## SUGGESTED READING

American Society for Public Administration. *The Administration of the New Federalism: Objectives and Issues.* Washington, D.C.: ASPA, 1973.

Beard, Charles A. *The Enduring Federalist.* Garden City: Doubleday & Co., 1948.

Colman, William G. *Cities, Suburbs, and States: Governing and Financing Urban America.* New York: The Free Press, 1975.

Elazer, Daniel J. *American Federalism: A View from the States.* New York: Thomas Y. Crowell, 1966.

Goldwin, Robert A., ed. *A Nation of States: Essays on the American Federal System.* Chicago: Rand McNally, 1974.

Michels, Robert. *Political Parties.* Glencoe: Free Press, 1949.

Porter, David O., and Olsen, Eugene A. "Some Critical Issues in Government Centralization and Decentralization." *Public Administration Review,* January-February 1976, pp. 72–84.

Reagan, Michael D. *The New Federalism.* New York: Oxford University Press, 1972.

Speer, Albert. *Inside the Third Reich.* New York: Macmillan, 1970.

"Symposium on General Revenue Sharing." *Public Administration Review,* March-April 1975, pp. 130–157.

*

# Down with Spoils? 5

# Down with Spoils? 5

## SPOILS

If one were to ask people at random on a street corner what they think of the spoils system for hiring civil servants, they might unanimously condemn it. (Could anything called "spoils" be good?). Although the spoils system is often thought to be a thing of the past, in truth, it is still robust in some states and localities, and even survives to a debatable extent at the federal level. Furthermore, we do not have to go back to Andrew Jackson to find defenders of the spoils system; it has modern advocates. Of course, they seldom use the term "spoils;" but more of that later.

### Jackson

Andrew Jackson, seventh president of the United States from 1829 to 1837, was the loudest and most outspoken early American advocate of spoils, though not the first to practice it. Jackson was something of a crude street-brawler type. As a young man he had gone to Tennessee where he grew up and won laurels in warfare with the Creek Indians. During the War of 1812 Jackson gained fame as a leader of savage military campaigns against Creeks and Seminoles who, unfortunately, had allied themselves with the British. General Jackson's style of leadership was somewhat lusty. He was not timid about hanging and shooting people. For example, in the Creek wars he executed several militiamen under his command to spur obedience, discipline, and enthusiasm among the other troops. In later years his will to insure obedience of subordinates was applied to the civil service.

As a consequence of his military exploits, Jackson became a national hero, and in 1828 was nominated for president by the recently formed Democratic Party, which then consisted of a collection of state politicians

91

seeking national power. Their election strategy was a demogogic appeal to the many propertyless voters recently enfranchized by abolition of property qualifications for voting, and an appeal to genuine left-liberal types of that era who favored a leveling down of political inequalities. A pugnacious, intolerant, unlearned frontiersman, General Andrew Jackson was an ideal leader for these democratic forces. John Q. Adams, the stiff and scrupulous Whig Party candidate was rejected by the electorate which voted for a personality more of its own image.

Jackson's presidency is usually remembered for two things that happened on his first day in office: (1) his inauguration speech in which he defended the spoils system, and (2) his inaugural ball attended by anyone who could crowd into the White House (a mob of people spilled food and drink on the floor, broke china, stood on chairs with muddy boots, and wiped their hands on the drapery).

In his inaugural address, Jackson defended the principle of rotation in office and said the duties of all public offices are plain and simple and no one has any more intrinsic right to official station than another. Jackson argued that the people had voted for reform when they elected him, and in order to have reform it was necessary to put reform-minded people in the bureaucracy: the people expect reform—they shall not be disappointed he said.

Identification of Jackson with the spoils system arises more from what he said than from what he did. Actually he did not remove many more people from office for political reasons, nor appoint many more new people to office for political reasons than had previous presidents. During his eight years in office he removed only about one employee out of six. And, if by defending the spoils system Jackson intended to increase his power for the purpose of bringing about democratic reforms, the result must have been disappointing. Evidence suggests that most of the power derived from his political appointments fell not to the President but to party professionals who had little interest in reform.

## Forces of Reform

Jackson's open advocacy of spoils drew public attention to this system of filling public offices, and every subsequent instance of misbehavior by a politically appointed civil servant attracted still more attention to the system, and encouraged reformers. It is not certain whether corruption associated with the spoils system increased in the half-century following Jackson's inauguration in 1828, or whether the press simply exposed it with greater ardor, or whether there was both more corruption and more exposure of it. In any case, the spoils system became a favorite target of reformers, and ultimately these reform efforts condensed into civil service reform leagues. The cry for reform grew shriller after the Civil War partly as a consequence of corruptions in the presidency of Ulysses S. Grant. Navy Department officials were receiving kickbacks from navy contractors; Interior Department officials were secretly collaborating with land speculators; the American minister to England lent his name to a mine swindle; the American minister to Brazil swindled a hundred thousand dollars from the Brazilian government and fled to Europe; there was skullduggery in the collection of customs duties at the ports of New York and New Orleans; officials of the Treasury Department were defrauding the government of millions of dollars in taxes collected on distilled whiskey; the Secretary of War was discovered selling Indian post-traderships. Corruption extended to state and local governments. Much of this activity was blamed, rightly or wrongly, on the spoils system.

Scandals and corruptions of the Ulysses S. Grant administration gave resolve and determination to reformers. President Rutherford B. Hayes, who succeeded Grant in 1877, worked hard to cleanse his party of corruption and to fulfill his pledge to reform the civil service. For example, he appointd Carl Schurz, the German-American political leader and well-known civil service reformer, to be Secretary of the Interior. But the Hayes administration itself was not without taint resulting in part from the President's determination to reward as richly as possible those who had helped him reach the presidency—spoils still had sway in civil service appointments. Civil service leagues were active in the cause of reform. Many writers connected with important newspapers and journals such as *The Nation* and *Harper's Weekly* also pressed for reform. But the reform efforts of President Hayes angered numerous important politicians such as Roscoe Conkling of New York who thought the so-called civil service reformers were really a group of self-seeking scoundrels masquerading as reformers. Conkling observed that when Dr. Samuel Johnson, the often quoted eighteenth-century English writer, defined patriotism as the last refuge of a scoundrel, he ignored the enormous possibilities of the word *reform.* Party regulars, self-styled "the Stalwarts," wanted to get back to old time spoils, and tried to put an end to reform.

The Republican Convention of 1880 featured a determined effort by Stalwarts to put up Grant for a third term, but the convention was not willing, and settled for the Ohio dark horse, General James A. Garfield, but threw a sop to Stalwarts by nominating Chester A. Arthur to the vice-presidency.

Garfield and Arthur were elected, and, as usual, patronage matters occupied much of the new President's time. After four months in office Garfield was still spending hours trying to satisfy countless demands of party workers for positions in the government. Not all could be satisfied. One dissatisfied office seeker was Charles J. Guiteau who had worked hard in the Stalwart camp for the nomination of Grant to a third term. However, once Garfield was nominated Guiteau changed his allegiance and worked for Garfield's election, and after the election he moved to

Washington in pursuit of a position in the Garfield administration. Guiteau particularly wanted an appointment as general consul to Paris. He hung around the State Department, bombarded the President with letters, and made numerous personal visits to the White House, where he was soon forbidden entrance by wary secretaries. He continued to haunt the State Department in pursuit of the Paris consulship. One day in May 1881 he was met in the hall by Secretary of State James G. Blaine who said to Guiteau, "Never bother me again about the Paris consulship so long as you live." Shortly thereafter Guiteau, depressed, unemployed, and hungry, decided to remove Garfield from office and clear the way for a Stalwart, Vice-President Arthur, to become president. On borrowed money he bought an elegant revolver and stalked the President. One day he read in the newspaper that Garfield would be leaving a Washington D.C. train station at 9:30 in the morning, July 2. Guiteau went to the station, managed to get close to the President, and shot him in the back just above the hip near the spine. Guiteau was apprehended on the spot and taken to jail. Garfield was felled, but did not die at once. He was moved to the White House, and lingered on in great pain through six weeks of the hottest summer weather.

The bullet that killed Garfield also killed the federal spoils system, although, like Garfield, it lingered on for a considerable time after the fatal blow. Garfield's lingering death made it appropriate for the press all the while to run editorials deploring the motives of Guiteau and condemning the spoils system. The assassination gave civil service reformers powerful new ammunition; they seized the opportunity, and pushed hard for a reform bill. Meanwhile, Arthur, once in the White House, became something of a reformer himself. In 1883 Congress passed, and Arthur signed, the Pendleton Civil Service Bill. The act created a civil service commission and required the commission to make rules for the appointment of civil servants on the basis of merit after competitive exams open to all. Money assessments on office holders for political purposes were prohibited. The act applied to only about 14,000 positions (roughly twelve percent of the total federal civil service in 1883), but provision was made to bring in other positions at the discretion of the President. Successive presidents have brought most positions under civil service rules. By 1940 approximately 700,000 out of 1,000,000 were in the classified service. Today more than 95 percent of all federal civil servants are under some kind of merit system.

## Criticism of Spoils

At the height of their attack, reformers blamed spoils for almost every evil in American life, even prostitution. But the central criticisms were (and are) alleged to be these. First, a spoils system discourages bright young people from embarking on careers in government employment—no matter how well they might do their jobs they could still be fired at any stage of life for purely political reasons. The low moral tone and poor reputation of a public service based on spoils also deters many from aspiring to associate themselves with it. Secondly, appointment of political favorites by the thousand to public office means filling the civil service with shifty and corrupt people because those are the type, it was (and is) commonly believed, who soil their hands with partisan politics. Thirdly, having only four years to exploit federal offices, those "shifty" people seek to reap financial benefit as rapidly as possible by influence peddling, favoritism, and outright graft. Fourthly, spoils is expensive owing to the loss of experienced employees and the cost of training new employees at the start of every new presidency. Fifthly, this vast turnover of personnel is costly in terms of administrative efficiency because each new presidency brings with it a sudden breakdown of administration as thousands leave and as other thousands take their place. Sixthly, a political appointee in the civil service is naturally going to be more responsive to those who got him the appointment than to those who are supposed to be his superiors in the administrative hierarchy. Thus, the spoils system blurs and confuses lines of administrative authority; an agency head may find himself in charge of a collection of unmanageable subordinates. Seventhly, a spoils system leads to creation of unnecessary jobs in the civil service; the more jobs the more patronage. Furthermore, political appointees are expected to do political work for their benefactors, which means they may not have time to be very useful civil servants. This fact results in pressure to create still more new positions to lighten the workload of political appointees. And finally, the spoils system is a terrible personal burden on a president. He is constantly besieged by faithful campaign workers for patronage jobs, as was Garfield by Guiteau. A president, especially a modern president, should give his time and attention to important international and domestic affairs, not to filling thousands of subpolicy-making positions. Of course, a president can subdelegate the work of finding jobs for office seekers, but it is understandably difficult for any politician, especially one so long in the political thicket as a president, to suddenly terminate all direct personal contact with his hundreds of fellow political workers. Not only is a president's time robbed by patronage seekers, but also his peace of mind— he can't please everybody, and this leads to sleepless nights. Nor is the dignity of the presidency enhanced by constant involvement in distribution of political plums. Many similar criticisms apply to state and local spoils systems.

## The Pendleton Act

When Congress embarked on an attempt to write civil service reform legislation it faced a legal annoyance: Congress could not give the President's constitutional power to appoint officers away to a civil service commission. The Constitution says the President shall appoint (albeit in some cases with advice and consent of the Senate). Therefore, in passing civil service reform legislation, Congress had to content itself with "permitting" the President and department heads to appoint according to the rules and regulations of the commission. It has usually been good politics for a president to favor a nonpartisan civil service and to do what he is "permitted" to do.

Several main provisions of the Pendleton Act are these. First, it created a bipartisan civil service commission of three members appointed by the President with consent of the Senate, and removable at any time by him. Second, the commission was directed to help the President prepare rules for the governance of the competitive civil service; the competitive civil service was to consist of those civil servants brought under the rules and regulations of the civil service commission. Third, the act permitted the President by executive order to bring positions into the competitive service which were previously outside, and likewise the President was permitted to remove any positions from the competitive service whenever he saw fit. Fourth, jobs in the competitive service were to be filled by persons who had passed open competitive examinations. Fifth, the exams were to be practical, meaning they were to test for skills required to do the job. Sixth, entry into the competitive civil service was to be by persons of any age, and they were to be allowed to enter at any grade or rank for which qualified. Seventh, the act forbade removals of employees for their refusal to contribute money or services to a political party.

## GROWTH OF THE MERIT SYSTEM

Although only ten percent of the civil service were brought into (or under) the merit system in 1883, successive presidents have added to that number. Today less than ten percent are *not* within one or another of the federal merit systems. In some ways it is remarkable how the scope of the federal merit system has grown. Almost every president has brought new groups of employees under merit procedures. Why? Certainly we must give some presidents such as Theodore Roosevelt (who was himself formerly a member of the United States Civil Service Commission) credit for believing in merit. Still, as Mark Twain said, each of us is like the moon, with a dark side, and some presidents, especially lame duck presidents at the end of their terms blanketed in thousands of patronage appointees to give them protection of the competitive service before they could be fired by a new administration. By 1900 almost half of all federal employees were under some form of merit system; by 1930 almost 80 percent; today over 90 percent.

It should be kept in mind that the general merit system administered by the Civil Service Commission is not the only federal merit system. Congress has provided special systems for several agencies such as the Atomic Energy Commission, the commissioned corps of the Public Health Service, the Federal Bureau of Investigation, the Foreign Service, the Library of Congress, the Panama Canal Company, the Tennessee Valley Authority, and the medical and nursing employees of the Veterans Administration.

The general principles and procedures laid down in the Pendleton Act of 1883 remain in effect today, although since 1883 there have been amendments to the original law, and numerous general policies have been developed by the Civil Service Commission governing personnel practices in the federal government.

Over two-thirds of the states have adopted statewide merit systems. Partly, this is the result of the example set by the federal government, and partly it is the result of the same antispoils forces that produced the federal merit system. The Social Security Act of 1940 shoved all states into adopting merit systems for at least those agencies administering federally supported social security programs—such was a condition which had to be met before a state could receive federal assistance for those programs. The dark continent of American public personnel practice is local government. Only a few local jurisdictions excel in the use of modern personnel practices—notably several large cities and counties. Some, however, carry on very laudable merit systems.

Something like 250,000 federal civilian employees are not under any congressionally authorized merit system. Not all are patronage jobs; most are Schedule B employees of the intelligence agencies (which, for practical reasons, cannot be bound by usual civil service rules), or are Schedule A seasonal employees. Only about 2,500 federal jobs are patronage positions which the President may fill on a purely political basis. About 500 of these are executive level posts including department secretaries, assistant secretaries, agency heads, and ambassadors. An additional 1,500 are aids, assistants, and confidential secretaries to high level policy-making officials.

When Dwight D. Eisenhower became president he felt it was necessary to increase the President's leverage over certain key merit system employees as a means of making the bureaucracy more responsive to his policies. He therefore ordered the aforesaid 1,500 positions put into a special category called Schedule C. Schedule C positions are exempted from the testing and qualifications requirements of the civil service merit system. A "plum book," as old Washington hands call it, is published from time to time by the House Post Office and Civil Service Committee listing all Schedule C positions.

## AN OVERVIEW OF THE FEDERAL PERSONNEL SYSTEM

As applied to the federal government the term "civil service" includes all appointive positions except those in the uniformed services. Appointive positions in Congress and in the judicial system are no less a part of the civil service than those in the executive branch. Only part of the civil service is within what is termed the "competitive service," meaning those positions filled by means of competitive examinations under provisions of the civil service act. Although the term "classified service" means the same thing as "competitive service," we will use competitive service because classified is too easily confused with other common usages of the word—security classifications, and the like.

Appointive positions not in the competitive service are said to be in the "excepted service," sometimes called the "unclassified service." The excepted service includes, for example, all the positions to which appointments are made by nomination for confirmation by the Senate, such as ambassadors, department secretaries, and other high level executives.

In recent years the federal government has employed about three million civilians distributed among the various segments of the government as shown, by proportions, below:

| | |
|---|---|
| Legislative Branch | .0129 |
| Judicial Branch | .0034 |
| Executive Office of the President | .0006 |
| Agriculture Department | .0366 |
| Commerce Department | .0126 |
| Defense Department | .3641 |
| Health, Education and Welfare Department | .0503 |
| Housing and Urban Development Department | .0058 |
| Interior Department | .0257 |
| Justice Department | .0175 |
| Labor Department | .0048 |
| State Department | .0112 |
| Transportation Department | .0254 |
| Treasury Department | .0420 |
| General Services Administration | .0136 |
| U.S. Postal Service | .2456 |
| Veterans Administration | .0736 |
| 41 Other Agencies Taken Together | .0534 |

Among the three levels of government in the United States, the federal government is by no means the largest civilian employer. Only about twenty percent of all civil servants work for the federal government while state and local governments account for 80 percent (twenty percent work for state governments and 60 percent for local governments). All tolled, some 15,000,000 civilians work for all governments in the United States, and another 3,000,000 are uniformed military persons bringing the total number of government employees to around 18,000,000, or about twenty percent of the employed persons in the United States. Every fifth employed person works for some kind of government in the United States.

## Classification

All positions in the federal competitive service are "classified," that is, they are collected into classes sufficiently similar to warrant similar treatment in personnel and pay administration. Classes of positions are in turn put into ranks or "grades." A grade includes all classes of positions which, although different with respect to kinds or subject matter of work, are sufficiently equivalent in level of difficulty, level of responsibility, and level of qualification to warrant their inclusion within one range of basic pay in the general schedule. There are eighteen grades in the general competitive service GS–1 (meaning general service grade 1) is lowest, GS–18 highest. Grade GS–1 positions are those in which the duties are performed under immediate supervision, with little or no latitude for exercise of independent judgment, the simplest routine work. Other grades range up from there. Naturally, before any job can be put into a pay grade, the job has to be studied to determine what it involves.

The primary functions of job classification are: (1) to insure equal pay for equal work, preventing favorites from being given more than the job deserves (job titles are also standarized insofar as possible for the same reason), and (2) to provide information about jobs and classes of jobs so that reliable appointment and promotion examinations can be drafted. Within each GS grade there are ten pay steps. An employee advances one step every year providing his work is of an acceptable level of competence as determined by the agency head. But to be advanced from one GS grade level to another requires being hired or promoted to a different or higher level job. Rank (that is, GS grade level) goes with the job. One has rank so long as one has a job that calls for the particular rank. If, because of a personnel cut back (called a reduction in force—RIF), a GS–11 loses his or her federal job, but manages to find another federal job, that person's rank in the new job depends on the rank assigned to the new job and has nothing to do with rank in the old job. Although the employees dismissed because of an RIF have certain priority rights to other jobs of equal rank, rank is not automatically carried over from one job to another as it is in the uniformed services. A captain in the army remains a captain no matter what his assignment, although, of course, there are duties appropriate to the rank of captain.

## Recruitment Process in the General Service

When a vacancy exists (or is anticipated) in a position, announcements are posted describing the position and stating when and where the examination may be taken by applicants. The exam may be "assembled" or "unassembled." An unassembled exam is really not so much an examination as it is preparation of a dossier: the applicant submits evidence of his or her education and experience qualifying him or her for the job. Exams for higher level positions are characteristically unassembled because of the impracticality of designing an exam for such positions. However, for lower level positions, which tend to be much more specific, assembled examinations are used, meaning the sort of exam students are accustomed to, a pencil and paper test, supplemented where appropriate by tests of practical skill. For example, a candidate for a typing job has to demonstrate typing skill.

Seventy points is a passing grade on an assembled examination. Veterans who pass the examination are given an extra five points; disabled veterans, ten points. This is called "veteran preference." The names of all applicants who passed the test are then arranged on a register according to their examination scores.

When a position vacancy occurs in an agency, the personnel office refers the top three names on the register to the official with authority to hire. This is known as the "rule of three." The three who are referred are said to be "certified." The hiring official may then choose one of the three certified candidates to fill the vacancy, and may base his selection on almost any reasonable criteria. The two candidates not chosen remain at the top of the register and are certified over and over again until they are hired or until the register expires.

This process of recruitment and selection is governed by statutes and by the rules, regulations, and policies drafted by the Civil Service Commission and promulgated by presidential executive order. All other federal personnel practices—promotion, dismissal, retirement, and so on—are similarly governed by statutes and rules. The Civil Service Commission plays a central guiding role in the whole merit system, particularly with regard to the general classified service.

## The Senior Federal Service Today

The law concerning federal appointments begins, obviously, with the United States Constitution which says the President "shall nominate, and by and with the advice and consent of the Senate, shall appoint ambassadors, other public ministers and consuls, judges of the Supreme Court, and all other officers of the United States, whose appointments are not herein otherwise provided for, and which shall be established by law: but the

Congress may by law vest the appointment of such inferior officers, as they think proper, in the President alone, in the courts of law, or in the heads of departments" (Article II, Section 2). By operation of this section, Congress determines which appointments (other than ambassadors, ministers, consuls, and supreme court judges) require consent of the Senate. Congress also decides which officers may be appointed by the President alone and which must be appointed by department heads. Congress has decided that most GS–16s, 17s, and 18s are to be appointed by department heads in accordance with civil service laws and regulations. But obviously, a president has influence over his department heads who exercise this power.

*Noncareer Executive Assignments:* When the President or the Civil Service Commission believes a position should be excepted from a career status and made subject to presidential appointment, the President may, under certain standards, except the position by executive order. These excepted GS–16s, 17s, and 18s are called noncareer executive assignments; they are not subject to merit staffing procedures. In order to put a position into that category, it must be demonstrated that the person holding the position would be deeply involved in the advocacy of administration programs or would participate significantly in the determination of major political policies, or would serve principally as a personal assistant or adviser to a presidential appointee or other key political figure.

These are not Schedule C appointments. A Schedule C appointment is to any position in a grade lower than GS–16, 17, or 18 which is excepted from the competitive service for reasons similar to those just described for noncareer executive assignment positions in the supergrades.

To appoint either a Schedule C person or a noncareer executive assignment person it is not necessary to pay much attention to competitive requirements. However, in the case of GS–16s, 17s, and 18s it is necessary to demonstrate to the Civil Service Commission that the candidate is at least eligible for the position to which he is to be appointed. In practice the only criteria of eligibility is the candidate's previous salary. If it was within a few thousand dollars of that for the grade to which he is being appointed then he is eligible, otherwise not. Apparently the commission is rather strict in its interpretation of a "few thousand dollars" which means probably within three or four thousand dollars. It is permissible to have made a lot more, but not a lot less than the salary for the position. Thus, a $20,000 a year professor is not eligible for appointment to a $50,000 a year noncareer executive supergrade position. There is no such monetary condition of eligibility for Schedule C positions, nor for a series of positions above GS–18 which are completely outside the competitive service called "executive levels," which we will discuss later.

A noncareer executive assignment position in one of the supergrades GS–16, 17, or 18 carries with it almost no protection against arbitrary dismissal. It is a risky position; there are no appeal rights. Nor is any advanced written notice required; they can be removed at any time.

*Executive Levels:* Coming back to that important layer of positions called the executive levels, these are a group of high policy-making patronage positions above the competitive service. They are arranged in five pay levels, the lowest of which (level 5) equals the pay of GS–18s and the remaining four levels (4, 3, 2, and 1) are each progressively higher paid. Executive level 1 is reserved exclusively for cabinet officers, that is, for secretaries of departments such as the secretary of agriculture or the secretary of commerce. Each of the other executive levels has within it a collection of diverse positions, but in general they can be categorized as follows. Level 2s are generally deputies to cabinet officers or are heads of independent agencies. Level 3s are usually undersecretaries in cabinet departments or in independent agencies. Level 4s are commonly assistant secretaries of departments, deputy directors of independent agencies, or administrators of bureaus. Level 5s are commonly deputies to administrators of bureaus. Each specific position is placed by statute (the executive level act) in one or another level with the exception of a block of a dozen or so given to the White House for the President to fill as he pleases (with assistants and secretaries to the President), and another block of several dozen also given to the President for use more or less where and how he sees fit in the executive branch outside the White House. All executive level positions are, to repeat, outside the competitive service and represent the political high command of the executive branch.

Advocates of a senior civil service corps with rank-in-corps generally contend that many of these positions held by executive level personnel should be included within the senior civil service corps, and that the so-called political high command should be more or less restricted to executive levels 1 and 2. This, of course, is hotly objected to by those who say the President needs more, not less, control of policy-making positions in the executive branch.

## RANK-IN-CORPS SENIOR CIVIL SERVICE IDEA

In the army a lieutenant is a lieutenant whatever his job, an he is still a lieutenant even if momentarily assigned to no duty whatsoever. So it is in all the uniformed services. One holds military rank in the corps regardless of job assignment; one does not hold rank by virtue of holding a particular job, as civil servants do.

In recent times it has been proposed that the top three grades of the United States federal competitive service, plus most executive level positions, be converted from the rank-in-job to the rank-in-corps system—that we have a corps of senior civil servants who, like the generals and admirals of the armed forces, hold their rank as they are shifted from job to job. Furthermore, it is said we need a corps of senior civil servants who are deliberately moved about from one assignment to another to make them generalists, and that this corps of generalists should be constantly on tap for assignment wherever they are needed. This idea was proposed by the Commission on Organization of the Executive Branch of Government in 1955 (the so-called Hoover Commission), and has been heard repeatedly since then.

Several steps have been taken to make senior generalists out of senior specialists. We have already touched on this in our discussion of the Federal Executive Institute and of the federal executive development program. The federal executive assignment system and the federal executive inventory are two other devices that should be mentioned here. The inventory is simply a list of upper crust federal competitive service executives with details of their experience, skills, education, special interests, and other background information kept by the United States Civil Service Commission. This, when taken together with increased emphasis on mobility of assignment in the senior grades, begins to resemble a "corps." However, rank is still in position, and senior civil servants can be demoted, or separated from their employment completely, when and if their positon disappears.

## Advantages of a Senior Civil Service Corps

The senior civil service corps idea is said to have a collection of advantages in addition to those mentioned above. It is said the corps would provide a politically neutral layer of civil servants immediately below the political high command. However, it is a rare president who wants "neutral" policymakers in his administration.

Another alleged advantage of a senior civil service corps is that it would attract more good people into the civil service because people contemplating such a career would know they could rise in the competitive service to positions just beneath the political top command. Furthermore, this knowledge would help keep ambitious competitive service people in the public service, and deter them from wandering off into high private sector positions. Also, it is said a senior civil service corps would have very high prestige, high recognition, and high pay, and this would help attract and keep top notch senior level people. Furthermore, the rank-in-corps principle would encourage good people to aspire to top positions—it is said many competent people shy away from top positions because they know the higher they go the riskier it becomes. More than one GS–16, 17, or 18 has found himself being eased out of his job and separated from the service because he disagrees with policies of the administration then in power.

## Criticisms of the Senior Civil Service Corps Idea

The proposal to have a senior civil service corps with rank-in-corps is not without its critics. First, as mentioned above, a president needs to control more than the heads of departments to manage the bureaucracy. It is not certain how deep into the bureaucracy presidential power must run to give him adequate control, perhaps considerably deeper than is now allowed; most, if not all, previous presidents of the United States might agree with this. A good argument could be made for putting all GS–15, 16, 17, and 18 positions under patronage.

The idea of having a politically neutral senior civil service corps in control of most policy positions strikes some people as bad not only because a president needs to control his own administration, but also because good management cannot be indifferent to objectives, cannot be neutral. The idea that neutral civil servants are better than committed civil servants is, they say, false. Nor is neutrality a good quality in policymakers. Should a doctor be neutral as between health and ill-health; should a teacher be neutral between truth and falsehood; should a welfare officer be neutral between welfare and the lack of welfare? Policy makers must make decisions, and good decision-making demands commitment to good goals. An administrator with no biases, no goals, is a poor administrator say the critics of neutrality. Therefore they say the idea of having a whole corps of senior civil servants with a virtual monopoly of policy-making positions, whose ideal is neutrality, cannot be a good idea.

However, defenders of the senior civil service corps idea answer that the cost of "political" involvement by senior civil servants is greater than its advantages: the cost consists of high turnover in the senior ranks, and a continual atmosphere of mutual suspicion and strife among the senior officials. Secondly, the defenders of a senior civil service corps say continuity in office and experience are more important than lateral entry.

Many GS–16s, 17s, and 18s look askance at the senior civil service corps idea. They wonder whether they would all be invited to join the corps, and if not, by what method members would be chosen. Secondly, many wonder whether they would want to be members of the corps even if chosen. If the basic idea of the corps is to generate a group of top executives with broad experience in many agencies who could be used anywhere in the civil service when and where they were needed, membership in the corps could involve frequent transfers. Thirdly, many GS–16s, 17s, and 18s are accustomed to their present mode of life, are pleased with their present position, like to work in their specialty, and do not want a reform that would upset all this.

Many people have other reservations about the senior civil service corps idea. One criticism is that the corps might discourage lateral entry into high policy-making posts, and this would discourage the introduction of new blood and new ideas at policy-making levels. Furthermore, the whole idea of a senior corps seems elitist and undemocratic to many. Not only would the corps develop a sense of superiority and a tendency toward intolerance of lay opinion, but also the corps might be difficult to control because its members would be tenured and at the same time have a monopoly of policy-making positions that should be responsive to the President.

Many countries around the world whose democratic traditions are less fixed than our own have used a kind of class system for filling senior administrative posts. The class system reserves the highest merit system posts to those who belong to a group of civil servants who make their whole career in that one class. Young people enter the senior class and move from rank to rank within that class, just as young people in the military might enter the officer class and progress from rank to rank, while others might enter the enlisted class and make their career in that class.

There is much to be said for cultivating a class of civil servants whose entire career is aimed at developing executive skill. Those who advocate a senior civil service corps in the United States employ many of the same arguments used in some foreign countries to defend their civil service class system. Likewise, critics of the corps idea are motivated by some of the same feelings that motivate critics of the class system.

## THE UNITED STATES CIVIL SERVICE COMMISSION

The original United States Civil Service Commission in 1883 was composed of three members and remains so today; a chairman, vice-chairman, and one other, all appointed by the President with consent of the Senate. No more than two commissioners may belong to the same political party—the intent being to maintain a nonpartisan commission. Commissioners serve at the pleasure of the President who may remove any of them at will, but commissioners are by statute given six-year terms; this means they have a right to serve six years unless fired by the President before their term ends. The purpose of the statutory six-year term is to discourage presidential manipulation of terms. It is hoped that if commissioners serve six-year terms, and if terms are overlapping, as they are required by law to be, then no president can pack the commission, at least not suddenly. This protection against presidential power is in some ways fanciful, for any president who really wants to get rid of a commissioner without firing him can no doubt arrange to have that commissioner presented with attractive offers he cannot refuse elsewhere. However, commissioners in recent years have characteristically served long periods, some even exceeding six years, and presidents have gingerly tried to avoid doing anything overt that would leave them open to the charge of attempting to improperly manipulate the commission or corrupt the merit system. Undoubtedly, the strength and integrity of the merit system depends on public support of that system, and the United States Civil Service Commission has benefited by such public support.

The chairman of the commission is named by the President, and this gives the President further influence over the commission. The chairman serves as chief administrator of the commission, but the commission also employs an executive director who plays a very prominent leadership role in federal personnel administration by virtue of his job.

There is, of course, more to the commission than its three commissioners and its executive director. Numerous other officials and employees (roughly 10,000) compose the many bureaus, offices, and programs of the commission, including the following subdivisions listed here to show some of the commission's major interests and activities.

> Office of Federal Equal Employment Opportunity
> Spanish Speaking Program
> Federal Women's Program
> Office of Labor-Management Relations
> Office of Public Affairs
> Appeals Examining Office
> Office of Hearing Examiners
> Office of Incentive Systems
> Bureau of Policies and Standards
> Bureau of Recruiting and Examining
> Bureau of Executive Manpower
> Bureau of Personnel Investigations
> Bureau of Training
> Bureau of Retirement, Insurance and Occupational Health
> Bureau of Personnel Management Evaluation
> Bureau of Manpower Information Systems
> Bureau of Management Services
> Bureau of Intergovernmental Personnel Programs

## The Commission's Major Functions

In the early years the Civil Service Commission kept itself busy with classifying positions, designing and administering examinations, maintaining registers of eligibles, certifying candidates to hiring agencies, and hearing complaints. Today the commission has largely quit doing most of that work itself, having turned it over to the agencies. Now the commission holds itself more or less above the scene, confining itself largely to making rules and policies for agencies to follow, and watching over the agencies to see that they adhere to correct procedures and standards. Agencies hire, promote, fire, and classify, by Civil Service Commission rules found in the *Federal Personnel Manual*. The commission conducts inspections of personnel management in the agencies; however, these inspections are not carried on quite like a Saturday morning barracks inspection in the infantry. Far from lording it over the agencies, the commission sees itself as lacking political clout and goes about the business of inspecting agencies almost as if it were an invited guest. The commission is more likely to bargain than to command. If it spots imperfections in agency personnel practices the commission invites offending officials to sit down and talk the matter over. Inspectors rarely pull unannounced inspections. On the contrary, inspectors are often permanently assigned to agencies, have their offices right within the agency, and are frequently very well acquainted with the people they inspect. Inspectors normally give agency officials an itinerary showing when and where inspections will occur. There may be frenzied preparation for it, but it does not come as a bolt from the blue.

This seeming timidity not only mirrors the commission's weakness versus the agencies, but also reflects the commission's view that it is not supposed to be an enemy, but an ally of the bureaucracy. The commission does not wish to work against the President, but for the President—commissioners are, to repeat, appointed and removable by the President, and it is the President who promulgates commission rules. The Civil Service Commission is the President's personnel office, and does not see itself as a competitor with the President, nor as a competitior with the agencies. It sees itself as a management consulting "firm" for the federal government, giving service more than acting as cop. In practice the commission's power is more political than legal—no one wants to be accused of corrupting the merit system, certainly not the President. The commission has the ear of the President, or at least of the Office of Management and Budget which assists the President in making his budget, and which therefore has leverage with agency officials.

The commission does not seek to embarrass agency officials by publishing the reports of its inspections. These reports have in the past customarily been kept secret, and have the status of interoffice memorandums insofar as the Freedom of Information Act is concerned. The commission feels the exchange of views between the agency and the commission will be more candid, honest, and productive if both parties are assured that the reports are not going to be published in the newspapers. Of course, this makes these reports all the more enticing for newspapers to ferret out and expose.

The Civil Service Commission does have regulatory power, and does have the power to withdraw various personnel functions from offending agencies. But the commission prefers to work through consultation and persuasion, prefers to behave like a consulting firm rather than as a regulatory agency. This attitude is almost forced on it by the small size of its staff and annual appropriations. The commission simply does not have enough manpower to repossess any significant part of the vast personnel functions now execised directly by federal agencies. The commission is overextended even under its current policy of turning as many personnel functions as possible over to the agencies and has little choice but to confine itself largely to inspecting agencies. Even its inspection duties are more than the commission can comfortably bear. Current plans call for turning those critical functions over to the agencies so that agencies will inspect themselves; the Civil Service Commission will ultimately confine itself to teaching agencies how to inspect themselves and will then inspect only the self-inspections.

Among its other duties, the Civil Service Commission is a "court." The board of appeals and review adjudicates appeals filed under the laws, rules and regulations administered by the commission. Before these appeals reach the appeals board, individual plaintiffs must exhaust their remedies within the agency which has supposedly wronged them. Exhausting one's agency remedies can be an exhausting process, and some plaintiffs think it is a process stacked in favor of the agency.

## SOME ABUSES OF MERIT SYSTEMS

### Illegal Patronage

The cardinal, original purpose of the federal merit system was to keep partisan politics out of personnel administration. Today the system successfully bars most political intrusion, but not all. Over the years some illegal patronage operations have been conducted in the guise of merit operations. Merit systems in some state and local governments are notorious for illegal patronage. The federal government is not presently "notorious," but illegal federal patronage is known to exist in the shadows, accomplished by various perversions of regular merit procedures. Some noteworthy forms of illegal patronage found in the federal system as well as in state and local merit systems are as follows.

*Temporary Appointments:* Characteristically merit system rules permit temporary appointments without the usual competitive procedures so that work can get done while the search goes on for a permanent employee. However, in some state and local governments, political favorites have held temporary appointments for twenty or more years, their appointments renewed every 180 days or so. When and if the holder of a temporary appointment ultimately competes in an exam for the job, he will very likely get the highest score because he learned the requirements of the job during his temporary service. And if the exam is unassembled, experience gained as a temporary employee will place him high on the register. Also, it should not be overlooked that a temporary employee may make useful contacts within the agency greatly favoring his ultimate selection for permanent employment.

*Job Description:* It is not uncommon for a position to be created for a particular person, and the job description written to fit that one single politically favored candidate like a glove. If the candidate speaks Swahili, Chinese, and Greek; has five years experience as a professional baseball player; and can repair television sets, a job description including those specific qualities might exclude everyone else in the world.

*Testing:* The nature of the testing process for many upper level merit system jobs invites mischief. First, there are usually no written exams. Responsible jobs are often so complex and ill-defined there is almost no way to find out whether someone can do the job except to look at experience and schooling. It would be hard to design a test for, say, the duties of an administrator. Tests are supposed to be specific and job related, but since nobody has yet been able to say specifically what an administrator does, it is not entirely clear what job related questions should be on a test for such a position. The same is true of numerous other upper level positions. Consequently, there is room for political favoritism in selection at this level. A point system is used in some jurisdictions to measure a candidate's education and experience, but point systems are occasionally foiled by drafting flexible qualifications for the job and then interpreting those qualifications to fit a favored candidate. Not all flexible qualifications are a clever attempt to upset the merit system; on the contrary, flexible qualifications usually make good sense, and this is why it is so difficult to close this particular door to favoritism.

In some circumstances an agency may feel it must have the unique talents of one special person. Occasionally civil service rules allow an agency to make what is called a "name certification," closing competition for the job. This practice is not common, but is a temptation to illegal patronage.

"Selective certification" is somewhat comparable to "name certification." An agency may insist that it must have a very special kind of person to fill a certain job, someone with an exact kind of experience not commonly found. This narrows the field of applicants to the point where competition is virtually closed to all but a handful, thus bringing the favored candidate within reach.

*Waiting Out the Register:* Sometimes an employer seeking to fill a certain job with a political favorite will play a game of watchful waiting until everyone above that candidate on the register has been hired. At that moment the employer declares his vacancy, just in time for the favored candidate to be certified among the top three on the list.

*Consultants:* Agencies have money to hire the temporary services of experts whose job is to advise. This not the same thing as a temporary employee; a consultant fills only a temporary position, he is not the temporary occupant of a permanent position. Usual competitive procedures are dispensed with and the agency simply hires anyone fit to give the advice sought. This is such a wide open door to old-fashioned spoilsmanship that one recent president instructed that all consultants must first receive political clearance from the White House before being hired.

*Ignoring the Job Description:* One way of seeing to it that political favorites occupy positions of power in an agency is to get them into the agency under cover of one position, but assign them duties of another, more powerful position. There could hardly be a greater violation of the principle of position classification than this, but in many large bureaucracies such violations may go for months or years before detection by anyone who has power and determination to do anything about it.

*Capture of the Civil Service Commission:* If a civil service commission (the supposed watchdog of the merit system) should happen to be captured by one political faction, clique, ring, or party, then clearly the whole merit system could be subverted and changed into an elaborate camouflage beneath which a spoils system thrives unchecked and unadvertized. This is most likely to happen where political machines are in strong control (most frequently in local governments), and/or where the mass media is unable or unwilling to unveil corruption in the civil service. At the federal level, the media is ready, willing, and able to glare down on any such capture or threat of capture. The United States Civil Service Commission is compelled by the stare of multitudinous eyes to hew more or less to the high road if it wishes to retain its moral authority as protector and defender of the merit system. This is why recent charges that the commission has from time to time cooperated with certain presidential efforts to fill several competitive service positions with political appointees have proved so embarrassing to the commission.

The various avenues of illegal patronage described above are by no means a complete catalog. Further ideas might be found in a manual circulated several years ago by the White House to cabinet level officials which explained how to manipulate the civil service for political purposes. Nothing in the so-called *Malek Manual* recommends anything overtly illegal, but it does point out what can be done within the law, and outlines to federal officials the broad boundaries of their appointment authority.

## IS THE COMPETITIVE SERVICE MANAGEMENT ORIENTED?

Are merit systems management oriented? Are they too little concerned with protecting employees and workers? Some observers say so, and point to the numerous ways by which politically objectionable employees under the supposed protection of a merit system can be fired or persecuted without regard to their merit.

## Dismissal or Forced Resignation

Ordinarily it is not easy to remove a member of the competitive service. Managers usually hesitate even to begin removal proceedings against a subordinate because it is such a nasty business personally. Furthermore, it takes a lot of time to build a case against an employee, and prosecute it. For those and other reasons, there are few removals. However, it is worth mentioning that the percentage of removals in private business is not much greater than the percentage in public employment—both run about one percent a year. Nevertheless every year thousands are, in fact, removed from the public service; a determined manager willing to take the time and face the unpleasantness, can successfully remove an offender.

Some critics of managerial "power" allege that a manager can, if he works at it, build a case for removal of any employee, and that some employees are removed simply because they are an irritant to the manager, not because of poor work. A manager who wants to "get" an employee, can, it is alleged, take advantage of all the technical rules and regulations which are supposed to govern everyday activities of employees, but which are routinely violated to some degree by most employees—the 30-minute lunch rule, the ten minute break, and so on.

To immediately remove an offending employee from sight, a manager can in some jurisdictions give a 30-day suspension at the same time a removal notice is given. Without the suspension, an employee who chooses to contest his removal through channels of appeal remains on the job, a greater irritant than ever.

A public employee holding a dismissal notice in his hand, immediately faces a terrible decision: whether to fight the dismissal, or swallow his pride and resign. Nearly everyone's first impulse is to fight, but fighting is exhausting and expensive, and may end in defeat. Defeat itself can be even more expensive; a dismissed competitive service employee may in some jurisdictions lose his pension and insurance rights as well as the possibility of future employment with the government. An employee who resigns before being fired retains his pension and insurance, and may find other employment in the competitive service, or in fact, end up in happier circumstances than before. Any employee who pauses to calculate the cost of defeat in a dismissal proceeding is tempted to avoid the proceeding altogether and resign.

Also, the cost of fighting a dismissal can be financially and psychologically crushing. Appeal through various hearing mechanisms may take months or years. An employee must first exhaust his remedies within the agency that employed him, and these "remedies" may be numerous. Finally he may (as in the federal system) appeal to the civil service commission or to its appeals board. Beyond that is the ultimate possibility of appeal to court. All this is time consuming—data must be gathered and packaged in a form suitable for presentation to hearing officers. Furthermore, it is psychologically consuming. The struggle against dismissal constantly occupies the victim's mind; there are sleepless nights and there is the gnawing self-destructive hatred of his persecutors. Meanwhile, as appellate procedures slowly move from stage to stage, the employee is without a job. Loss of pay checks aggravated by his own increasingly distraught behavior draws his family into the maelstrom, and there is the expense of lawyers, paper work, travel, and witnesses, just when money and patience are running low. The temptation to capitulate is great; sooner or later even an employee who knows he is being railroaded may fold his tent, hand in his resignation, save what can be saved from the debacle, and go on to new employment with a "resignation" on his record rather than a "dismissal." Thus it is alleged the scales are tipped too much in favor of a manager who, armed only with a flimsy case, may frighten an employee into resignation.

A timid employee might resign if the manager simply calls him in, tells him he is no longer wanted, and asks for his resignation. An employee who is both timid and proud may more easily be pushed to resign if the request for resignation is accompanied by a hint that failure to do so would be reflected in his employment references and personnel file. Of course, managers are usually careful not to allow witnesses to hear any of these unauthorized threats.

## Reduction in Force

Understandably, public agencies sometimes find they do not need a particular job done any more, or perhaps don't have the money for it. Sometimes whole offices, programs, or bureaus are eliminated, and sometimes the reduction in force is pinpointed on one single position. Keep in mind that technically what is eliminated is the position, not the person. But by eliminating the position you also eliminate (so to speak) the one who holds that position.

The charming thing about reductions in force from the point of view of a manager who is out to get somebody, is that the merit of the employee has nothing to do with it. A manager, through an RIF, can remove an employee who could not otherwise be removed for lack of merit. Need for a particular position in an agency is usually determined by the agency's chief executive; he can trump up a case for abolishing a particular position. It is easier to remove a high level competitive service employee than a low level competitive service employee. This is because in the federal service (and in some state and local governments as well) there is a bumping system: an employee who gets a "reduction in force" may take the job of someone in the same competitive category who has less seniority, and that person may in turn bump someone else, and so on down the line until the least senior person in the competitive class has no one to bump and becomes the victim of the RIF. High level positions may stand alone, that is, there may be no one else in the agency in the same competitive class, and therefore no one to bump. Since management determines which positions are in the same competitive class, management can jeopardize the bumping rights of employees, particularly of high level employees. If an employee does have bumping rights he may learn to his dismay that the person he can bump holds a position in a different city or state, which means moving. Reduction in force is a potent weapon in the hands of any manager.

## Layering

An employee can be removed from his duties even if he is not removed from his employment—he can be layered over by others who are hired to do the same job. The victim finds his duties steadily transferred to a new person. Of course, this procedure can be expensive. Federal agencies are budgeted for only so many slots (positions), and it may be necessary to borrow a temporarily unfilled slot from some other part of the agency to create a new position to layer over an objectionable employee. The victim may resign in disgust or boredom, but if he does not, the agency head will want to eliminate (RIF) the layered over position as soon as possible, and dismiss the unfortunate target of this operation. However, since a RIFed federal employee has bumping rights against someone doing the same kind of work, there is danger the intended victim will succeed in bumping the new man. To avoid this danger, the agency head may give the new person an executive level appointment not within the competitive service. In the federal service a competitive service employee has no bumping rights against anyone holding an executive level position. Naturally, there is no point in going to all this trouble unless the person to be layered over and perhaps ultimately removed by RIF holds a policy-making position and policy preferences contrary to those of the agency head.

Chief executives must be alert to the danger that a layered over employee might begin formal appeal proceedings alleging that he was deliberately reduced in status without cause. To avoid this it may even be necessary to "promote" the victim in grade or title, while leaving him substantially without significant policy-determining responsibility.

Whole organizations can be layered over and by-passed. Sometimes an agency head discovers there is an organization in his agency staffed completely, or almost completely, with persons holding views, sentiments, and preferences contrary to his own. As a consequence he may not want any dealings whatsoever with that organization, nor wish to be held responsible for its work. Under these circumstances the agency head can set up a new organization parallel to the one already in existence, and siphon the duties of the one to the other, trusting the new organization will do its work more "sensibly." Setting up a parallel organization can be very expensive, and the agency head will therefore want to RIF the entire old organization. But the problem here is comparable to the problem of RIFing an isolated individual position—people in the old organization would have bumping rights against the new people in the new organization. Therefore, the agency head would have to apply his genius to designing positions in the new organization which are not comparable to positions in the old organization. This is a terrible headache, but possible.

Layering is used most often after a change of presidents—the new president wanting to layer over and ultimately get rid of policy makers who do not respond to his leadership.

## Exile

When FBI Director J. Edgar Hoover didn't like one of his agents he sometimes banished him to an unpleasant duty station. In Hoover's eyes, the worst places in the United States were Butte, Oklahoma City, and New Orleans. Apparently it didn't occur to him that some agents just loved those places.

Exile as a way of provoking someone to resign will not work without a little advance spy work to determine where the victim and/or his wife could not bear to live. Some people can be happy just about anywhere, others rebel at the thought of living in certain states, regions, or cities. Some cannot bear to live anywhere but in one (to them) exalted place, some would die before leaving Boston, others simply would not leave "the Coast," and so on. The object is to confront an unwanted employee with a choice of being transferred to an unacceptable place, or resigning. This technique is less feasible in local government, and somewhat less feasible in state government, but the federal government has a wide choice of miserable duty stations.

In the federal service a manager must be cautious in the use of transfer to get rid of somebody: the victim might commence an appeal against the transfer, on grounds it constitutes an "adverse action" motivated by some prohibited purpose. To avoid such a charge, the transfer may be accompanied by a promotion, and by a silent prayer that promotion will not sweeten the transfer to the point of toleration by the victim.

## Special Assignment

Exile need not be geographic—it may also include banishment to a distasteful job calculated to provoke the employee-victim to resign. These two forms of exile (geographic and job) might be combined to maximize an employee's distress: assign him to an intolerable job in an intolerable region. Of course, it is important to design the "special assignment" to the special aversions of the candidate; for example, a family man who dislikes travel might be given a traveling job (beware of trying this on a man one step from divorce who would go for a traveling job like a trout after bait). Research is important in order to invent just the right job for the right person.

Some achievement-oriented people are most annoyed by the absence of significant work. For such a person, assignment to meaningless tasks such as organizing departmental beauty contests, would be ideal. But caution is again useful here. The victim may commence an appeal against his new special assignment on grounds it diminishes his status, or constitutes a retaliatory "adverse action." To forestall that move, the manager may accompany a "special assignment" with a promotion and even with letters pointing out that the new assignment constitutes a recognition of his outstanding abilities and that because of these unique talents he is being assigned to the new project.

## Deep Freeze

Deep freeze is comparable to solitary confinement in the penitentiary. Managers hope that by physically isolating an unwanted employee and giving him boring assignments a resignation will soon follow. The victim can be cut off from the outside world during working hours—his telephone removed, his secretary taken away. He might be assigned a new office in some remote and inaccessible place, perhaps even in a security area to which armed guards forbid entrance to almost everyone except the "special" employee and his supervisor. Meanwhile the employee is given no work to do, or perhaps only demeaning and boring work. Rules may be made forbidding employees to bring magazines or radio to work, and the supervisor may drop in unannounced from time to time to see that his unwelcome subordinate is properly on the job, violating no rules during work hours.

## Probationary Employees

It should be kept in mind that not all employees are tenured. Many civil service systems, including the federal, require employees to serve an initial one-year probationary period before acquiring tenure. The formal procedures for dismissing an employee still serving his year of probation are much simpler. Upon taking office a new manager may want to immediately survey the list of probationary employees, and be prepared to act against those who are unwanted.

## Is There Need for Chicanery?

All the above techniques are designed to deal with unwanted competitive service employees. Naturally, this list of techniques is only partial—seasoned managers could no doubt add many grim and creative suggestions. Some public employee unions regard these oblique methods as proof unions are needed to protect public employees. Champions of the merit system point to such practices as proof that merit procedures need tightening up. But some managers argue that these underhanded techniques are absolutely essential for the good of the public service: to get rid of poor employees who are excessively protected by civil service rules. And other managers, defending the right of a president to control policy making (and policy makers) within his administration, also defend these methods as appropriate to that end.

## IS MERIT A FRAUD?

The foregoing discussion should not lead one to the pessimistic conclusion that merit is basically a fraud. Merit is, of course, hard to define in high level administrative positions, and may be less important there than the policy bias of those who hold the positions. Bias may, in fact, be a dimension of merit in high policy-making positions—maybe even the most important dimension. But for the great mass of positions in governmental bureaucracies, merit can be reasonably well defined and measured. The federal merit system, and the systems of numerous states and localities, are by and large characterized by integrity, and work very well despite the fraudulency that slips into every human institution.

## POLITICAL PARTICIPATION BY PUBLIC EMPLOYEES

Sometimes we talk about "the people" and "the public servants" as if they were two separate species. But public servants are also citizens, they are part of the people and have the same wish to participate in the American political process that is customary and usual among the rest of the population. Still, there has always been a lurking suspicion that the people's servants would prefer to be the people's masters. This has caused legislators in most Western democracies, including the United States, to put special restrictions on political participation by public employees.

## THE HATCH ACTS

In the 1930s the federal civil service grew by leaps and bounds as first one then another New Deal program was added to cope with the Great Depression. As it grew, so also grew the fear that these vast numbers of federal employees would become political activists for the regime. Congress decided in 1939 to pass a law forbidding federal employees from taking any active part in political management or in political campaigns. This law, called the Hatch Act after a senator from New Mexico, prohibits civil servants from running for public office, distributing campaign literature, playing an active role in political meetings, circulating nominating petitions, attending a political convention (except as spectator), publishing letters soliciting votes for a candidate, and all similar activity.

A second Hatch Act was passed in 1940 applying these restrictions to state and local officials employed in activities financed by federal funds. However, much of the second act was revoked in 1974 by the Federal Elections Campaign Act, leaving the 1939 restrictions on federal employees still in force. Many states have enacted little Hatch Acts patterned more or less on the federal model, but often lacking the same severity.

These Hatch Act restrictions did not spring newborn in 1939 from the fertile brain of Senator Carl Hatch. Most were already implied in President Theodore Roosevelt's 1907 executive order which prohibited activity in political management or in political campaigns by federal employees in the competitive service. And the Pendleton Act of 1883 had provided that no federal civil servant could be punished or threatened with punishment for refusing to make a political contribution. As a matter of fact, the idea that certain kinds of political activity are incompatible with certain kinds of government employment goes back at least as far as the English cannon law. The Hatch Act was little more than a congressional enactment of what had already preceded it.

Since enactment of the two Hatch Acts, the United States Civil Service Commission has decided around 3,000 cases in which it interpreted various provisions of the acts. In the process of doing this, the commission has spelled out in considerable detail exactly what the slightly vague provisions of the law mean in concrete practice.

### In Defense of the Hatch Acts

When, in a democracy, a certain class of citizens are excluded from participation in the usual democratic processes and even denied some basic freedoms enjoyed by other citizens, such as freedom of speech and assembly, the reason would have to be compelling. The great controversy raging around the Hatch Acts today is whether the public interest served by these denials of civil rights to public employees is compelling enough to justify the denial. The issue has always been discussed, but discussion in recent years has grown more intense as the idea has grown that roadblocks to participation in the political system should be removed. Twenty percent of all employed persons work for government. Is there a compelling public interest in keeping them out of active politics? Here are some arguments by those who say there is.

*A Neutral Civil Service:* First, it is argued that when vast numbers of people are employed by government, there is danger they will side with the administration in power and establish an unbeatable machine of party workers who will become masters instead of servants.

An openly and actively partisan public employee can, it is claimed, subject the beneficiaries of public services to political coersion. Applicants for various government grants—scholars, for example, applying for research money, farmers for agricultural subsidies, or ordinary citizens for common benefits such as social security or veterans benefits—may come to believe their success or failure in such applications depends on their "correct" political behavior. Even if actively partisan bureaucrats do not carry their partisanship over into the realm of their official duties (and it assumes a fantastically beautiful view of human nature to think they wouldn't) citizens would still suspect it, fear it, and resent it. Active partisanship by, say, FBI agents, CIA agents, or internal revenue service agents, would not only threaten the peace of mind of people registered with the other party (or the wrong faction of the same party), but would also seriously impair public confidence in these agencies and make their work more difficult. An actively partisan public employee would find it difficult to convince the public that he is impartial in the conduct of official duties. It is as important for a public official to appear neutral as to be neutral.

*An Honest Civil Service:* Not only is it claimed that the image of a *neutral* civil service is protected by the Hatch Act, but also it is claimed that the image of an *honest* civil service is protected by the Act. Partisan politics in the United States does not have a completely clean and honest image, nor do those who actively participate in it, although there are some who claim the image is improving. The good character of the public service at large is said to be protected by keeping its members above the machinations of partisan politics. The effectiveness, security, and reputation of a governmental regime, no matter what kind of government, or what kind of regime, or in what nation, depends to some degree on the image projected by its civil servants. An image of corruption does not help, and has brought down more than one regime, here and abroad.

If civil servants including competitive service employees are permitted to be active politically, this will make competitive service positions very attractive to party wheelers and dealers. Agency heads will naturally be slow to remove political soldiers working hard for the "right" causes. Even when this political work begins to intrude into the working day, or when a civil service job has been turned into a sinecure supporting a political worker, the tendency will be for politically appointed top officials of the agency to look the other way. The Hatch Act is, say its defenders, a dike against reintroduction of the spoils system. Removal of the Hatch Act will open the door to still further assaults on the merit system by making the competitive service an attractive base of operations for party workers.

*Coersion:* The Hatch Act not only protects the merit system in general, according to its defenders, but also protects individual civil servants from coercion. When the law forbids an employee from doing active political work, the effect is to protect that employee from being coerced into political work by his superior. A manager will hesitate to coerce his subordinates to commit illegalities, but once those illegalities have been made legal, then the door to coercion is wide open, and thus the beginning of a new chapter in the history of American spoils.

Because the lives of bureaucrats are so intimately involved with government, it is natural that they take a keen interest in political developments that control the government. As bureaucrats see it, the outcome of an election determines who their next boss will be, and has a lot to do with the course of events at their workplace. For employees working for private enterprise, the outcome of an election may not have quite the same personal impact, nor are private-sector employees as likely to be as knowledgeable about, or as concerned about political developments. This keen interest which public servants naturally have in political developments will have the effect of drawing an unusually high percentage of them into active politics once it is permitted by law, say Hatch Act defenders. When competitive service employees sense that their promotion and careers depend to any degree upon active politics, masses of them will be drawn into it (where not prohibited by law), and the evil effects will invade and infect the entire merit system.

*Time:* Finally, defenders of the Hatch Act point to the time many public employees would spend on politics if not prohibited, sapping their performance of official duties. It being difficult beyond words to fire a tenured public employee, many will get away with excesses of political activity, devoting untold on-hours and off-hours to political work, and nobody will have the guts, the time or the interest to institute proceedings against them.

## In Opposition to the Hatch Acts

But there is another side. There are those who say, "the Hatch Act is the most archaic and un-American law on the statute books." Here are some of their arguments.

The worst charge that can be made against the Hatch Act is simply that it denies to government workers a large part of what is supposed to be the central right of citizenship in a democracy, namely the right to participate politically. In democratic theory, political participation is the most important of all imaginable civic duties. It is true, the Hatch Act permits public employees to vote, and permits them to participate in nonpartisan politics, even to the point of running for nonpartisan offices and managing nonpartisan campaigns. But, why, ask the enemies of the Hatch Act, should any citizen of a democracy, public employee or not, be excluded from any form of political activity considered routine and normal for other citizens?

Not only does the Hatch Act partially exclude public employees from the central civic duty in a democracy, but it also partially excludes them from two of the most important civil rights of a free and democratic country—freedom of speech and assembly.

If it is true, as is so often claimed, that many occupations in the private sector are as critical to the public welfare as occupations in the public sector, then why is it more justified to curb the civic duties and civil rights of one group than the other? The public interest is no more jeopardized by the political activity of private citizens than by the political activities of public employees, except possibly in a few fields like police, fire, and military. So argue the defenders of free public employee political participation.

Enemies of the Hatch Act say the Act is simply unconstitutional—you cannot constitutionally make laws in this country that tell people they can't make a political speech, or they can't peaceably assemble with others to petition their government, or they can't write and distribute political literature. Such restrictions violate three of the most fundamental civil rights in the United States Constitution, freedom of speech, press, and assembly. The United States Supreme Court has labeled these First Amendment freedoms essential to any system of ordered liberty, and gives them a preferred position among all other civil rights. So important are these freedoms that the Court has taken the unusual step of putting the burden of proof upon the government to show that any law limiting freedom of speech, press, assembly, and religion is constitutional when a plaintiff brings an action alleging the unconstitutionality of such a law. In all other cases, that is, in cases not involving an allegation of unconstitutionality under the First Amendment, the burden of proof is routinely upon the plaintiff, not the defendant.

## Legality of the Hatch Acts

How then has the Hatch Act survived challenges in court that it violates the First Amendment? First, let it be said, its survival at the hands of the court has been less certain in recent years than previously, and, given the course of judicial opinions, many constitutional lawyers predict the Hatch Act will be struck down as unconstitutional in the near future, providing Congress does not beat it to the punch by revoking or revising the Act. As these paragraphs are written, Congress is on the verge of doing just that.

Since its passage the Hatch Act has come under two frontal assaults before the United States Supreme Court, one in 1947 and another in 1973. In 1947 the Hatch Act came under attack by the United Public Workers of America defending an employee of the Mint who had engaged in political activities prohibited by the Act. The Union argued that the Act was an unconstitutional violation of First Amendment and other constitutional guarantees. But the Mint employee lost; the Court, in a four to three decision, ruled in *United Public Workers* v. *Mitchell* that while the Hatch Act did indeed impair First Amendment and other constitutional rights, nevertheless, those rights are not absolute. It is permissible, said the Court, to limit the constitutional freedoms of individuals when exercise of those freedoms interfere with certain compelling public interests. The Court thought there was a compelling public interest in restricting the political activities of public employees, and that interest outweighed the First Amendment in importance. However, since 1947 the Court has modified its view concerning the permissibility of requiring public employees to surrender constitutional rights as a condition of holding a government job. In 1968 the Court said, "For if the government could deny a benefit to a person because of his constitutionally protected speech or associations, his exercise of those freedoms would in effect be penalized and inhibited. This would allow the government to produce a result which it could not command directly.... Such interference with constitutional rights is impermissible." (See *Pickering* v. *Board of Education.*)

In the 1973 attack on the Hatch Act, the National Association of Letter Carriers brought suit declaring among other things that the act was unconstitutional because it was so vague that government employees could not tell what was permitted and what was forbidden. The Court in a six to three decision conceded that the Act was somewhat vague, but that Congress had intended for the United States Civil Service Commission to interpret the Act and to flesh it out by the process of case by case adjudication of individual controversies. This the commission has done. (See *Civil Service Commission* v. *National Association of Letter Carriers.*) At the same time the Court upheld its previous ruling in the *Mitchell* case.

At present the Hatch Act is a treed fox. Whatever its fate, the great issue will remain: should the law prohibit public employees from active partisan participation in politics?

Basically the proposed revision of the Hatch Act by Congress in 1977 would give public employees substantially the same political rights as possessed by other citizens—the right to run for partisan office, to manage partisan campaigns, to speak and write in behalf of candidates and causes, and so on. However, the revision would retain a prohibition against use by an employee of his or her official authority to influence voting or for other partisan purposes. A manager would, thus, be prohibited from using his position to influence subordinates, and no public employee would be permitted to use his office or authority to influence other employees or the public. The Act would prohibit solicitation of funds by superiors, and would prohibit political activity while on duty in a federal building or in uniform. Employees who become candidates would be put on leave. An independent three-member Board on Political Activities of Government Employees would be set up to hear and adjudicate alleged violations of the law, and the Civil Service Commission would have power to investigate and prosecute alleged violations of the law.

Provisions of the 1977 bill somewhat resemble the earlier (1967) recommendations of the Commission on Political Activity of Government Personnel set up in 1966 by Congress to probe the permissible area of political activity by federal employees.

Opponents of the new liberalization policy reassert all the previously asserted arguments against partisan political activity by public employees. Furthermore, they argue that the remaining prohibitions under the 1977 bill would not be worth the paper they are written on because it is impossible to prevent a superior from influencing and even coercing subordinates into "approved" political activity. All the boss has to do is let his political preferences be known; eager subordinates will, it is claimed, try to make points by joining with him in campaigns and political management. Unscrupulous bosses may deliberately favor subordinates who are politically cooperative, and other bosses may unconsciously do the same thing. It may be nearly impossible to pin a violation of law on anybody, and very few would be motivated to try.

## SUMMARY

Although patronage played no greater part in Jackson's administration than in those of his predecessors, he did openly defend patronage, thereby drawing critical attention to the spoils system as a method of filling public offices. Criticism of spoils grew louder in decades following Jackson. Civil service leagues were formed and ultimately led the charge against spoils; they were strengthened by revelations of scandal, especially during the Grant administration. By 1881, when Garfield was assassinated by a man he had turned down for a patronage appointment, the stage was set for passage of the Pendleton Act of 1883 which established the basic structure of the federal merit system prevailing yet today. Successive presidents brought new categories of federal workers into the competitive service; today about 90 percent are within some form of merit system. About two-thirds of the states and a number of local governments also have merit systems modeled somewhat on the federal pattern.

Some illegal patronage exists beneath the facade of merit systems. While not notorious at the federal level, it is known to lurk in the shadows. Abuses can creep in through temporary appointments, slanted job descriptions, improper testing, and various other avenues. Merit systems are also occasionally abused by managers who succeed in firing (or forcing the resignation of) certain persons for political or other nonmerit reasons. Struggle for improvement and extension of merit systems is a battle that continues in our time.

A rank-in-corps senior civil service has been suggested as the best system for employing and training top level career managers. According to its advocates, such a system would provide a politically neutral layer of civil servants immediately below the political high command, and would have high pay, high prestige, and job security. By rotation of job assignment they would become generalists with broad understanding of high level administration. Opponents of the senior civil service corps idea argue that a politically neutral senior civil service corps would make it difficult for the President to control the bureaucracy, and would become an elitist corps with a monopoly on high career positions. Among other evils, this would discourage lateral entry and block the inflow of fresh ideas and new talent.

Much of the senior federal service today is composed of political appointees including the so-called executive level appointees, the noncareer executive assignment appointees, and the Schedule C appointees. While this gives the President leverage over a considerable number of policy-making officials, the careers of those officials are usually confined to a single agency, often only for the term of a single president.

Public servants are also citizens, but under the federal Hatch Acts and comparable state and local laws many of them have been by virtue of their occupation excluded from certain forms of political participation open to other citizens. The Hatch Acts undoubtedly will be modified by Congress or declared unconstitutional by the United States Supreme Court. But the issue whether special restrictions should or should not be put on political participation by public employees will remain alive so long as democracy as we know it survives. The issue is particularly perplexing, for on the one hand the fear that public employees will become political activists in support of a regime is balanced on the other by the idea that no citizen in a democracy should be denied the most important right of every citizen, the right to participate actively in the political system.

## SUGGESTED READING

Civil Service Commission v. National Association of Letter Carriers, 413 U.S. 548 (1973).

Gerhart, Paul. *Political Activity by Public Employee Organizations at the Local Level: Threat or Promise.* Chicago: IPMA, 1973.

Golembiewski, Robert T. and Cohen, Michael. *People in Public Service.* Itasca, Ill.: F. E. Peacock, 1976.

Harvey, Donald R. *The Civil Service Commission.* New York: Praeger, 1970.

Hatch Acts. 53 Stat. 1147; 54 Stat. 767.

Leich, Harold H. "Rank in Man or Job? Both!" *Public Administration Review,* Spring 1960, pp. 92–99.

"Malek Manual." *Federal Times,* October 16, (p. 12) 23 (p. 12), 30 (p. 12), November 6 (p. 12), 13 (p. 19), 20 (p. 12), 27 (p. 12), December 4 (p. 12), 11 (p. 12), 18 (p. 12), 1974.

Martin, Philip L. "The Hatch Act in Court: Some Recent Developments." *Public Administration Review,* September-October 1973, pp. 443–447.

Pickering v. Board of Education, 391 U.S. 563 (1968).

Rapp, Michael T. and Wible, Roger L. "Freedom of Political Activity for Civil Servants: An Alternative to Section 9 (a) of the Hatch Act." *George Washington Law Review,* March 1973, pp. 626–645.

Rosen, Bernard. *The Merit System in the United States Civil Service.* Washington, D.C.: U.S. Government Printing Office (Committee on Post Office and Civil Service of the United States House of Representatives), 1975.

Shafritz, Jay M. *Position Classification: A Behavioral Analysis for the Public Service.* New York: Praeger, 1973.

Shafritz, Jay M. *Public Personnel Management: The Heritage of Civil Service Reform.* New York: Praeger, 1975.

Stahl, O. Glenn. *Public Personnel Administration.* New York: Harper & Row, 1976.

"Symposium on the Merit Principle Today." *Public Administration Review,* September-October 1974, pp. 425–452.

Tolchin, Martin and Tolchin, Susan. *To the Victor—Political Patronage from the Club House to the White House.* New York: Vintage, 1971.

United Public Workers v. Mitchell, 330 U.S. 75 (1947).

United States Civil Service Commission. *Personnel Manual.* Washington, D.C.: U.S. Government Printing Office.

Van Riper, Paul T. *History of the United States Civil Service.* Evanston, Ill.: Row, Peterson, 1958.

Wilson, Woodrow. "The Study of Administration" *Political Science Quarterly,* June 1887, pp. 197–222.

*

# Getting Hired 6

# Getting Hired 6

## RECRUITMENT

"Look before you leap" can be good advice for an employer about to hire someone. As veteran managers know, it's easier to guard against making a poor appointment in the first place than to correct the mistake afterward. Here an ounce of prevention is truly worth a pound of cure. Hiring, in fact, has some things in common with marrying, and perhaps William Congreve's line "married in haste, we may repent at leisure," carries a message for recruiters.

In the jargon of administration the word "recruitment" means something quite different from the word "selection." Recruitment is the process of attracting a pool of qualified applicants for a vacant position; selection is the process of choosing from among that pool the individual for the job.

Unless a manager already knows exactly who he wants to hire, it only makes sense to locate through recruitment as many potential takers as possible. Often this is done by advertising the position and waiting for applications, but it may also be done by directly approaching various individuals known to have the qualities sought.

Aggressive recruitment is hard work, and many public employers don't bother to do it very well, or to do it at all. It is much easier and more pleasant to fall back on the buddy system for filling vacancies, or to select from among those who just happen to be in the neighborhood when competitive examinations are given.

Affirmative action has had the great virtue of compelling employers to advertise vacancies far and wide, and to go through the miserable but necessary chore of soliciting and evaluating dozens or hundreds of applications. This process not only contributes to equal opportunity, but also casts the widest possible net for qualified candidates; the more candidates the better the ultimate choice is likely to be.

## Job Related Qualifications

Naturally, before one recruits for a position, it is important to know just what work the person to be hired is supposed to do and the qualifications needed to do it. However, employers are often compelled against their will to set nonjob related qualifications for positions they seek to fill. "Professional" qualifications sometimes fall into this category. Statutes often prohibit persons from entering certain trades or professions without a license. Practically every state prohibits the practice of barbering without a license, no matter how skilled a nonlicensed barber might be. Although it may take only 72 hours to become a skilled barber, still, to get a barber's license one may be compelled by law to attend barber's school for six months, learn not only how to cut hair, but what a hair is, and how it grows. Barbers have mounted campaigns in every state to make it as difficult as possible to become a barber, their purpose being to control the number of barbers and keep the price of haircuts high. Employers cannot simply recruit for a skilled barber.

Many occupations and professions in the United States have conspired to protect their economic interest by imposing superfluous requirements upon those who would enter the field. These usually take the form of excessive educational requirements, and commonly they are masked as measures necessary for the "health, safety, and welfare" of the public.

Nor are employers always free to give in-service-training in order to qualify the unqualified. An agency might like to hire a few alert young recruits and teach them how to practice law. But the organized bar does not look kindly upon in-service-training for the purpose of manufacturing lawyers. The same is true of the medical profession. Probably three-quarters of what most doctors do could be done by nurses, but the doctors' lobby would not sit still while nurses are recruited to do "doctors' work." We are a credential-happy society. Credentials do, of course, like licenses have some socially useful purposes—the case for them is not presented here—but the point striven for is that employers cannot always avoid imposing nonjob-related qualifications.

We cannot place the entire blame for these excessive qualifications on trade associationism. Nor is there much evidence that they are inspired by bigots determined to keep minorities out of jobs. On the contrary, the most likely villain (other than trade associationism) is just plain thoughtlessness, mixed with pride. Why would a city require applicants for the position of dogcatcher to have a high school diploma? A thing like that could easily escape the attention of aldermen in a reasonably self-respecting city.

Affirmative action programs which seek to clear paths to jobs by disadvantaged persons, run head-on into these nonjob-related qualifications which work a special hardship on the disadvantaged. Militancy by women and minorities has done much in recent years to force employers to pay attention to excessive qualifications, and to validate their recruitment tests.

Agencies (at least managers within agencies) commonly have secret, unannounced, and unspoken recruitment goals. For example, an employer might have a deep horror of people with beards. Although he might hesitate to write "must not have a beard" in the vacancy announcement, it remains a very real, if secret, qualification for the job. Or this same manager may picture himself a conservative dedicated to keeping liberals out of his organization, or vice versa.

Most agencies will consciously or subconsciously try to recruit candidates who share enthusiasm for the goals of the agency: welfare offices want candidates who believe in welfare; civil rights offices want civil rights fans, and so on. There may be some value in this; agencies are said to function better when they are staffed with persons who are agreed on goals—goal consensus may, in fact, be a valid recruiting goal or bias, but it is seldom mentioned as a job requirement.

Many managers are intensely interested in attracting candidates who show promise of joining whatever office clique the manager himself belongs to. Of course, the manager keeps this to himself and may not breath a word of it for general circulation. This could even happen at a university where faculty members live exhausting lives of internecine warfare, sometimes fought out on the terrain of recruitment and selection. New candidates for faculty positions may be carefully interviewed and screened to see whether they are smart enough, if hired, to join the right side in the campus war. Of course, all this is can be disguised as a lofty search for true merit in candidates. Success in recruitment for a clique consists of paving the way for selection of reinforcements; to this end it may apply numerous secret qualifications unknown to the candidate.

## SELECTION

### When Does Selection Begin?

Selection is said to follow recruitment, but actually it does not always follow. Sometimes managers know exactly who they intend to hire before recruitment ever begins, and recruitment is reduced to an after-the-fact series of empty motions demanded by law or good taste. Of course, where there is a properly functioning merit system, it is somewhat difficult to put selection entirely ahead of recruitment.

Also, the process of recruitment is in essence a process of selection, a screening out of all but the qualified. When a position is announced and described, this in itself deters applications from most who do not meet the stated requirements. Recruitment exams screen out still others. A form of selection also occurs when the manager decides whether to fill the position from inside or from outside the agency, for in many merit systems, he may exclude from competition all persons outside the agency and fill the position by promotion, transfer, reassignment, or reinstatement from within.

### Selection From Within or From Without?

In deciding whether to fill a position from within or without, bureaucratic self-protection is often a governing principle. Thus, merit in candidates may be measured by the defensive or offensive needs of the employer, especially in candidates for high level positions where merit is hard to define anyway. From the point of view of a manager who wants to fill a position with someone sympathetic to his own goals, appointment from within may have its advantages. This is because most managers know who the friendly Indians are within their agency, and know them better than they know the average applicant from outside.

Some managers, especially those whose own positions are slightly precarious, see their self-interest in filling positions by whatever method is most likely to keep subordinates happy. Subordinates usually favor filling positions from within because it gives them opportunities that might otherwise be lost to outsiders. However, if a manager is going to fill a position from inside, especially if it involves a promotion, he has to worry about making enemies out of every member of his organization who thinks he should have had the job but did not get it. A manager looking out for his own security, and who finds it in the contentment of subordinates, may find it helpful to apply seniority when selecting from within. Seniority is a readily understandable and completely objective way to make an otherwise touchy decision. Although it penalizes merit, merit is often hard to define. Civil service rules, however, usually prohibit much use of seniority.

A manager may find it impossible to locate within his organization the talent sought, and may have to look beyond the organization. Also a manager may want to look beyond the organization to find a fresh face, a candidate unscarred by office or agency politics.

### Rule of Three

The rule of three is sometimes thought to be an unreasonable limitation on an employer's freedom of choice. Its purpose, of course, is to limit his opportunity to subvert the merit system, but at the same time allow him some freedom of choice. His choice is limited to three persons at the top of the list of eligibles. Changing the rule of three to a rule of six, eight, or ten might bear some benefits. Differences in merit between the third and fourth person may not be significant, nor even between the third and tenth. Since merit is sometimes hard to define, and since management does have a justifiable wish for latitude and flexibility in filling vacancies, good arguments can be made for presenting employers with a larger group of candidates from which to make a final selection.

## Veteran Preference

Veterans groups, such as the American Legion, have long cultivated centers of power to see that veterans are treated fairly. Among the major veteran benefits provided by the federal government are educational benefits such as the G.I. bill of rights that put so many of us through college, life insurance, loan guarantees, disability compensation, pensions, and medical rehabilitation at clinics and hospitals throughout the nation. State and local governments also provide benefits to veterans, as does the private sector. The Veterans Administration, established in 1930 to bring under one hat administration of federal benefits, is one of the biggest federal agencies. Past commanders of the American Legion and other potentates of the veterans lobby are commonly appointed to high positions in the Veterans Administration.

To further assist veterans, the Federal Veterans Preference Act was passed in 1944, giving veterans preference in federal employment. The law adds points to the scores veterans make on civil service examinations, gives veterans a monopoly of certain positions such as elevator operator and chauffeur, and gives veterans a preferred position when an agency must reduce its staff. Under present federal law, any veteran who passes a competitive examination is given a five point bonus, disabled veterans get ten. Some state and local governments give absolute preference to veterans who pass competitive exams; that is, if they pass the exam they are put at the head of the list of eligibles.

At first glance, veteran preference seems to be a fully justified response to the risks and sacrifices endured by veterans. But the question is sometimes asked whether veteran preference should be given to *all* veterans. Military service seldom results in injury, although it does generally involve sacrifice of time and money, and always creates difficulties at the point of discharge and transition back to civilian life. Veteran preference in civil service employment is very helpful to veterans readjusting to civilian life. But should ordinary veterans who suffered no wounds or serious disabilities be given job preference ten, twenty, thirty, forty years after their discharge?

The essential idea of a merit system is that it is based on merit and nothing but merit. To the extent jobs are given on any other basis, the system is less a merit system. If exceptions to the competitive principle are to be made to accommodate the needs of veterans, this sets a precedent for similar exceptions to accommodate the needs of various other groups— the culturally deprived for instance. And many Americans besides veterans make sacrifices in war. Albert Einstein gave his time and talent to development of atomic weapons. And it is not unusual for civilians to be bombed, machine gunned, starved, and raped. Why single out those in uniform for special reward in the civil service, especially when, far from being disabled, many veterans actually benefited during their service, some even learning a civilian trade.

Hardly anyone questions the right of a veteran, especially of disabled veterans, to be cared for, rewarded, and rehabilitated. But is it a good policy to give such benefits at the expense of the merit system? Most critics of veteran preference for civil service jobs heartily support other ways and means of benefiting veterans.

## RECRUITMENT AND SELECTION TESTS

### Validation

The process of validating tests (and qualifications) begins with "job analysis." It hardly makes sense to give a test for a job that has not been studied to identify exactly what work that job involves, and what knowledge, skills, traits, and characteristics its holder should have. Only after job analysis can one make a sensible set of qualifications, and design tests to probe whether a candidate has those qualifications. But those qualifications and tests need to be validated. They need to be studied in actual practice to see whether there is in fact a correlation between them and success at the job. It is often difficult to identify just what knowledge, skills, and traits are needed to perform a job. No one, for example, can say exactly what mysterious brew of talents makes a good supervisor. It is easier to identify traits needed for low level technical jobs than for high level managerial jobs.

### Objective and Subjective Tests

Most competitive service examinations are of a type familiar to students, and have shortcomings and advantages also well known to students. Basically there are four types of exams used in most merit systems: (1) written, paper and pencil tests; (2) performance tests used to measure skill in operating machinery, such as typewriters; (3) oral tests and interviews; and (4) evaluation of education and experience and references. The latter can hardly be said to be a test, but is used in lieu of written tests for higher level jobs. Generally, several of these forms of testing are used in combination with each other.

Written tests come in two forms, as students well know: objective (such as multiple choice) and subjective (essay). From the point of view of a teacher or of a civil service examiner, multiple-choice examinations have certain distinct advantages; they can be rapidly graded by machine, and they can probe a candidate's knowledge over a wide span of subject matter. Multiple choice exams are often criticised for hitting too many details and too few important points. However, correctly drawn multiple-choice exams need not suffer that shortcoming. For example, if a candidate is asked whether Congress has one, two, three, four, or five houses, that is not an insignificant question if the object of the test is to measure knowledge and understanding of American government. Unless a candidate knows that specific fact, then one can fairly conclude he doesn't know anything about Congress. Furthermore, even if a multiple-choice exam were guilty of asking for knowledge of insignificant details, it could still be a valid indicator of a candidate's knowledge of large matters, for large matters are composed of small matters. A multiple-choice exam can be designed on the assumption that nobody will get all the details right, but that he who knows the most details is likely to have the best grasp of the large issues as well. Multiple-choice exams are thought to be "multiple guess." This is bad if guessing is forced upon candidates by poorly written and unclear questions. But if the questions are clear, and the candidate still has to guess, this is not necessarily bad—it might be good, for, after all, the best guessers are the people who know most about a subject. If one were to ask, "Will the stock market go up or down tomorrow," a stockbroker might have to guess, but his informed guess has a higher probability of being correct than the uninformed guess of someone else. When candidates are asked to make dozens of informed guesses on multiple-choice exams, then clearly those who are best informed will probably do best.

Multiple-choice and other objective tests also have the advantage of seeming to be free of bias in the grading process. Even when the designer of the exam insinuates his own subtle biases into it by the questions he chooses to include and by the way he writes those questions, nevertheless, a multiple-choice exam is largely free of bias insofar as the mechanics of grading it are concerned.

This contrasts with an essay examination which requires subjective evaluation by a grader. Evaluations are always tinged with bias. Nevertheless, an essay exam has virtues. For one thing, candidates normally have to demonstrate some ability to handle language and organize ideas. If the job calls for such ability (most administrative jobs do), then an essay exam may be valid. A multiple-choice exam is almost totally lacking as a measure of a candidate's ability to write, nor does it ordinarily have much to say about a candidate's ability to organize ideas. But if the job does not require intellectual talents of that sort, then an essay exam could work a terrible injustice. All written exams, whether objective or subjective, discriminate against culturally deprived minorities who tend to be weak in reading and writing. This is why minority group spokesmen sometimes charge public agencies with practicing bias when written exams are used. However, every exam is biased and discriminatory insofar as it discriminates between those who have the desired qualities and those who do not. The goal is to invent exams which efficiently and precisely discriminate for the desired purpose but which do not inadvertently discriminate for undesired purposes.

The passing grade on federal competitive examinations is 70. But O. Glenn Stahl, author of Public Personnel Administration says, "The passing point is more properly a function of how many eligible candidates are needed and at how stringent a point it is desired to cut off eligibility." (p. 131). The first thing a federal employer does is decide how many people he wants to pass his exam, then he puts the passing score low enough to yield as many people as needed, and arbitrarily calls that score 70. Then he arranges candidates on a register of eligibles according to their score. Actually the highest score is not 100, but 110, because a disabled veteran may score 100, and receive a 10 point veteran preference.

## Professional and Administrative Career Examination

One federal exam that may be of particular interest to recent college graduates is the Professional and Administrative Career Examination, successor to the Federal Service Entrance Examination. PACE is designed for people who want to begin a career in responsible administrative and professional jobs, and is designed to measure potential for advancement into such jobs. Most positions are filled at grade GS–5 and do not require specialized education or experience. Some who do particularly well on the exam or who have taken graduate work or have certain kinds of experience are appointed at the grade GS–7. However, positions filled through this examination are at trainee levels preparatory to advancement to grade levels GS–9 and above. Since the initial appointment is to trainee positions, it is not necessary to have education or experience in a specific field, although it is necessary to have a college degree of some sort to take the exam. These trainee positions are in a wide variety of occupational categories. Some positions are in areas such as taxation, immigration, importing, exporting, and business regulation—jobs such as customs inspector, revenue officer, immigration inspector, tax technician, and so forth. Other positions involve staff specialties in such areas as computer science, personnel administration, management analysis, contract and procurement, supply, budget, and general administration. There are some positions which involve processing claims and applications for pensions, insurance, and disability payments. Other positions involve investigations such as special drug enforcement agents and criminal investigators. Also, there are some jobs as writers, editors, and economists. Still other positions involve social service.

The Professional and Administrative Career Examination is, to repeat, a gateway to trainee positions in a wide variety of occupations. This internship program has attracted many young persons of high managerial potential to federal service. Information about when and where to take the exam can be obtained from any one of the many outposts maintained by the United States Civil Service Commission; in addition to its ten regional offices located in Atlanta, Boston, Chicago, Dallas, Denver, New York, Philadelphia, St. Louis, San Francisco, and Seattle, the commission maintains over 100 Federal Job Information Centers in cities across the nation. They are listed in phone books, and there is a toll-free number for each state which may be used by persons phoning from within that state. It is possible to take examinations for many different federal positions at these information centers, and to find out what federal job vacancies exist, qualifications required, and how to apply.

Federal Job Information Centers are part of an attempt by the federal government to actively recruit candidates. The centers make applying for federal jobs much easier than previously, because now, instead of having to contact each federal agency separately at some distant address, the centers consolidate job information from almost all federal agencies, and bring that information to the public at numerous locations where actual applications may be taken, and exams given.

## Examination for Mid-Level Positions

An examination for persons interested in administrative, management, technical, or other professional positions in the middle ranks of the federal service (GS–9 through GS–12) is the so-called Examination for Mid-Level Positions. The examination is not a paper and pencil test, but is an examination by the United States Civil Service Commission of the applicant's background and qualifications. You apply by first contacting an office of the Civil Service Commission where you are given application forms. The completed forms, together with other relevant material, are then returned to the office. An initial review is then made to determine whether you meet the minimum qualifications. If these are met, your application goes on a mid-level referral list held by the commission. When a federal agency has a mid-level vacancy in an appropriate occupational field, it requests the commission to refer some candidates from the list. The commission looks through the whole mid-level list to find candidates qualified for the position, and then determines which three among those qualified are the best qualified. Those three names are sent to the requesting agency for consideration. After the agency selects an applicant for employment, the other names are returned to the list for consideration when other vacancies occur.

## A REPRESENTATIVE BUREAUCRACY

Do we want a bureaucracy that operates strictly on merit principles? Are there other considerations more important? Some think giving jobs to veterans very important; some think giving minorities and women positions at all levels of the bureaucracy is very important; some put union membership high on the scale of values and some put seniority very high.

Today there are some vocal advocates of the idea that bureaucracies should be "representative," and that representativeness should precede technical proficiency as a job qualification. They argue that the more a bureaucracy resembles the public, the better it can serve that public—therefore, the bureaucracy should mirror the social, economic, racial, and sex characteristics of the population. This not only makes the bureaucracy more sensitive in application of law, but also more sensitive in adjudicating disputes and in making law. Because bureaucracies do a great deal of legislating (by rule-making and by influencing legislatures) they should, according to this theory, be representative.

To some degree the federal bureaucracy, like the Congress, is supposed to be geographically representative. The Pendleton Act apportions appointments to jobs in Washington, D.C. according to the population of the states and territories. But what about social, economic, racial, and sex representation?

Bureaucracies are actually a better mirror of the nation's class structure today than the average legislative body. Most state and federal legislators are better educated and better off financially than the average voter in his district. The same is usually true of local boards, councils, and commissions. Bureaucracies, on the other hand, include a high percentage of custodians, guards, messengers, typists, blue collar workers, minorities, and others commonly thought to be in the lower economic strata. As a whole, therefore, the bureaucracy does substantially mirror the nation's class structure. But perhaps it is inaccurate to compare an *entire* bureaucracy with a legislative body to determine which is most representative of the public. Perhaps only senior level bureaucrats should be compared with legislators; senior bureaucrats after all are the main policy makers within the bureaucracy. If one compares senior level bureaucrats as a whole with legislators as a whole, we find that both groups are well above the national average in education, wealth, and in most other indicators of status.

Those interested in nurturing a bureaucracy which understands and responds to the whole public, are prone to insist on a senior civil service composed of persons who stem from all the nation's major classes, high and low. This would be difficult to achieve unless some senior civil servants were deliberately hired on the basis of their class and economic condition, whether or not they are proficient in the job. This would constitute an affirmative action program of sorts for all deprived persons, not just those who by their race or sex are assumed to be deprived. Today affirmative action, to make the senior ranks more representative racially and by sex, seems to be having some effect. But this alone does not assure a bureaucracy representative of groups whose deprivation stems from causes other than race or sex.

A truly representative bureaucracy may be impossible to achieve if theories of "acculturation" are correct. Once a lower class person is elevated to a new class, that person gradually acquires the attitudes of his new surroundings, and sheds the attitudes of his old environment.

One approach to increasing the representation of deprived groups in the bureaucracy is to inaugurate massive in-service training programs, opening the bureaucracy to those who may not have a skill, but who are capable of being trained. How this could be made to work for senior positions in the government is not clear. The talents and qualities needed by persons who want to be successful supervisors are almost indefinable, especially the talents of high level policy-making supervisors. Senior ranks are most likely to be staffed with people who have traits lacking in the deprived. One thing that drives certain people to the top of any hierarchy is what sociologists call "achievement orientation." Parents in the middle and upper classes tend unconsciously to teach their children to compete and achieve. "Achievement orientation" is less characteristic of lower class parents, and hence of their children. It seems to be very difficult to implant "achievement orientation" after a child has reached adulthood. Thus, while in-service training may teach skills that qualify individuals for low level jobs, it probably cannot instill the will to achieve, cannot implant that mysterious quality that drives achievers toward the top of the bureaucracy.

## RACE IN PUBLIC EMPLOYMENT

While the percentage of black employees in the federal civil service exceeds the percentage of blacks in the total United States population, those blacks are heavily concentrated in lower ranks. In senior grades blacks hold a far lower percentage of positions than their percentage in the general population. What is true of blacks is also true of Spanish surnamed persons and several other minorities. And what is true of minorities in the federal service is also true of minorities in some state and local services. In many states and local governments, the percentage of minority employees at both the upper and lower levels falls far short of their percentage of the population served by those governments.

### Equality and the Constitution

After the Civil War, states began passing laws discriminating against blacks, depriving them of many basic rights of citizenship including the right to vote and sit on juries. In response to this, and to a concern what might happen if federal troops were withdrawn from the South, the 14th Amendment was added to the United States Constitution. The 14th Amendment, among other things, prohibited states to deny "equal protection of the laws" to any of their citizens. Equal protection is a rather vague term, and the courts have had to interpret it and say what it means over the course of time in countless law suits. We will not trouble to recount the circuitous path of court decisions before 1954 touching on the equal protection clause; most litigation concerning it did not relate to race, but to money. Corporations used the clause to attack laws that seemed to single them out for special treatment. For example, if a law were passed requiring all hotels with more than 50 rooms to employ a night watchman, the owners of such hotels might argue in court that the law discriminates between big hotels and little hotels and therefore denies "equal protection." (In 1915 it was decided that such discrimination does not violate the 14th Amendment.)

The equal protection clause does not prohibit all discrimination, but only, as courts say, "unreasonable discrimination." The difference between reasonable and unreasonable is for judges, who are presumed to be reasonable, to decide.

Although the purpose of the 14th Amendment was to protect blacks (not corporations) from discrimination, it was not until 1896 that the first case came to the United States Supreme Court involving racial discrimination. That was the case of *Plessy* v. *Ferguson* concerning a law in Louisiana requiring blacks and whites to ride on separate railroad cars. Plessy, who was only one-eighth black, and who usually passed for white, got on a car for whites, and when asked to move to a car for blacks refused. He was arrested by Ferguson, the sheriff. Plessy argued that the law requiring segregation of blacks and whites on the train amounted to discrimination against blacks—a violation of the equal protection clause. The Supreme Court upheld the Louisiana law; it is not discriminatory, said the Court, to segregate races so long as the facilities for each race are equal. This became known as the "separate but equal doctrine;" it prevailed until 1954. Dozens of cases concerning segregation in parks, schools, busses, and what not were decided under the separate but equal doctrine. Under that doctrine, no segregation law violated equal protection so long as equal facilities for the races were provided. Slowly the Court demanded stricter compliance with the "equal" part of the separate but equal doctrine.

Finally, in 1954 the Court abandoned separate but equal altogether. In the famous case of *Brown* v. *Board of Education* the Court held that any and all school segregation laws are unconstitutional because all such laws produce a sense of inequality in the minority race even if facilities are equal. The Brown doctrine has been extended to all other kinds of discrimination based on race imposed or fostered by governmental action.

The 14th Amendment does not apply to the federal government; only to the states. There is no equal protection clause applying to the federal government. However, the "due process clause" of the 5th Amendment to the United States Constitution does apply to the federal government and says no person may be denied life, liberty, or property without due process of law. The term "due process of law" is another one of those vague phrases which abound in the United States Constitution. It has been litigated more than any other phrase, and if one boils all those cases down, "due process of law" appears to mean "fair." Therefore, anything "unfair" done by the federal government is unconstitutional. In a Washington, D.C. segregation case, the Court simply found racial segregation to be "unfair." There is also a due process clause in the 14th Amendment. Therefore, almost anything done by either the federal government or by any state (or by any state agency or local government) based on race is illegal.

## Unintentional Discrimination

What if a government (state, local, or federal) does something that unintentionally produces an adverse effect on a minority race? Suppose a school board, for example, divides up school attendance zones adhering to the "neighborhood school" concept, and ends up with some schools attended almost wholly by blacks or some other minority race because such schools are located in neighborhoods where all or most of the inhabitants happen to be of one minority? Suppose the school board had no intention of producing an all-minority school, but it just worked out that way? The Court does not now seem to consider that a violation of equal protection and due process of law. In some other areas and situations the Court will give greater weight to discriminatory intent than to discriminatory result. Whether result is weighed more heavily than intent depends partly on where the Court thinks the public interest lies.

## Civil Service Testing

Does the merit system unintentionally discriminate against minority races insofar as they, being in some cases culturally deprived, are as a group sometimes unable to demonstrate merit as successfully as mainstream Americans? No, the United States Supreme Court does not now consider insistance on merit to be racially discriminatory, and is not ready yet to strike down the merit system. Courts find greater public interest in maintaining a merit system, than in avoiding this unintended and unfortunate side effect of merit.

Courts, however, have not hesitated to strike down supposed "merit" requirements which actually are not job related. For example, in 1972 a black golf pro contested the City of Atlanta's use of an IQ test to fill golf-pro positions. The court found there was no substantial relationship between the test and the work of a golf pro. Most lawsuits in recent years alleging discrimination in pubic employment have challenged the validity of tests. Recently, for example, a district court enjoined the New York City Board of Examiners from continuing its use of an invalid examination to fill supervisory positions in the New York City schools. The board of examiners was unable to prove to an appeals court that the examination was job related. However, in an attack upon examinations for police officers in the District of Columbia, black applicants claimed the examinations were discriminatory against them, and that the examinations bore no relationship to subsequent job performance. The court held that the examinations accurately measured those qualifications necessary for success in police work. But, in another case a district court found that written tests given by the City of Philadelphia did discriminate against black applicants for positions in the police department.

Written exams have usually been the target of suits against racially "discriminatory" examinations. Inability to read and write is one of the chief marks of cultural deprivation. All written tests are claimed to be discriminatory against most minority groups. Practical, job-related tests, such as a typing test for those applying for typing jobs, are considered fairer by minorities.

However, courts do not reject all written exams as discriminatory against minorities. Recently a black in the District of Columbia Police Department claimed in court that the written exam used by the department in making promotions discriminated against blacks. The exam was a multiple choice critical-incident test of judgment. The court found the test had been "content validated" by current professional standards insofar as possible in the present state of the art of testing, and upheld it.

Written tests are not required for all government jobs. Only about half of the jobs in the federal competitive service require written tests. Courts today are taking the position that the use of any test (written or practical) which adversely affects minorities is discriminatory unless the test has been validated and evidences a high degree of utility. A leading United States Supreme Court decision addressing itself to the subject of examinations and their validity is *Griggs* v. *Duke Power Co.* 401 U.S. 424 (1971). The court said that nonjob-related employment selection devices which exclude a disproportionate number of minority group applicants from employment are unlawful, but that a test which is validly job related and has a high degree of utility, and no alternative procedures are available for use, is valid even though it does have an adverse impact on the employment of minorities.

## Quotas

It is easier to forbid "racial discrimination" than to tell anybody exactly what it is. Congress has passed several laws forbidding racial discrimination in public employment (beginning with the Civil Rights Act of 1883), and these acts have been backed up by executive orders issued by various presidents, for example, President Richard M. Nixon's executive order 11478 (issued in 1969 based on the Civil Rights Act of 1964) requiring "affirmative action" to end racial discrimination in hiring. Do these laws mean employers should simply stop discriminating, or do they mean employers must take affirmative action which goes beyond simple nondiscrimination? Courts generally say that agencies should aim to employ enough minorities in each type of job so that the percentage of minorities on board at least equals the percentage of qualified minority applicants for each type of job. Courts do not generally say that the percentage of minority employees in each job type must equal the percentage of minorities in the total population; courts do not, for example, say that if twenty percent of the population is composed of racial minorities, then twenty percent of the brain surgeons in a hospital must be minorities. Courts do not demand the employment of unqualified brain surgeons just to meet a twenty percent quota, nor apparently would they order such a thing with any other occupation, for the courts have clung to the idea that no employer should be required to employ an unqualified employee to meet the requirements of nondescrimination. The percentage used by courts in most cases is not the percentage of minorities in the total American population, but the percentage of qualified minorities among the total number of qualified persons in each field.

Nor do courts generally permit use of any sort of quota system requiring employers to employ such and such a number of minorities by such and such a date. Quotas are simple to understand and easy to enforce, but most judges frown on them because a quota might be interpreted to mean that an employer must hire so many minorities by a certain date whether or not qualified candidates can be found. Furthermore, a quota seems to say, "Once you've got your quota you can quit hiring minorities if you want to." Also, quotas worry some minorities such as Jews who remember the old "Jewish quota" once used in some quarters to keep out Jews rather than bring them in. A quota is a two-edged sword.

Courts prefer "goals and timetables." But it's hard to enforce a goal or a timetable, because the instant you enforce it, it magically changes into a quota. However, while courts shun quota systems they at times seem willing to order certain agencies which are below average in their percentage of minority employees to employ a certain number of qualified minority applicants by a certain date (whether *best* qualified or not). The United States Supreme Court has kept out of most of these issues concerning the exact meaning of nondescrimination and has let the lower courts deal with them case by case. There are, consequently, conflicting judicial opinions among and between lower courts.

## Is Affirmative Action Hostile to Merit?

Many advocates of affirmative action deny that it conflicts with the merit system. On the contrary, they claim affirmative action is an aid to merit, and represents a firm determination to let nothing enter into hiring except merit when merit can be determined. Affirmative action means, they say, a conscious effort to cleanse the civil service of racism and sexism, both of which run counter to merit. A booklet published by the United States Civil Service Commission's Equal Employment Opportunity Training Center advises instructors at the center to define affirmative action as a "conscious effort to root out every vestige of inequality of employment opportunity, such as unrealistic job requirements, selection instruments and procedures which are not job related, insufficient opportunity for upward mobility, inadequate publicity about job openings." The training manual asserts that "affirmative action, when properly carried out, reinforces state and local merit systems by assuring that all segments of our society, not just some, have an opportunity to enter and advance in the public service on the basis of open competition." A memorandum issued jointly in 1973 by four federal agencies charged with enforcing laws designed to keep government personnel systems free from racial discrimination says that minority hiring goals are fully in accord with the merit system: "Under a system of goals, an employer is never required to hire a person who does not have qualifications needed to perform the job successfully; and an employer is never required to hire such an unqualified person in preference to another applicant who is qualified; nor is an employer required to hire a less qualified person in preference to a better qualified person, provided that the qualifications used to make such relative judgments realistically measure the person's ability to do the job in question, or other jobs to which he is likely to progress."

The term affirmative action can be difficult to understand. Some of its advocates insist it means going beyond a passive policy of nondiscrimination. But the differences between passive nondiscrimination, and active nondescrimination is not always clear. Suspicions have occasionally been voiced that the phrase "active nondiscrimination" is code for outright discrimination in favor of minorities to make up for past decades of neglect. Yet many advocates of affirmative action deny they have any secret goals, deny they favor substitution of new victims of discrimination (white males) for old victims, and insist affirmative action simply means making double sure personnel actions are taken totally and completely without regard to race or sex.

## WOMEN IN PUBLIC EMPLOYMENT

Women have been discriminated against in employment during our entire history as a civilization. In this they have shared the fate of racial minorities and are therefore included with minorities in the basic laws against job discrimination. Employers today are required by law to take affirmative action to root out every vestige of inequality of employment opportunity for women, as well as for racial minorities.

### Discriminations Against Women

How have women been discriminated against? The forms of sex discrimination are numerous, varied, and colorful. The first problem, and one of the worst, is the idea that certain jobs are men's jobs and other jobs are women's jobs: auto mechanics and house painters are supposed to be men, nurses and secretaries women, and so on. Until recently most newspapers listed jobs by sex: "help wanted: women;" "help wanted: men." Naturally, women hesitated to apply for men's jobs, and men shrank from applying for women's jobs. This stereotyping of jobs would obviously have a bad effect on recruitment, for there are some good male typists and good female house painters.

Not only have jobs been advertised by sex (less so today than previously) but each sex is itself stereotyped—men are assumed to have certain characteristics and women others. Men, for example, are thought to be less capable of assembling intricate equipment, women less capable of aggressive salesmanship. The correctness of such stereotypes is questionable, yet they often hurt an individual's job opportunities, especially those of women. Even if the stereotypes are true of men and women in general, they are not true of all women or of all men; there are exceptions. It may be that most women are less muscular than most men, but many women are very muscular, so muscular in fact that they might make successful loading dock workers, or even star football players. Women's rights advocates insist that all people should be considered for jobs on the basis of their individual capacities, not on the basis of any characteristics generally attributed to their sex or to any other group to which they might belong.

No one denies that sex is in some cases an almost ironclad qualification for certain jobs. For example, the Metropolitan Opera might forcefully argue that in searching for someone to play the role of Juliet, women applicants should be favored over men; and when it comes to selecting someone to play Romeo, men should be favored. Where sex is a bona fide occupational qualification it is permitted under federal sex discrimination guidelines, but enforcement agencies narrowly interpret them.

Women are sometimes injured by laws designed to protect them. Many states have special laws governing the employment of females. In some cases these laws flatly prohibit employment of females in certain occupations, for example, in jobs requiring lifting or carrying weights exceeding certain limits, or prohibiting females to work during certain hours of the night, or limiting the number of hours per day or per week they can work, and so on. These, to repeat, were often enacted by compassionate legislators to safeguard women whom they stereotyped as frail and in need of protection. While women may appreciate this concern for their welfare, many find these laws burdensome to their employment opportunities. To exclude women from jobs requiring lifting weights excludes those who don't mind lifting weights; laws that limit the number of hours per day or per week a woman may work, discriminate against women who want to work more hours and are perfectly capable of it. Furthermore, these protective laws make women less attractive as potential candidates for jobs because it forces employers to be constantly on the lookout for a plethora of special women's laws.

Some states require special rest periods for women, special rest areas, special meals, special this, special that. Some states have had laws requiring that women but not men be paid overtime for work beyond a certain number of hours. This, of course, makes women employees more expensive. Other laws have required payment of minimum wages to women, and these have the same depressing effect on job opportunities for women. Some employers have maintained separate "male" and "female" seniority lists and when there is a reduction in force a woman can only bump a woman and a man a man. Likewise, some employers have maintained separate lines of promotion for men and for women, so that no woman's promotion can interfere with a man's. Both the seniority lists and the promotion lists amount to creation of separate men's and women's jobs.

Some employers have set up admirable fringe benefits for their employees and then turned around and said they are only for "heads of households" or for persons who are the "principal wage earner" in the family, thus excluding a high proportion of women employees. Also, some employers have set different compulsory retirement ages for men and women.

Another collection of discriminatory practices against women clusters around rules excluding pregnant women from employment altogether, and/or excluding them from health insurance, disability insurance, or sick leave for disabilities caused by pregnancy such as miscarriage, abortion, and childbirth. Various other rules injure the employment benefits of pregnant women: loss of seniority, for example, while off the job because of pregnancy, or loss of retirement benefits for the same reason.

This does not exhaust the list of discriminations against women in employment. It is a notorious fact that women have regularly been paid less for doing the same work as men. Women are often not given promotions because it is thought promotions are for men. Women are often denied opportunities for training which would make them eligible for higher pay and higher rank. Women are often denied membership in man-dominated unions, or if not denied, then discouraged from joining. Women are routinely discouraged from numerous jobs even when they are not barred outright.

Many of these discriminations, and others, are now prohibited under federal (and most state) laws. Much of what was described above is now passing into history and women, through their own insistance and militancy, are finding new avenues opening up—not only new kinds of work, but advancement as well.

## AGE IN PUBLIC EMPLOYMENT

Close to one-third of all Americans are between the ages of 40 and 65. They are commonly discriminated against in employment, perhaps more so than minorities or women. Federal law prohibits employers (including governments) from discriminating on the basis of age against anyone between 40 and 65. The law permits certain bona fide hiring on the basis of age when age is manifestly a job qualification—it is not a violation of law to hire only young persons to model "junior miss fashions."

## SUMMARY

Possibly nothing in administration is more important than good recruitment and selection. Mistakes in hiring are hard to correct and can seriously wound an organization and haunt it for years. No matter how painful the recruitment and selection process, it is less painful than errors arising from neglect of that process. To the maximum degree possible, searches for new employees should focus only on job-related qualifications. Every effort should be made to detect nonjob-related requirements and remove them from the recruitment and selection process. However, some nonjob-related requirements are imposed by law and cannot be avoided. Also, the defensive or offensive needs of employers often creep into the search and it is difficult to know whether these attempts by employers to arm themselves with allies are altogether beyond the proper scope of recruiting and selecting.

Several typical merit system recruitment and selection practices are of debatable value. The rule of three, for example, may unreasonably limit the flexibility of employers. Veteran preference may in some circumstances unreasonably negate the competitive principle of merit systems.

Advocates of a "representative bureaucracy" present us with the problem of how to achieve a bureaucracy which mirrors the class structure of society, while at the same time being competitive.

Despite the equal protection and due process clauses of the United

States Constitution, job discrimination by race, sex, and age has long abounded. Affirmative action programs in recent years have sought to end such discrimination, but the meaning of the term affirmative action is somewhat unclear. In general, courts have rejected race and sex "quotas" and have preferred "goals and timetables" as a guide for ending discrimination; however, the difference between a quota and a goal is not always great at the point of enforcement. Insofar as affirmative action in recruitment and selection amounts to taking special pains to ensure that no one is discriminated against by race or sex, then it is in no way hostile to a merit system, and, in fact, supports and champions the idea of merit—merit freed from the impediments of sex and race discrimination.

## SUGGESTED READING

Brown v. Board of Education, 349 U.S. 294 (1955).

Corson, John J., and Paul, R. Shale. *Men Near the Top: Filling Key Posts in the Federal Service.* Baltimore: The Johns Hopkins Press, 1966.

Djilas, Milovan. *The New Class.* New York: Frederick A. Praeger, 1957.

Donovan, J. J., ed. *Recruiting and Selection in the Public Service.* Chicago: Public Personnel Association, 1968.

Ghiselli, Edwin E. *The Validity of Occupational Aptitude Tests.* New York: Wiley, 1966.

Griggs v. Duke Power Co., 401 U.S. 424 (1971).

Glazer, Nathan. *Affirmative Discrimination: Ethnic Inequality and Public Policy.* New York: Basic Books, 1975.

Hellriegel, Don and Short, Larry. "Equal Employment Opportunity in the Federal Government: A Comparative Analysis." *Public Administration Review,* November-December 1972, pp. 851–858.

Kranz, Harry. "How Representative is the Public Service?" *Public Personnel Management,* July-August, 1973, pp. 242–255.

Krislov, Samuel. *Representative Bureaucracy.* Englewood Cliffs, N.J.: Prentice-Hall, 1974.

Lawshe, C. H., and Balma, Michael J. *Principles of Personnel Testing.* New York: McGraw-Hill, 1966.

Meier, Kenneth J. and Nigro, Lloyd G. "Representative Bureaucracy and Policy Preferences: A Study in the Attitudes of Federal Executives." *Public Administration Review,* July-August 1976, pp. 458–469.

Newgarden, Peggy. "Establishing Affirmative Action Goals for Women."

*Public Administration Review*, July-August 1976, pp. 369–374.

Plessy v. Ferguson, 163 U.S. 537 (1896).

President's Commission on Veterans' Pensions. *Veterans' Benefits in the United States: A Report to the President.* Washington, D.C.: April 1956.

Stahl, O. Glenn. *Public Personnel Administration.* New York: Harper & Row, 1976.

Subramanian, V. "Representative Bureaucracy: A Reassessment." *American Political Science Review,* December 1967, pp. 1010–1019.

"Symposium on Minorities in Public Administration." *Public Administration Review,* November-December 1974, pp. 519–563.

"Symposium on Women in the Public Service". *Public Administration Review,* July-August 1976, pp. 347–389.

United States Civil Service Commission. *The EEO Act: Implications for Public Employees: A Trainer's Module.* Washington, D.C.: U.S. Government Printing Office, 1974.

United States Department of Health, Education and Welfare, Office of State Merit Systems. *An Equal Opportunity Program for State and Local Government Employment.* Washington, D.C.: 1970.

United States Department of Labor. *A Working Woman's Guide to Her Job Rights.* Washington, D.C.: U.S. Government Printing Office, 1975.

*

# Bureaucrats Unite! 7

# Bureaucrats Unite! 7

Neither unions nor strikes are new to the American public service. As long ago as 1836 there was a walkout by workers at the Philadelphia Navy Shipyard. The earliest attempts to unionize federal workers focused on skilled workers in various crafts—printers and bookbinders in the Government Printing Office, machinists in government arsenals, and so on. Craftsmen employed by government naturally felt common cause with similar craftsmen working in private employment; they often enrolled in the same union.

Among noncraft federal workers, the first to organize were postal workers. In 1890 the National Association of Letter Carriers was formed. Various other groups of postal workers (clerks, for example) organized between 1890 and 1920. In more recent years unsuccessful attempts have been made to lure all postal employees into a single union.

Among the earliest associations of nonpostal, noncraft federal employees was the National Federation of Federal Employees (NFFE), organized in 1917. Soon other unions were competing in the lush federal field; the American Federation of Government Employees (AFGE) was formed in 1932 and the United Federal Workers of America (UFWA) in 1937. However, very few federal employees bothered to join any of these general noncraft unions which catered to people who had little in common except a common employer. In the course of time numerous other unions have formed to represent employees of particular agencies, functions or departments: for example, the National Association of Federal Veterinarians and the National Association of Internal Revenue Employees to mention only two. Well over a hundred employee organizations today represent various categories of federal employees.

Of all the people who work for all levels of government in the United States (this includes uniformed military), 80 percent work for state and local governments. Numerous unions and Associations representing state and local employees now flourish. Perhaps the greatest of these is the

American Federation of State, County, and Municipal Employees (AFSCME) with close to a million members. It is one of the fastest growing unions in the nation. Two other unions also enroll numerous state and local employees: Service Employees International Union (SEIU), which caters primarily to white collar and hospital employees, and Laborers International Union (LIU), which caters mainly to unskilled labor. Other unions such as the Teamsters Union and many building trades unions have also been aggressively recruiting public employees. Some unions such as AFSCME represent only public employees, while others such as the building trades unions represent both public and private sector employees.

In addition to regular unions there are many associations. They are sometimes accused of being bargain-basement unions. Their dues are much lower, and their purpose is often partly social, partly to serve as a vehicle for group insurance and running cooperative stores, partly for organized lobbying, and partly for collective bargaining—the latter being in many cases least important.

Among teachers there has been a sharp rise in union affiliation and militancy. Early in the 1960s one could search in vain for a written contract between a teachers' union and a school board. Today hundreds of such contracts exist. Over a million of the nation's four million teachers are covered and the trend suggests millions more will soon be covered. Elementary and secondary teachers spearhead this movement; college teachers are less rapid. Two national unions compete to represent teachers, the American Federation of Teachers (AFT) and the National Education Association (NEA).

The American Federation of Teachers was launched in 1919 and ever since has been a competitor to NEA, although at present NEA has by far the largest following among teachers. Both AFT and NEA chiefly represent classroom teachers. School administrators have their own organizations such as the American Association of School Administrators and the National Association of Secondary School Principles. Both these associations of administrators are loosely associated with NEA, but operate independently for the most part.

## WHAT DO PUBLIC EMPLOYEES' UNIONS DO?

### Tactics for the Public Sector

There are several important differences between tactics used by unions against governmental employers and tactics used against private employers. Methods successful against one may not be appropriate for the other.

However, the differences between public and private employers are sometimes overestimated. Very few business enterprises are *entirely* "private" in the United States today; public regulation of business, or threat of regulation, is an ever increasing fact of life which blurs the line between private and public. A strike against a telephone company is hardly distinguishable from a strike against a government: phone service is no less vital than, say, school service, and phone rates are hardly less fixed by government than are school district tax rates. Increasingly, unions find themselves negotiating with government no matter whether the employer is "public" or "private." It is worth mentioning here also that in some cases a governmental employer is so dominated by private interests that the agency can hardly be said to be governmental: the Federal Communications Commission, for example, is alleged to be regulated by the broadcasting networks, rather than the other way around. This further blurs the line between public and private, and suggests that union tactics for one may be appropriate for the other. However, having noted these similarities, it must be said that unions as a general policy find it useful to go about the business of representing public employees somewhat differently than they go about the business of representing employees in the "private" sector, the difference is chiefly one of emphasis, not of kind.

## Lobbying

Lobbying is a cardinal technique employed by unions to satisfy the aspirations of their members. Some public employee unions are among the biggest spenders in the United States for lobbying. Public employee unions can be rather skilled at lobbying because public employees, by the nature of their work, tend to know where power is located and how it is used.

The term "lobbying" includes much more than wining and dining important people and more than promises to contribute or withhold contributions from campaigns. The term does include all that, of course, because office holders, together with the rest of humanity, like to be liked, and to be smiled upon at dinner parties, and to receive generous donations of time, money, and effort in election years. Many unions certainly have the money, the manpower, and the know-how to wine, dine, contribute, and/ or threaten if they wish to do so.

But lobbying by most successful lobbyists today also includes what one might call "indirect lobbying," that is, drumming up support with the general public so that elected officials will find it easier to accept, or harder to deny, the wage or other demands of unions. This indirect lobbying is sometimes called "public education" or "public relations." Fundamentally it is propaganda aimed at the mass public. It can be so smooth and sophisticated that nobody recognizes it, as when a union fields a community baseball team or stages a drive to raise money for that community chest. Good deeds are always good propaganda. On the other hand, public relations might be a direct attempt to influence public opinion for or against some particular piece of legislation of interest to the union, such as a bill legalizing strikes by public employees, or legalizing binding arbitration.

Another somewhat related form of lobbying is the "education" of legislators and other government decision makers. Legislators, one must confess *are* often influenced by facts. Where political risks do not preclude a legislator from voting "right" he will no doubt be inclined to do so if he knows what is right. Legislators vote on multitudes of subjects, yet they cannot be universal geniuses on all subjects; they welcome expert opinion from people deeply concerned about a given piece of proposed legislation. Union lobbyists may be able to present a great deal of technical information, and maybe analyze the long- and short-range consequences of legislation—social and economic as well as political consequences. Lobbyists contribute a great deal to the work of American legislative bodies by supplying information. They particularly help state and local lawmakers who often lack staff to get needed information. Lobbyists, of course, give slanted opinions—their presentation of information is often stacked to serve their bias. But, by the time legislators have heard lobbyists from several sides of an issue, the truth often emerges much as it hopefully does in a jury trial, even though jurors hear only the carefully staged arguments of competing parties. Lobbyists, by the way, have the same value to administrators as to legislators.

Lobbying has another function: it helps a legislator or administrator justify what he wants to do anyway. A legislator who wants, let us say, to vote for a "right to strike" bill, or who dare not vote against it, finds it useful to fortify himself with good arguments for defense of his position when he goes back home to face the people. In short, lobbying can make it easier for power holders to accept union demands. To that end unions supply information to the public, and directiy to legislators and administrators.

## Bargaining

A second fundamental union tactic is to provide teams of skilled and knowledgeable negotiators to represent the interests of union members in negotiations with employers. A good union negotiator should know everything there is to know about the employer and his agency. Unfortunately (or sometimes fortunately), a great many public officials don't really know very much about the agency they are supposed to be in charge of. A school board may be composed of amateurs who have only superficial knowledge of the multimillion dollar school system—they may be quite unaware how and where inefficiencies exist in the system. Correction of these inefficiencies might make possible teacher salary increases. Or to take another example, one can easily imagine a board of county commissioners consisting perhaps of five or so commissioners, similarly ill-informed and in charge of a large county with thousands of employees and a sixty-million-dollar budget. These commissioners may know nothing about cost accounting, may have never heard of performance budgeting, and may have no idea whether county operations are efficient or wasteful. One can imagine all sorts of government bureaucrats—local, state, or national—who lack technical training to improve operations of their agency. One great weapon a union can bring to bear in negotiations with public officials is the weapon of superior knowledge (professional knowledge) to point out wasteful inefficiencies and show officeholders how these can be corrected to free money for such things as higher wages, better working conditions, or new (union-favored) programs. Public employee unionism could become a mighty force for efficiency in government through application of union employed expertise. On the other hand, economies thus achieved could be negated by excessive wage demands, and by the natural tendency of organized labor to fight for anything that increases the number of jobs and the security of incumbents in those jobs.

*Bargaining versus Lobbying:* Bargaining and lobbying sometimes get in each other's way. If an employees' organization finds the process slow and difficult during collective negotiations it may resort to "end run" lobbying with elected officials to bring pressure on the government's negotiators. While such a tactic may momentarily pay off, it could have a negative long-range effect because it torpedoes the bargaining process, demoralizes negotiators, and leaves the agency with less inclination to embark on future efforts at collective negotiation. These ill-effects are even worse if a union engages in lobbying with high elected or appointed officials to improve a package just agreed upon by the negotiators. This sort of thing frustrates the bargaining process, and leaves negotiators and many other people angry. It is better to avoid simultaneously lobbying and negotiating for the same things. It is best to leave each process to its separate sphere.

Lobbying and collective bargaining may, however, supplement each other. For example, a union may lobby to increase the number of negotiable issues. Governments commonly provide by law that certain issues may not be discussed or negotiated at the bargaining table: a school district may enact a rule against moonlighting by teachers and prohibit the subject from being negotiated. A teachers' association in that case may wish to lobby against the moonlighting rule, but if successful, then the association might find it wise to leave the exact circumstances under which moonlighting will be permitted to the negotiators at future bargaining sessions.

*Strikes and Coercive Tactics:* No idea is decaying faster in America than the notion that civil servants should never under any circumstances go on strike. Of course, the no-strike idea has not died completely, and it may never disappear. In fact, it is still against the law for federal civil servants to strike, and until 1970 the United States Civil Service Commission would not recruit anyone for a federal job who confessed a belief in the right of civil servants to strike. Most state and local governments, as well as the federal government, outlaw strikes by civil servants. However, it is perfectly clear that vast numbers of civil servants are prepared to withhold their services whenever they feel like it, and in recent years there have been four or five hundred work stoppages annually by government employees. These have occurred in a wide array of public services including education, police, fire, health, and sanitation.

The fact that a strike may be illegal does not appear to have much effect on whether or not there is a strike. It is very difficult to enforce antistrike legislation. Clearly it would be impolitic to round up five thousand-striking teachers and throw them in jail, and it would bog down the court system to haul them through elaborate and expensive legal procedures. When there is legal action it usually focusses upon the union itself—its officers and financial resources. But arresting, fining, and jailing union officers only makes them martyrs and angers strikers, and strengthens their resolve so that they often become more militant and intractable than before. If a union is fined, this may, of course, deprive it of money to pay striking workers and thus dampen their will to prolong a walkout, but fines against a union also tend to anger and unify the strikers.

Because it is often impolitic and impractical to punish strikers and their leaders, it is hard to find public officials willing to enforce the law against a strike. An elected judge hesitates to jeopardize his continuance in office by issuing an injunction to halt an illegal strike, nor do judges like to punish strikers or union leaders who violate court injunctions. A police chief hesitates to accumulate vast numbers of implacable enemies by vigorously enforcing strike-related laws and injunctions. Vandalism and violence may go unchecked by police.

For these reasons, it is perhaps safe to dismiss antistrike laws as almost meaningless, except for the moral sanction they represent. But that moral sanction is powerful in some cases. When police walk out illegally they are subject to the accusation that they, of all people, are setting an example of lawlessness. Teachers who strike illegally are subject to the wrath of parents who resent the spectacle of teachers behaving lawlessly, of teachers flaunting this lawlessness by picketing even elementary schools and participating sometimes in vandalism against their own schools. These striking teachers may also become antagonistic toward teachers not on strike, toward parents who bring their children to school despite the strike, and toward students themselves (even very young students) for attending schools kept open in spite of the strike.

The main deterrents against strikes by public employees are not so much the laws which prohibit strikes, but other factors having to do with the suitability and practicality of strikes. Strikes are expensive—for both parties. An employee on strike may lose an entire day's wages for every day on strike, unless, of course, the union, as a condition for settling the strike can bludgeon employers into paying strikers their usual wages even for time on strike. However, this is not likely to happen, especially if the public is aggravated by a strike, political officers are not likely to compound that aggravation by paying civil servants for refusing to work. Furthermore, strikers always run the risk of losing their jobs, especially if demands are unreasonable and/or unpopular with the electorate and if there is unemployment and if skeleton crews of nonstrikers can manage to keep the agency functioning during the crisis.

Strikes by civil servants can be expensive in various other subtle but important ways. If a walkout is unpopular with the electorate, say a police or teachers' strike, it raises barriers of hostility between those civil servants and the public, and can result in all sorts of backlashes. A teachers strike may reap the whirlwind of defeated school bond issues, and public hostility to new school taxes. As for a police strike, it may seriously damage the rapport and cooperation between public and police so important to law enforcement.

A union, of course, has other pressure tactics at its disposal besides strikes. Informal picketing sometimes helps, and various kinds of work slowdowns can be used. Courts might classify a mass sick call as a strike if a union leads it. Work slowdowns, on the other hand, are difficult to prove, and some are entirely legal—for example, if every employee should start meticulously following every work rule, performing every task by the book, taking no shortcuts, and getting next to nothing done because everything is done "exactly right."

## Social and Psychological Functions

Union membership may provide some human associations that help fill a void caused by bureaucratic impersonality at the work place. Also, unions give members a sense of power. The superior-subordinate relationship of modern bureaucracy tends to reduce employees to an inferior status. In a union subordinates feel less helpless before the boss; a union gives members rights and power, and a sense of being on top some of the time instead of always on the bottom.

## IS COLLECTIVE BARGAINING COMPATIBLE WITH PUBLIC EMPLOYMENT?

Opponents of public employee unionism sometimes argue that it conflicts with the sovereignty of the state, that governmental services are too essential to permit union interference, and that public service unionism is at bottom a conspiracy against the public.

The sovereignty argument runs briefly as follows: if a government, whether local, state, or national, is to remain sovereign, then it cannot bow to the demands of unions or anyone else. This argument may sound better than it is. Many scholars doubt there is any such thing as sovereignty, if by the word one means a power that cannot be influenced by any other power. Certainly governments are influenced—what is politics but an effort to influence. If by sovereignty one means an organization without legal superior, then it is logical to say sovereignty exists and to say that governments cannot negotiate labor contracts (or any other sort of contract) because, alas, there is no legal superior to enforce such contracts upon the sovereign. Technically it is true that the United States government, for example, cannot be irrevocably bound by any contract which the three branches of government—executive, legislative, and judicial—working in concert choose not to honor. But, of course, governments do enter into contracts, thousands upon thousands of them, and courts do tend to honor them. The United States Constitution expressly forbids states (but not the federal government) to pass any law impairing the obligation of contracts (Article 1, Section 10). However, in various leading United States Supreme Court decisions the police power of the state is ranked higher than the obligation of contract, meaning, a contract will not be allowed to stand in the face of the general welfare. Aside from all this, a contract carries a certain moral and political suasion, no matter what its legal status may be, and is therefore likely to be adhered to.

The opponents of public employee unions also say that government services are essential and no union should have the right to interfere with those services. Defenders of public employee unions counter with the claim that many government services are not more important than private services—a city owned swimming pool is no more essential than a privately owned swimming pool, city trash collection is no more essential than private trash collection, public transportation is no more important than private transportation, and so on. Usually, the antiunionists point to police, fire, and hospital workers as examples of services so essential that interruption can not be permitted. However, some recent police strikes or slowdowns have caused some people to ponder whether there is much relationship between police service and crime rate. Skeptics whisper that the crime rate goes down when police disappear. Firemen do seem to be essential, although the history of volunteer fire departments suggests the public is not entirely helpless without professional firepersons. As for hospital workers, no one disputes their essentiality, but one may question whether the workers in a public hospital are more essential than the workers in a private hospital.

It is also argued by antiunionists that collective bargaining by public employees is a conspiracy against the general public. The public, they say, is not making money by employing civil servants, and cannot pass the cost of increased wages on to buyers of public services because, except in the case of utilities, there are, generally speaking, no "buyers" of public services. However, this argument is countered by the contention that public employees can, nevertheless, be exploited—that the public does gain by the services of public employees such as teachers whose services are used by students and their parents to increase the students' earning power. Defenders of unionism argue that the general public does, in fact, buy the services of public servants, profits by those services, and has no more right to obtain free or underpaid service than does a private firm to free or underpaid service from private employees.

## IS UNIONISM COMPATIBLE WITH MERIT SYSTEMS?

If public service unionism is compatible with public employment, is it also compatible with a merit system? Here again we find heavy contention on both sides.

### A Nonmerit Condition of Employment

At heart, the idea of a merit system is that merit and only merit should govern appointments, promotions, dismissals, and so on. But what if a union turns around and says, "We want to negotiate an agreement under which every applicant for a civil service job must belong to the union before he can be hired, or at least must join the union as a condition of keeping his job after he is hired." Such a thing would constitute imposition of a wholly nonmerit condition on civil service hiring. At present the Taft-Hartley Act forbids both the "closed shop" and the "union shop" in federal employment. A closed shop requires a prospective employee to be a member of the union before being hired and to remain a member so long as he is employed by the shop. A union shop requires a new employee to join the union within a certain period after being hired, but does not require him to be a member before being hired. Most unionists, while preferring a closed shop, are adamant that a union shop is completely and entirely justified. After all, say union advocates, victories won by unions are profitable to everybody in the agency, not just to union members. Why shouldn't everybody be compelled to join, and to share the cost as well as the benefit—negotiations cost money, the apparatus of a union has to be paid for. Under a union shop this is done by requiring new employees to join the union which is fighting for "their" interests. So say the unionists.

Unionists also point out that compulsory union membership would not be the *only* nonmerit condition of public employment. The federal government (and many state and local governments) already have a collection of nonmerit conditions. For instance, they commonly require civil servants to be citizens; many state and local governments also require civil servants to be residents of the city, town, or county that employs them. Perhaps these requirements seem reasonable, but they have little to do with merit. Veteran preference laws give nonmerit advantages to veterans for appointment to federal and many state and local civil service jobs. Affirmative action programs and the so-called equal employment opportunity programs have in recent years given nonmerit advantages to certain groups. Unionists argue that nonmerit conditions for public employment are by no means unheard of, that those which exist are claimed to be justified sufficiently to override merit considerations. Thus, compulsory union membership would also be justified.

### Right of Nonassociation

Nonunionists may or may not admit the value of unions to their economic well-being, but they often insist there are other values besides economic well-being to consider. One such value is the right of nonassociation. The First Amendment to the United States Constitution guarantees the right to associate, and this would seem to imply a right not to associate. The issue has been brought to the United States Supreme Court whether compulsory union membership in the private sector violates the right of association. The Court has not chosen to decide the issue, but in 1961 did hold *(International Association of Machinists* v. *Street)* that Congress in passing the National Labor Relations Act (Par 8 (a) (3) (61 Stat. 140), which authorized union shops in firms doing business in interstate commerce, had intended that dues money obtained through union shop agreements should be used only to support collective bargaining and not to support other causes. However, to repeat, no federal employee is compelled to join a union, and, in fact, Executive Order 11491 expressly guarantees the right of federal employees to refrain from organizing for employee representation.

At the state and local level, states with "right to work" laws also prohibit both the closed and union shop in both public and private employment; elsewhere very few union shop agreements have been negotiated.

Unions, recognizing the resistance to compulsory union membership in public employment, have hit upon a middle road, the so-called "agency shop" which, if adopted in a particular jurisdiction, requires all public employees in that jurisdiction to pay fees to the union to cover its representational expenses, but does not require actual membership in the union. This is permissible in some state and local jurisdictions, but not in the federal civil service.

Unionists could argue that the constitutional right of nonassociation has no bearing on the issue of compulsory union membership—no person is compelled to associate, because no person is compelled to remain a government employee who does not like the conditions of employment. Or, as Justice Oliver W. Holmes put it in 1892, "The petitioner may have a constitutional right to talk politics, but he has no constitutional right to be a policeman" *(McAuliffe v. Mayor of New Bedford).* Or as the United States Supreme Court put it in 1952, "The First Amendment guarantees free speech and assembly, but it does not guarantee government employ" *(Adler v. Board of Education).*

However, in recent years the United States Supreme Court has modified its position, and now seems to hold that governments may not deny employment to any person for any reason that infringes on that person's constitutionally protected interests. (See *Perry v. Sinderman.*) If that is the position of the Court, it would seem unconstitutional for any government to deny employment to any person who, asserting freedom of association and nonassociation under the First Amendment, refuses to associate with a union.

## Partisan Politics

Many who oppose public service unionism argue that employee organizations are bringing partisan politics back into the public service. Unions, it is claimed, play politics to win benefits for their members because those benefits can only be granted by politicians in control of a government. Bargaining with politicians draws one, naturally, into politics, just as bargaining with the devil is said to draw one into sin. From the point of view of some politicians, alliances with unions can be attractive—unions have money, unions have lots of people to work in campaigns and to vote. All this irresistably sucks the unionized civil service back into the murky waters of partisan politics from whence it with such difficulty emerged. It makes overt or covert party politicians out of what should be a nonpartisan civil service. At least, that is what the antiunionists claim.

This point of view is not shared by unionists, some of whom claim that while unions will naturally support their friends and oppose their enemies, this is (or should be) done on an individual basis and not on a party basis. That is, a union will support or oppose this or that individual politician, but will not support or oppose a political party. It is, as Samuel Gompers said, poor practice for a union to attach itself to a party, because there is no certainty that every member of that party is a "friend of labor." Unions should be political insofar as they support their friends and punish their enemies, but not in a partisan sense. Furthermore, the defenders of public unionism point out that one of the cardinal purposes of a union is to protect its members from arbitrary dismissals, and from nonwork-connected, nonmerit-connected personnel actions of almost every kind. In fact, they argue that public employee unions are the strongest defenders of the merit system.

## Seniority

Unions almost always favor heavy reliance on seniority for determining who should be promoted, laid off, recalled, transferred, given job or work assignments, given shift preference, get days off, allowed overtime, and so on. This hardly seems to square with the love professed by unions for merit principles, but it does square with the hostility of unions to capricious and arbitrary personnel actions. Seniority is arbitrary, but not capricious. Prounionists defend their seniority idea against the claim that it conflicts with the merit idea. First, they claim seniority and merit are frequently identical—those on the job longest are likely to know as much about the job, and therefore have as much merit as any person in the organization. Secondly, merit is hard to define and is often not quantifiable. What constitutes merit in a teacher, for example, or in an administrator?—Very often "merit" boils down to somebody's personal opinion of who has it and what it is. In many cases seniority is just as efficient at pinpointing merit as any other system, and much less distressing to those found lacking in merit. And if seniority should give a reward to someone less meritorious than others, what is lost is gained again in morale; seniority makes clear-cut decisions, on a clear-cut, universally understood principle, and leaves in its wake much less internecine strife, jealousy, tension, and muttering.

Seniority, though under attack, has been used for generations in the United States Congress for making all sorts of personnel decisions which, if not made by seniority, would result in a ceaseless war of all against all. Senators and representatives are assigned such things as space in office buildings, seats on the floor of the house or senate, and most importantly, chairmanships of most committees on the basis of seniority. Even within civil service career systems, seniority may determine one's salary within each grade, and seniority is generally considered as one among various measures for determining a candidate's qualification for promotion. Some jurisdictions bring seniority into the promotion system by doing such things as selecting for promotion one of the three senior employees in length of service qualified for the job.

## Equal Pay for Equal Work

The opponents of public service unionism insist that collective bargaining destroys the principle of equal pay for equal work, and without that principle, the whole merit system comes crashing down. Merit demands that everybody with the same general type (classification) of job be paid about the same amount of money. If people are going to be paid on the basis of how much political or union muscle they have, then we are back to where we began—bogged down in politics. So say the opponents of public unionism. But defenders argue, as they did in the case of seniority, that merit is hard to define, and all sorts of personal values go into determining what jobs are equal to what other jobs, what occupations are equal to, or above, or below other occupations. Management has considerable freedom to determine grade levels for public service jobs; there is no mathematically precise way of determining these things. Collective bargaining may be as good a way as any, especially when you consider that market forces have a great deal to do with merit-system job classification. Market forces, as much as anything, dictate that a dentist be classified higher than an auto mechanic.

## Impartiality of the Civil Service Commission

Opponents of public service unionism sometimes argue that civil servants do not need a union to look after their interests if there is a properly established civil service commission like the United States Civil Service Commission. The commission, they say, will be evenhnded and fair and will make personnel rules which fairly balance the interest of subordinates with the interest of superiors. It will also fairly balance the interest of the general public and of the government on the one hand with the interest of public employees on the other.

Many unions emphatically deny this claim of evenhandedness by civil service commissions, even the United States Civil Service Commission. Unions say the commissions often represent primarily the interests of management, and point to the United States Civil Service Commission as an example of one considered the "personnel office of the President," whose members are appointed by the President and can be removed by him at will, whose record has allegedly been one of "see no evil, hear no evil" when it comes to manipulation of merit procedures by agency heads, which has been accused of sometimes cooperating with those manipulations. At the state and local level unionists argue that the situation in many places is worse—political control is all too evident in a great many state and local civil service commissions, and it is folly to think the interest of state and local civil servants can be left to the tender care of such commissions.

## PUBLIC SERVICE UNIONISM AND THE LAW

### The Private Sector

Federal law governing labor relations in the private sector does not govern labor relations in the public sector, although it does provide an interesting backdrop. Looking briefly at federal law governing labor relations in the private sector, the picture is this. Before the New Deal, unionism was a risky business because employers could fire employees for organizing or participating in a union, and could pull all sorts of other dirty tricks on unions and their members. Courts could and did freely issue antistrike injunctions—a judicial command ordering a strike halted on grounds it worked irreparable harm to the employer (by damaging his business in ways that could never be recouped).

Antistrike injunctions were considered by unions to be doubly troublesome because judges were thought to be more sympathetic to management than to labor. In 1932 the Norris-LaGuardia Act outlawed the antistrike injunction in labor disputes involving firms doing business in interstate commerce. Courts could still issue injunctions to stop certain kinds of misbehavior connected with a strike, such as window breaking and tire slashing, but were forbidden to enjoin a whole strike. This was a great step forward in the eyes of unionists, but a greater step forward occurred with passage of the National Labor Relations Act of 1935 (29 U.S.C. Par 151 et seq.) commonly called the Wagner Act. The law, thought of as organized labor's bill of rights, prohibited a whole series of dirty tricks ("unfair labor practices") which for generations had annoyed unions and injured their development. Among these outlawed practices was laying off people solely for union activity. To interpret and apply this law, a National Labor Relations Board was established to hear complaints and determine whether an unfair labor practice had been committed.

Unions flourished under protection of the Wagner Act, but the act was thought to be too one-sided. It prohibited employers to be unfair but did not prohibit labor unions to be unfair. Therefore in 1947 Congress passed the Labor Management Relations Act (an amendment to the Wagner Act) which balanced the scales by listing and outlawing numerous "unfair" labor union practices. This list was expanded by the Labor Reform Act of 1959 (the Landrum-Griffen Act), a law which also regulated various internal organizational affairs of labor unions.

## The Public Sector

None of this federal legislation for the private sector applied to federal employees. The Wagner Act and the Taft-Hartley Act specifically exclude federal employees from coverage, and the Taft-Hartley Act forbids federal employees to strike: any employee who does "shall be discharged immediately from his employment, and shall forfeit his civil service status, if any, and shall not be eligible for reemployment for three years by the United States." And in 1955 Public Law 330 made it a felony for federal employees to strike or assert the right to strike, and required them to sign promises they would not do either of those things. However, this does not mean federal employees are forbidden to join unions. On the contrary, Congress long ago (1912) in the Lloyd-LaFollette Act permitted federal employees to join unions and lobby Congress so long as those unions do not advocate the right to strike.

State legislation in these matters tends to run more or less parallel with federal legislation, and in recent years many states have passed laws requiring local governments and state agencies to recognize and bargain with employee organizations, while at the same time outlawing public employee strikes.

The Lloyd-LaFollette Act was not a Wagner Act for federal employees. While it permitted employee organization and lobbying, it did not encourage those things, it did not acknowledge that employee organizations had any legitimate role in the formulation and implementation of personnel policies, it set no standards for recognition of employee organizations, made no rules concerning matters upon which employee organizations should appropriately be consulted, said nothing about employee representation in appeals and grievance proceedings. Nor has Congress in subsequent years enacted any bills to fill this void, although at present Congress is studying such a bill.

Consequently, a task force of high executive officials in the John F. Kennedy administration studied the situation and found an absence of government policy in labor-management relations in the civil service, and noted the tremendously diverse policies followed in the various agencies and subagencies of the federal bureaucracy. It recommended to President Kennedy a series of proposals dealing with various aspects of federal employee collective bargaining including unit determination and representation procedures, arbitration, recognition, scope of bargaining, conduct of negotiations, grievances, and impass procedures. Shortly thereafter, in 1962, President Kennedy promulgated Executive Orders 10987 and 10988 setting forth collective bargaining and grievance procedures in the executive branch. After several years experience with Kennedy's executive orders several inadequacies were noted, and in 1967 President Lyndon B. Johnson ordered another task force to study how things were going under Kennedy's orders. By the time the review committee finished its study, Richard M. Nixon had become President. He promptly issued a new Executive Order 11491 revoking Kennedy's Executive Order 10988, and then repromulgated most of the Kennedy provisions, adding various changes suggested as a result of the study made by the review committee appointed by Johnson.

## BASIC FEATURES OF FEDERAL COLLECTIVE BARGAINING

A Federal Labor Relations Council oversees the labor-management relations program of the federal service. The council administers and interprets the executive orders pertaining to labor relations in the federal service, decides major policy issues, prescribes regulations, and reports with recommendations to the President.

The Assistant Secretary of Labor for Labor-Management Relations plays a role comparable to that of the National Labor Relations Board in the private sector. He decides appropriate bargaining units, supervises representation elections, and rules on unfair labor practice complaints. As with labor organizations in the private sector, unions of federal employees are required to file annual financial reports for disclosure to the public, and to observe standards of conduct in respect to election of union officers, administration of trusteeships, handling of money, and the rights of union members.

In determining the unit to be represented by employee organizations, the assistant secretary of labor for Labor Management Relations is to establish units that will ensure a clear and identifiable community of interest among the employees concerned and which will promote effective dealing and efficiency of agency operations.

An employee organization selected in a secret ballot election, by a majority of the employees in an appropriate unit as their representative is given exclusive recognition. When a labor organization has been accorded exclusive recognition, it is the exclusive representative of employees in the unit and is entitled to act for and to negotiate agreements covering all employees in the unit without discrimination and without regard to labor organization membership. The labor organization must be given the opportunity to be represented at formal discussions between management and employees concerning grievances, personnel policies and practices, or other matters affecting general working conditions of employees in the unit.

Unions are always concerned about something they call "union security." It has to do with the danger to their security posed by people who are not members of the union, for example, the threat to a teachers' union out on strike presented by teachers who are not members of the union and not on strike and managing to keep the schools open. Whenever they can, unions try to win contracts which include "security clauses," meaning provisions forcing people to join the union as a condition of employment—union shop, closed shop, agency shop, payroll withholding of union dues, and similar things. However, under federal rules, payroll deduction of dues is entirely voluntary with the employee, and nothing may be negotiated with an agency which requires an employee to become or to remain a member of a labor organization, or to pay money to the organization.

A great many things are not bargainable at all under the federal rules. This is partly because Congress determines many conditions of labor by law: levels of pay, hours of work, retirement age, the merit principle in hiring and promotion, job classification, performance rating, and many other personnel policies. A mandatory management rights clause must be in every contract negotiated: this means everyone is governed first by the laws of the land and second by the negotiated agreements; and it also means that management officials of the agency retain the right, in accordance with those laws to direct employees of the agency, to hire, promote, transfer, assign, and retain employees in positions within the agency, and to suspend, demote, discharge, or take other disciplinary action against employees; to relieve employees from duties because of lack of work or for other legitimate reasons; to maintain the efficiency of the government operations entrusted to them; to determine the methods, means, and personnel by which such operations are to be conducted; and to take whatever actions may be necessary to carry out the mission of the agency in situations of emergency.

If negotiations between a union and federal agency reach an impass, the Federal Mediation and Conciliation Service may help the parties reach an agreement, and if it fails, either party may ask the Federal Service Impasses Panel to decide the matter.

## SUMMARY

Though still the subject of heated debate, collective negotiations in the public sector are increasingly common, and numerous public employee unions function today in the United States. The debate over public employee unionism turns partly on whether unionism conflicts with the sovereignty of the state, whether governmental services are too essential to permit union interference, and whether unionism is compatible with merit systems. Under federal law, which is mirrored by the law in many states and localities, no employee is required to become or remain a member of a labor organization or pay money to it; and a great many things are not bargainable, because Congress determines many conditions of labor by law. Nevertheless, employee unions effectively serve their members in a variety of ways. Strikes are growing more frequent but continue to be illegal almost everywhere. Although the strike weapon is at present rejected by most public employee unions, there are many tactics other than strikes regularly used in dealing with governmental employers. Some of these tactics are similar to those used by unions in the private sector; they include direct lobbying of employers, indirect lobbying through public relations or public education, and bargaining by teams of skilled and knowledgeable negotiators.

## SUGGESTED READING

Adler v. Board of Education, 342 U.S. 458 (1952).

Berle, Adolf A. *Power.* New York: Harcourt Brace Javanovich, 1969.

International Association of Machinists v. Street, 367 U.S. 740 (1961).

McAuliffe v. Mayor of New Bedford, 155 Mass. 216 (1892).

Nigro, Felix A. *Management-Employee Relations in the Public Service.* Chicago: Public Personnel Association, 1969.

Perry v. Sinderman, 408 U.S. 593 (1972).

Stieber, Jack. *Public Employee Unionism, Growth, Policy.* Washington, D.C.: The Brookings Institution, 1973.

"Symposium on Collective Bargaining in the Public Service: A Reappraisal." *Public Administration Review,* March-April 1972, pp. 97–126.

Tax Foundation. *Unions and Government Employment.* New York: Tax Foundation, 1972.

United States Civil Service Commission, Bureau of Training, Labor Relations Training Center. *Collective Bargaining in the Federal Sector: Where We Are: Where We May Be Going: Implications for Managers.* 1973.

United States Civil Service Commission, Personnel Bibliography Series No. 44, *Labor Management Relations in the Public Service.* 1972.

Weitzman, Joan. *The Scope of Bargaining in Public Employment.* New York: Praeger, 1975.

Zagoria, Sam, ed. *Public Workers and Public Unions.* Englewood Cliffs, New Jersey: Prentice-Hall, 1972.

# Internal Communications 8

# Internal Communications 8

An organization without communications is as unthinkable as a book without pages. Organization and communication may, in fact, be identical substances; where there is organization there is communication; where there is communication there is organization. An organization may be nothing more and nothing less than a communications network. The various parts of an organization must necessarily be in some sort of communication with one another. Insofar as organizations are controlled by hierarchies, such control can be exercised only through communication.

Any stimulus could logically be defined as "communication." An organization could perhaps be defined as two or more bodies directly or indirectly stimulating and responding to one another.

The shape, structure, and procedures of every organization are greatly affected (if not dictated) by the shape, structure, and type of communication network within an organization. Likewise, organizational structure affects the communications network. To repeat, it is difficult to distinguish between organization and communication.

## VARIETIES OF HUMAN COMMUNICATION

Five persons filed into the public library in Clinton, Louisiana and staged a sit-in. Three high school students attended school in Des Moines, Iowa wearing black armbands to protest a war. In New York a draft card was publically burned, elsewhere a United States flag was publically desecrated. The perpetrators of all these actions were prosecuted; their defense rested on the first amendment to the United States Constitution which guarantees freedom of speech. Federal courts had to decide what, if anything, besides verbal utterance constitutes speech protected by the first amendment. Picketing, wearing long hair, topless dancing, and many other actions raise the question whether they constitute communication pro-

173

tected by the first amendment. These actions which are intended to be speech are called "symbolic speech," and there is probably more symbolic speech in the world and within every organization than any other kind of speech. We constantly speak through our actions; we speak with our clothing, with facial expression, with general demeanor, with the interior and exterior of our houses, with the professions we follow, with the manner in which we pursue those professions, and with many other acts. There is a constant and ceaseless flow of symbolic speech from each of us. Our verbal utterances by comparison are rare.

## THE EXECUTIVE'S VERBAL ENVIRONMENT

A large part (perhaps all) of an executive's job has to do with giving and receiving communications. Managers are nerve centers in the organizational communications network; they receive, process, and transmit all sorts of memoranda, letters, policy statements, instructions, reports, face-to-face communications, and what not. Perhaps nothing is more important to successful administration than successful communication. Yet one rarely finds any systematic attempt to teach communication skills in schools of public administration.

Communications in organizations are often characterized by the direction they flow in relation to the hierarchy—"upward" from subordinates to bosses, "downward" from bosses to subordinates, or "laterally" across hierarchies. Communications have about as much difficulty flowing upward as water; a pump may be needed. Downward communications also exhibit some of the characteristics of downward flowing water; they can become a sloppy, unruly torrent. Lateral communications are sometimes the most successful and least disturbed of all communications.

## UPWARD COMMUNICATIONS

Subordinates generally expect to be told what to do by bosses, not the other way around. The natural flow of communications is downward, not upward. Yet it is important for a manager to receive information from those beneath him. An upward flow of communications is as important to him as an upward flow of nerve signals to the brain; without it he will soon fall unconscious of happenings in the branches and limbs of his organization. But the obstacles to this imperative flow of intelligence from the bottom are numerous and complex. Few managers ever succeed in overcoming them, and must wage constant warfare to keep lines of upward communications open. Total success at this is not possible. The best one can hope for is partial success; even under the best of circumstances, much of what is communicated whether up, down, or laterally is unreliable, misleading, and distorted.

## Hindrances to Upward Communications

*Inferior Status of Subordinates:* The prestige of managers is one of the great hindrances to upward communication. The word "prestige" has an interesting origin. It stems from the Latin *praestigium*, meaning illusion, and from *praestigiae*, meaning jugglers' tricks. From rank there radiates an illusion similar to the illusion produced by a juggler—that something is there which is not. Rank gives the illusion that the holder of that rank has mysterious, awesome, and slightly frightening qualities. Of course, there is some substance to prestige, it's not all illusion. The juggler does in actuality perform, but there is a gap between what the juggler actually does and what he appears to do, just as there is a gap between the actual qualities of a person holding rank and the shimmering qualities which he seems to have (his prestige).

The prestige surrounding persons of rank is an intimidating barrier to persons of lower status. Managers often feel they need to magnify this intimidating prestige by surrounding themselves with signs, symbols, and trappings of rank.

The inferior status of subordinates makes them feel uncomfortable in the presence of superiors, reluctant to initiate conversations, and tongue tied and nervous in the great one's presence. Managers who value communications from below must do what they can to put subordinates at ease about approaching them, and at ease during conversations. This, of course, presents a dilemma to managers who believe "familiarity breeds contempt," and who are insecure to the point of requiring emphasis rather than deemphasis on the symbols and mannerisms of rank. How can one scare the wits out of subordinates, and at the same time put them at ease?

A manager who values upward communication more than he values full emphasis on his status, may find it useful to take at least a few steps to de-imperialize himself. First he might find it useful to seek out occasions and situations for visiting with subordinates outside his office, away from the intimidating status symbols with which many managers like to adorn their inner and outer offices. Secure administrators might also find it useful to tone down their offices, get rid of the carpet, the silver set, the oak desk, and establish themselves in less overpowering surroundings. Second, if at all possible, a manager might want to try having a really open door, try to ease that feeling so many subordinates have that they must "petition" for an audience with the manager and that such a petition is an annoyance to him.

One of the most common fears of subordinates is that they are intruding on the "great one's" time when they visit him. Students sometimes exhibit this feeling when they dare to knock on a professor's door for a conference. How often they begin with apologies for taking the professor's time and after a moment hasten away with more apologies! Students seldom have the "affrontery" to view professors as people paid to confer with students. Likewise, a manager is paid to manage, and no part of management is more important than listening to the managed.

Some managers are very poor listeners, and compound the uneasiness of subordinates by seeming tense, nervous, and tied up with their own problems. A manager who wants to put subordinates at ease should quit fidgeting, quit moving papers around on the desk, quit taking phone calls, quit looking at his watch, and start giving full undivided attention to what a subordinate who has ventured into his office has to say. And rather than butting in, changing the subject, and playing big shot, a manager might try keeping his own mouth reasonably shut except for giving his visitor encouragement and opportunity to say what he wants to say. The manager's attitude and demeanor will make a great difference in how much his visitor ventures to say, now and in the future.

*Distortion:* Receiving messages from below is not enough. Equally important is that those messages be accurate. It is notoriously difficult for superiors to get the truth from subordinates. Some of this distortion of upward communications is intentional, some not.

The intentional distortion comes from those who want to win favor with the boss. This is a perfectly natural desire, but some are more willing to lie for it than others. Perhaps everyone in the organization colors the news somewhat, but ambitious climbers and empire builders will commit the worst crimes of coloration: everything unfavorable is minimized, everything favorable is maximized. Sometimes this distortion is magnified as it goes through channels. An infantry squad exaggerates, say, the number of enemy troops killed in a day. This exaggerated report is further exaggerated at division headquarters, and further exaggerated at army headquarters and so on, until the enemy dead is astronomical. Every administrator has to beware of good news; it may be largely fluff and falsehood. Cumulative distortion can be found in the reports of many agencies including universities.

Armies have been defeated, battles lost, and nations brought to disaster by the deceptions of subordinates who want to improve their personal status with the boss by bearing good news or who fear to bear bad news. Managers such as Adolf Hitler often seal their own fate by allowing themselves to be surrounded by "yes" men.

Some dilutions and distortions of upward communications are quite unintentional, but no less hurtful. Nearly everyone prefers to bear good news, and a great many basically innocent people unconsciously edit out or deemphasize that which would displease the hearer, and unconsciously emphasize that which pleases. Some, as noted earlier, do this systematically, consciously, and maliciously, while others do it almost out of their own goodness of heart, often wholly unintentionally.

Another unintentional distortion occurs as news is edited by each successive level of the hierarchy. Top level managers don't have time to see or hear all the information generated at the lower reaches of the organization, especially of a large organization. The mass of data must be (and is) edited, condensed, shortened, packaged, and repackaged at successive levels, until what finally reaches the desk of the top manager is a sculptured work at which many hands below have carefully chipped and carved. Editing of communications can produce a bias: he who structures a problem and the decision maker's perception of it can virtually make a decision.

## DOWNWARD COMMUNICATIONS

Few of the psychological roadblocks to free flowing upward communications afflict downward communications—bosses have less hesitancy communicating with subordinates, and there is less need for superiors to impress subordinates by altering messages. Still, there is distortion in downward communications caused partly by the inevitable distortion resulting from repetition of a message as it reaches each level of the organization and is passed on. This can be illustrated in the classroom by a practical demonstration: a short story is told to the first student who whispers it to a second student who in turn whispers it to a third and so on through a collection of persons. When the story reaches the last student it may be quite different from the story given the first student. So notoriously unreliable are witnesses, that judicial rules of evidence generally prohibit introduction of "hearsay." Hearsay is what a witness says he heard another person say, it is evidence not proceeding from the personal knowledge of the witness, but from mere repetition of what he has heard others say. The inaccuracies of direct observation are bad enough without compounding them by further inaccuracies of a second person reporting what he heard the first person say.

Of course, there is also much deliberate distortion of downward flowing messages. Subordinates who receive instructions they disagree with are prone to ignore or to deliberately "misunderstand" what they have been told. Nor is it unheard of for subordinates in the chain of command to deliberately disrupt or alter downward flowing communications with which they disagree.

## HOW TO CURB DISTORTION

A manager who wants to be sure a communication reaches everybody it is intended to reach without distortion or alteration might find it useful to send it by several routes, not relying solely on the chain of command. Important new policies or instructions might, for example, be communicated straight to the whole organization by means of mass meetings, in-house loudspeaker, and television, or by written communication sent directly to every member of the organization who is expected to play any part in carrying out the new instructions or policies. Briefing teams are also useful. A top level manager who wants to be sure every key subordinate receives an identical education about a new policy, might establish a briefing team to carry that education to every important point in the organization. Top level management can also conduct inspections at the bottom of the hierarchy to satisfy themselves whether instructions are being executed. They can also get a fairly good impression whether their orders are reaching the operating level by talking with clients of the agency who feel the ultimate effect of those orders.

But here it must be said that executives occupying steps on the hierarchical ladder beneath top managers are very sensitive and usually hostile to any attempt by their superiors to reach around them. Some managers are especially vigilant to see that nothing goes upward in the organization that does not first cross their desk. Unfortunately this kind of censorship is exactly the thing top managers have to fight against, yet, at the same time, they cannot afford to express lack of confidence in subordinate managers. However, a top manager simply must have a reasonably accurate flow of intelligence from the bottom, and must run checks to test the accuracy of what he is receiving through regular channels. If he must reach around subordinate managers for direct contact with operating level people, this must be done with caution and judgment. Just how this can be done varies with the situation, but in some cases a manager can learn a lot by strolling through the agency from time to time casually visiting with operating level people in the hall or in the snack bar. But it is probably ill-advised for a manager to permit subordinates to by-pass any steps in the chair of command to see him formally about an organizational matter. This infuriates the by-passed supervisors and also reduces their status and undermines their authority.

Top managers might consider reducing the number of hierarchical layers in their organization; that is, they might profit by having a flat organization instead of a tall one. The taller the organization the more levels through which upward and downward communications must pass, therefore the greater the accumulation of distortion of all messages. Of course, many considerations enter into whether to have a flat or tall organization other than the factor of distorted communications.

Some top managers combat distortion by giving the same job to two subordinates, and then sit back to enjoy the cockfight. Meanwhile he is bombarded with inspired and penetrating reports from both sides. President Franklin D. Roosevelt is said to have followed this practice with great success and personal pleasure among his immediate assistants in the White House.

Another antidote to distortion is the so-called "distortion-proof message." Perhaps there is no such immaculate thing as an absolutely distortion-proof message, but attempts can be made to design, for instance, field or shop reports that go direct from the bottom of the organization to the top without giving anyone in between a chance to distort it. While this may be useful for transmitting certain extremely important data such as the combat readiness of army tanks, top managers of large organizations would soon be swamped with data if there were no intermediate editing whatsoever of any upward communications. As for downward communications, one way to minimize distortion is to simplify and clarify messages. A message may be so lengthy, so poorly written, and such a coil of perplexity that no two people agree what it means.

## LATERAL COMMUNICATIONS

Communication between chairmen of several academic departments is an example of lateral communication in a university. Committee meetings commonly provide a setting for lateral communications between hierarchies, as do bull sessions. Few of the hang-ups troubling upward and downward communications severely affect lateral communications. Specialists in various adjacent organizations commonly keep in lateral contact with one another about mutual problems—finance officers to name one example. Lateral communications are occasionally impeded because the people in one organization don't know exactly where the power is located in the other organization; hence lateral communcations may miss the target.

## IMPEDIMENTS NOT RELATED TO HIERARCHY

The preceding paragraphs have emphasized hierarchy as an impediment to communication. There are, of course, numerous other obstacles to communication within and among organizations: class differences, language differences, personality differences, cultural differences, and countless other diversities. These often further complicate already existing hierarchical problems of communication.

## FORMAL AND INFORMAL COMMUNICATIONS

Most communications within an organization are informal—casual conversations, rumors, and so forth—and much (but not all) informal communication occurs outside the formal chain of command. One finds within most formal organizations one or more overlapping informal organizations bound together by informal networks of communication, occasionally referred to as "the grapevine." Information moves along the grapevine at incredible speed, and is usually accurate. When not accurate a rumor may express a subterranean and unexpressed wish of some sort, for example, the wish that something bad might happen to some unpopular person. False rumors floating around in an organization can be useful pointers to what subordinates are really thinking. If a manager hears of a false rumor that he has suffered a fatal heart attack, the discovery may be reason for having a real attack.

Perhaps the best way to define an informal communication is to say it is a communication made without any intent by the communicator to record it in any retrievable form for official use. A formal communication, on the other hand, is on-the-record, is generally written, but could be a verbal communication officially conveyed and so noted on appropriate records.

Formal, on-the-record communications have their advantages, especially written messages. They constitute evidence of exactly what was said to whom, when, and how. Any future disputes about the message or its meaning can be checked by pulling out the record. Copies of a formal, written communication can be made, including one for the sender's own file, and miscellaneous copies for any number of concerned parties. When the sender wants to communicate with several people at the same time, a written message addressed simultaneously to several people assures that everybody on the list gets exactly the same communication. It is not unusual for a bureaucrat to want to protect himself against false rumors about what he said in a certain communication by seeing to it that numerous copies are scattered about to interested parties.

Formal communications often save time because they do not involve the day-fracturing appointments and time-consuming social niceties of face to face communication. It may be quicker and cheaper to send a written communication if writing it doesn't take too long, but the sender always runs a risk that the formality of his message will be misunderstood. The written word can easily appear cold, unfriendly, and distant although the writer may not intend it to be. Written communications cannot be assisted by tone of voice, facial expression, and other subtle auxiliary modes of expression that accompany and clarify the spoken word.

Bureaucrats, in general, are passionate record keepers. Their files bulge with papers kept as proof of what they have or have not done. Very often letters are written less to benefit the recipient than the author. Formal communications are made and copies kept as proof that responsibilities were attended to, and how. This self-protective documentation is called "red tape." The less secure an administrator, the more his obsession with documentation.

Written communication also tends to be a form of self-advertising. One way to keep your name constantly in the boss's mind is to send him a memorandum every couple days. He will be compelled to think of you, and may come to picture you as an amazingly industrious and dedicated worker. On the other hand he may want to fire you if he ever discovers how much time you spend writing those memorandums. While it may take the recipient of a memo only four minutes to read it, it is not unusual for authorbureaucrats to spend half a day, a day, or even several days carefully wording a single page memo. Written communications are fearfully expensive when every cost of their production is considered: the author's time, the secretary's time, and, of course, the time of the recipient who not only has to read, think about, and file the letter, but also in many cases answer it.

Cost of communications is certainly one expense an accountant would want to weigh in analyzing the economy and efficiency of any organization. Formal communications rival the fruitfly in their power to spawn offspring. Memos call for answering memos which call for still further memos. One widely circulated and provocative memo can plunge the hierarchy of an organization into a frenzy of authorship, at outrageous cost to taxpayers who, mercifully, have no idea how much literary effort they support. Memo writing by public officials is the most richly subsidized and least esteemed of all the arts.

## SUMMARY

Where there is organization there is communication—some of it formal, some of it informal. An organization may be defined as a communications network, and a large part of any executive's job has to do with transmitting and receiving information. The natural flow of communications is downward, not upward, but managers must have both. Special efforts are required to remove obstacles to communications. Many obstacles to upward communications are to be found in the manager's own demeanor and receptivity to them. Messages that do reach a manager are often distorted by the deliberate or inadvertent editing of subordinates. Downward communications are also subject to distortion as they pass through various levels of bureaucracy. Managers should take steps to curb that distortion. Lateral communications are less troubled than upward and downward communications.

Most communications are informal, not intended to be recorded in retrievable form for official use. However, when evidence of exactly what was said to whom, when, and how, is needed, formal (usually written) communications are used. Under certain circumstances written communications can save time, but out-of-control red tape and rampant memo writing can be needlessly expensive and time-consuming.

## SUGGESTED READING

Anderson, John. "What's Blocking Upward Communications?" *Personnel Administration*, January-February 1968, pp. 5–8.

Bassett, Glenn A. *The New Face of Communication*. New York: American Management Association, Inc., 1968.

Bernard, Chester I. *The Functions of the Executive*. Cambridge: Harvard University Press, 1938.

Henry, William V. *Communication and Organizational Behavior: Text and Cases*. Homewood, Ill.: Richard D. Irwin, 1972.

Huseman, Richard C., Logue, Cal M., and Freshley, Dwight L., eds. *Readings in Interpersonal and Organizational Communication*. Boston: Holbrook Press, 1969.

# The Goebbels Touch 9

# The Goebbels Touch 9

Few if any agencies can thrive and grow without friends, nor even exist. Every agency is, of course, born with friends, those who fought for its creation in the first place, and with enemies, those who fought against its creation and who may continue their hostility far into the future.

Every agency, no matter the circumstances of its birth, is instantly thrust into combat, first for survival then for growth and expansion. So long as an agency lives this struggle continues. The mother-milk of survival and growth is power; power comes from political support; political support is won by serving the real or imagined interests of others. The process by which an agency convinces its sought-after friends that their interests are being served, or could be served, is called public relations.

## PUBLIC RELATIONS

Public agencies are obviously going to have relations with their clients, usually with the general public or some part of it. An agency's public may be a narrow clientele or a broad clientele, a handful of people or millions, but every agency deals with people important to its survival and growth. No agency can avoid public relations. The managers of each agency will know who its major present and potential benefactors are, and will actively work to keep and win their support. This is completely human and natural.

### Public-Relations Officers

Public relations is critical to agency survival and growth, and therefore is an activity the agency head himself should personally supervise. It is one of his cardinal functions. Most agencies have public-relations officers, but

**185**

public relations cannot be left to such officers, because, to repeat, this is a key function of the agency head himself. But a busy chief executive may well need someone to advise on public-relations strategy and do mechanical work such as preparing communications for the media, and keeping contact with media representatives. To call this officer a public-relations officer is poor public relations; enemies of the agency, by constantly quoting him and citing his title can lead people to believe the agency is intent on manipulating the public and even hires a professional manipulator to do it. The public-relations function should be camouflaged under a more innocent title, say, Vice-President for Production.

## Decentralized Public Relations

Furthermore, by highlighting the public-relations function of a single officer, the importance of others in the organization who also do (or should do) public-relations work is diminished. Quite often rank and file employees of an agency have more to do with winning and losing agency support than anything an agency head or his public-relations officer do directly.

The best public-relations program may be one that exudes from the daily behavior of rank and file agency employees toward clients of the agency. The behavior of sales clerks toward customers may have everything to do with success of a store. Clerks are public-relations officers no less than an officially sanctioned public-relations officer. Likewise, the behavior of professors toward students can have an effect on enrollment and community good will. It would be unfortunate if the appointment of a college public-relations officer leads teachers to think public relations is his business, not theirs. Normally, public relations should be decentralized, the more so the better.

Care should be taken not to let public relations interfere with the integrity of the agency's goals. A sales clerk should not decline to accept payment for goods just to be nice to customers. Nor should professors try to curry favor with students or with the community by giving unearned grades—a reputation for low standards can be self-defeating for a college. An organization can have good public relations while at the same time maintaining its integrity. A city building department does not necessarily improve public relations by neglecting to enforce the building codes. Perhaps the best public relations is by those who do a competent job, while at the same time being attentive, courteous, friendly, and fair.

The agency head should by all means try to convert each and every member of his organization into public-relations officers. Employees should be taught how to treat clients right (if they need teaching), and should be praised for their efforts. And (perhaps most importantly) employees should themselves be treated fairly by their superiors. Grumbling employees are going to be morose in their contacts with the public—hardly anything could be worse for public relations. A good public-relations program is founded on a good employee relations program.

## Are Public Relations Programs Democratic?

Should a government agency in a democratic country where government is supposed to be of, by, and for the people, engage in a conscious program of influencing public opinion? Should an agency propagandize the people it is supposed to be serving? Should it use taxpayers' money to prevail on taxpayers to supply more money and authority, or to support certain policies? Should public relations be confined to informing the public?

Unfortunately, it is not easy to segregate persuasion from information. Often the process of persuading the public goes on simultaneously with the process of informing the public. Suppose, for example, the park service made an official movie depicting its work. This could inform people how their tax money is being used, but it could also elevate the public's regard for the park service. It might be difficult to say whether the purpose of the movie is merely to inform, or whether its fundamental purpose is to justify bigger staff and larger appropriations for the park service. Information and propaganda are blood brothers.

One of the most irritating problems in Western democracies is how much latitude the government or any of its agencies should have to influence public opinion. The larger and wealthier the bureaucracy, the more serious the problem. Government publicity is potentially lethal to the democratic order. A large agency employing thousands of people with a budget of millions, could, if left free to do as it pleases, carry on a stupendous advertising campaign, building an ever more solid base of public support with which to claim still larger appropriations and power. A president could influence the public relations output of agencies to glorify the achievements of his administration. Governors, mayors, and other leading politicians could do likewise.

It may be impossible to draw a line between information on the one hand and propaganda on the other, but the attempt should probably be made because governments simply must inform. After all, the idea of democracy assumes a certain level of information by the public and its representatives about what the government is doing. Furthermore, agencies can not do their job without revealing at least the basic essentials what they are doing and when, where, and how. Any agency offering services would want at least to reveal its business hours, what services it offers, and how to apply. If a government agency were stopped from distributing public information on the grounds that information becomes propaganda, then social security officers could not tell old people what benefits they are entitled to or how to apply. Universities could not print catalogs to let students know what courses are being offered. Professors could not tell students when and where a course is being held, what books to buy, how often to attend the class. Degree requirements would be secret, because no one would be allowed to give information. The internal revenue service would not be allowed to explain the tax laws, describe how or where to get tax forms, how or when to file the tax return, how or when to get a refund. Veterans could not ask the veterans administration about their benefits, nor could farmers contact the department of agriculture for information about crop insurance and so on. But as we see in looking at some college catalogs, information imperceptibly merges into propaganda.

Governments at all levels in the United States distribute verbally or in print a staggering mass of information. Democracy could not exist nor government services be accomplished without a flow of information outward from the government and from its numerous agencies and officers. But it is also true that most bureaucrats seize opportunities to make self-serving public relations in the process of distributing "information." Government publicity belongs to that class of things capable of towering good if rightly used and of towering evil if wrongly used.

## SOME PRINCIPLES
## OF EXTERNAL COMMUNICATIONS

### Mass Audiences and Mass Media

Anyone trying to reach mass audiences can generally anticipate the public's ignorance, or, to be more precise their low level of information. A further characteristic of mass audiences is that they do not tend to think very deeply; they apparently feel more than they think, even an audience of college professors. We "think with our blood" as someone said.

The mass media in the United States is largely a private enterprise to which news is a stock-in-trade. The purpose of nearly every privately owned mass media—newspapers, television, films, magazines, books—is to make money. Education may be a by-product, but seldom is the central purpose. Even public television, and publically owned presses (such as university presses) have to give some thought to whether anybody is watching or reading. This dictates what the mass media covers; they cover stories that interest people. A reporter wants a "good story," one that has controversy, excitement, and drama. There is very little drama in a news release from a university public-relations office announcing that professor so-and-so put in another day's work as usual. However, if he came to work as usual after being shot and wounded by an angry student, that's news.

Reporters not only want a "good story" but they want it early; news is a perishable commodity. Professor Smith's speech to the Rotary Club makes a better story when it happens, than a month later.

While reporters love controversy, bureaucrats often do not. Bureaucrats win their spurs by smoothing over controversy. A reporter wins his spurs by sniffing out and highlighting controversy. This often puts reporters and bureaucrats at odds, but at the same time, a bureaucrat who understands a reporter's thirst for controversy can design his press releases to highlight whatever harmless drama he can dredge up or invent.

Anyone who deals with the mass media should keep in mind that news is rarely covered in depth. While there are occasionally some documentaries, some feature articles, some background studies, normally one can not hope for much more than the briefest possible mention of most stories. A newspaper might carry the appointment of, say, a new chancellor of a university, might state when and where he was born, his degrees, his major publications, his most recent employment. Television news may not go beyond mentioning his name. Rarely will the media delve into the significance of the appointment, unless it has been the center of public controversy. Yet, the appointment may signify an important rearrangement of power relationships within the university, may spell triumph or defeat for a faction or for a philosophy of education, or may have other ramifications, but none of this is likely to be reported.

The mass media generally reports only isolated fragments of news. A news program on television is little more than a grab-bag of splinters and snippets of news, isolated fragments without elucidation. What the public gets is froth, not substance. Therefore one must try to avoid giving anything to the press (especially to television) that demands explanation; the explanation may never see the light of day. It may not be reported, and if reported could easily be garbled by reporters who didn't understand the explanation, or by editors who shortened the story to accommodate space or time. And if by some miracle the explanation is accurately carried, then much of the public which is supposed to receive this explanation may not pay attention to it or will be confused.

It is easy to understand why bureaucrats tend to be secretive. They know the media deals mainly in splinters of news, which if not fully explained could lead to harmful misunderstandings. A report that an army chaplain visited a house of prostitution could be disasterous unless further explained that he went there to confer with a woman, which could also be disasterous unless further explained that he wished to confer about another chaplain known by the woman, which could also be disasterous unless further explained that . . . and so on. One reason judges do not want television coverage of trials is that the coverage of an all-day trial might end up as a 30-second fragment on the 10 P.M. news showing the defendant weeping, but leaving unexplained how that fits into the rest of the trial.

## Measuring the Success of Public Relations Efforts

It could be a mistake to measure the success of a public-relations program merely by the number of lines in the press or by the frequency with which the agency is mentioned by the media. Success should be measured by the effect of public relations on the people who count. While the general mass public counts to some extent for all public agencies, most agencies owe their fate to one or more client groups to whom the main thrust of public relations should be directed, for example, the Veterans Administration on veterans, the Agriculture Department on farmers, and so on. They are the agency's most important public-relations targets. The mass media may not be the best way to reach those targets. Certain specialized journals might reach farmers better than any newspaper, such as the house organ of a farmers' association. Still more effective are personal contacts with farmers by representatives of the agency, or by representatives of commercial firms in regular contact with farmers such as seed companies or fertilizer companies.

Mass media communication seems to be most useful in the initial stages of a campaign to introduce a new idea. After the target public is aware of the new idea or product then the most effective tactic of persuasion is through personal contact, testimony by peer sources, commercial sources, and authority sources (such as professors). Adoption of something new by a target group comes in three stages: (1) awareness; (2) information; and (3) trial. Mass media is most useful at the awareness stage, peers and authority sources at the information stage. The flow of ideas in this process is from the mass media to opinion leaders, and from opinion leaders to the target public. Effective public relations, like effective warfare, involves, first, careful target selection, and second, careful weapon (or tactic) selection. The mass media is a powerful weapon, but only with certain targets and at certain stages of the campaign.

## Propaganda

The word "propaganda" came into notoriety when Pope Gregory XV in 1622 established a College of Propaganda (congregatio de propaganda fide), a committee of cardinals in charge of training priests for foreign missions. Dictionaries usually define propaganda as ideas disseminated to support a doctrine. However, the word began to acquire an ominous reputation as a result of war propaganda such as the so-called "atrocity" stories of World War I. Since the time of Dr. Paul Joseph Goebbels, Adolf Hitler's propaganda minister, the word has acquired an especially sinister connotation. It now implies deceptive sleight of hand in communications designed to trick people into adopting certain ideas, attitudes, and beliefs. The word as used today suggests deception for evil purposes, however, the same sleight of hand used for evil purposes may also be used for good purposes.

We are all propagandists in everyday life to the extent we tailor communications to achieve some result. We are propagandists when we teach children not to steal, when we talk about our successes and forget our failures, when we dress up to meet the boss, when we watch our manners, and so on. The world is "a stage, where every man must play a part," as William Shakespeare said.

Propaganda techniques are ceaselessly used in administration, sometimes consciously, sometimes unconsciously, but always used. Bureaucrats constantly propagandize each other, as well as the public. Public relations officers are the visible institutionalization of propaganda, but are only the tip of the iceberg.

## Types of Propaganda

In the late 1930s the Institute for Propaganda Analysis published *The Fine Art of Propaganda* which analyzed seven propaganda devices: name calling, glittering generality, transfer, testimonial, plain folks, card stacking, and band wagon.

"Name calling" is attaching a bad label to something so that it will be condemned and rejected without examination. Name calling can be crude and direct, or it can be so sophisticated no one recognizes it. Clearly it is name calling to call someone stupid. But in the United States Senate this is done with some degree of polish; a senator who wishes to call his colleague stupid may refer to him as "my very learned" colleague.

A "glittering generality" is the reverse of name calling. It is bestowing virtue upon something so that it will be accepted or approved without examination. This, likewise, can be done in plain language ("hey, that's a 'super' idea") or with sophistication ("Professor Jones has given us some very 'positive' thoughts").

"Transfer" is an attempt to make an idea respectable and acceptable by associating it with something else respectable and acceptable. "For God and country, let us unite on this program" associates God and country (both respected) with a program. To call something Godly, by the way, is both transfer and glittering generality. Transfer is used by universities when they hire prominent people to give speeches on campus, or prominent professors to "reside" for a year. Transfer may also attempt to associate with something disrespectable to make us reject.

"Testimonial" is testimony by some well-esteemed (or loathed) person who claims that something is good or bad based on personal experience. Testimonials are used constantly in commercial advertising: dentists are hired to say they use a certain brand of mouth wash; athletes affirm the potency of an underarm deodorant, skinny girls testify to the wonderous effect of a diet pill. In public affairs, show business stars testify to the measureless virtues of candidates for president, lawyers hire psychologists to testify to the sanity or insanity of accused criminals, job applicants mobilize testimonials (letters of recommendation) for inclusion in their resumes, and the United States Forest Service uses a singed bear to testify that fire prevention is a good idea.

"Plain folks" is an attempt to convince people that something is good because it is something plain, ordinary folks would think or do. A president uses plain folks propaganda when he brings television cameras into the kitchen of the White House to show him fixing his own breakfast. County agents of the Department of Agriculture find it useful to dress like plain folks when making their rounds among farmers. Ideas can be expressed in an aura of plain folks, "Horse sense tells us," says the speaker, "that we should have fewer bureaucrats." ("Horse sense" is recognized as plain folksy.)

"Card stacking" is when one tries to make the best or worst possible case for a proposition by a one-sided presentation of evidence, or by use of outright falsehoods. The practice is so universal that anyone who does not card stack risks being considered a fool. A job seeker stacks cards when he designs and submits a personal resume that tells only good things about himself. The applicant does not list his failures, nor include letters of reference from enemies. Nor does an advertiser broadcast the shortcomings of a product. Nor does a public-relations officer of a university send out news releases listing all the professors who were recently rejected for promotion, describing their shortcomings, nor does he speculate on potential contributors who chose not to contribute to the university and their reasons. Lovers are among the greatest card stackers. Courtship can be systematic deception; divorce may result when the truth is finally disclosed. The adversary system for deciding cases at law invites attorneys for contesting parties to take turns stacking cards; it is hoped juries and judges will ultimately sort out the truth after opposing sides have finished.

Outright lying is, of course, a gross form of card stacking. Furthermore, it should be mentioned here that the bigger the lie the better (or worse), since a little bit of every falsehood is believed no matter how vehemently and thoroughly rebutted.

"Band wagon" relies on the herd instinct. When we see "everybody doing it" then we quite generally are motivated to "jump on the band wagon" ourselves. Even individualists who pride themselves on not going with the mob, nevertheless go with the mob in most things. Normally it is hard to sell a new idea, but once it begins to catch hold it may spread like wildfire as more and more people hasten to jump on the band wagon. We see this in the world of fashion and in the world of politics. Candidates for elective office try to sustain a band-wagon affect by claiming ever greater popularity with the electorate. Administrators may use band wagon to sell a new proposal by pointing to others who agree with the proposal.

Naturally, an ethical public administrator would not want to use propaganda tactics unethically. However, prevailing standards of administrative ethics seem somewhat permissive in the area of information manipulation.

## SECRECY

### Secrecy and Democracy

While an informed electorate may be essential to a democracy, the electorate can know too much about some things for its own good. This is because what the electorate knows, so does the foreign enemy. Some obvious examples of information that should be kept secret are troop deployments, weapons, plans, codes, and stock-piles. A multitude of other matters also directly relate to national defense; as a matter of fact, everything relates to national defense in one way or another.

The more a combatant knows about the enemy, the better he can fight. In a sense, the perfect national defense would include total secrecy if it were possible. Every good intelligence effort directed at another country becomes an effort to learn everything there is to know about that country. It is not necessary to get this information from spies. Most of it is obtained from libraries by studying the history, culture, politics, economy, manners, and customs of people. Intelligence officers are more apt to be reading foreign novels, newspapers, and magazines than sneaking around with cloak and dagger. Even the smallest item of information can be used in diplomacy or war. If we know, for example, that in the culture of a certain country there is a strong aversion and even horror of eating pork, then in friendly times we can avoid serving pork to their diplomats at state dinners, but in war time we might panic their troops by dropping leaflets "disclosing" that their field rations have been secretly augmented with pork fat.

All knowledge may be useful in war, but clearly a democratic, open society cannot begin to close the sources of information about itself, for when information is denied the enemy it is also denied to the people who cannot govern themselves without it. The question has often been asked whether democracy is a workable system under conditions of continuous external military threat when the very institutions that make democracy possible become tools in the hands of the enemy, especially public information. When a nation such as the United States today spends three-fourths its annual budget and does three-fourths its work in the area of defense and foreign affairs, this could draw the biggest part of the federal government's work behind a partial or total shroud of secrecy. The public is often barred from knowledge it needs to make judgments about the biggest, most expensive, most critical things their government is doing. Certainly, one of the most perplexing dilemmas in a country such as the United States is how to know when the people's need to know outweighs the security risk of informing them.

## Truman's Order

In 1951 President Harry S. Truman signed an executive order empowering heads of government agencies (or persons designated by them within an agency) to withhold from publication information in possession of the agency that might be useful to potential enemies. The order extended to nonmilitary agencies the classification scheme long used by the military: confidential, secret, top secret. Although Truman forbad use of the system to withhold nonsecurity information, no mechanism for review or appeal was provided. The American Society of Newspaper Editors protested Truman's order and kept trying for years to get it modified. In 1953 President Dwight D. Eisenhower corrected some of the deficiencies of Truman's order and restricted the power to classify to only seventeen agencies.

The law does not make reporters liable for reporting classified information, nor publishers liable for publishing it. Criminal liability falls only on the individual who knowingly releases classified information.

## Executive Privilege

Besides classification of security information, the doctrine of executive privilege is also used to withhold information. Under the doctrine of separation of powers, none of the three coequal branches of government has a right to compel another to disclose information. The doctrine was affirmed by the United States Supreme Court in the case of *Nixon* v. *United States*, although the court drew boundaries about the doctrine by limiting the power of a president to withhold evidence of criminal behavior from courts. Presidents frequently cloak their assistants with executive privilege, generally for the purpose of giving them the right to refuse to testify before congressional committees when subpoenaed. Some degree of confidentiality is needed. Administrators, especially cabinet level officials, ought to be able to discuss alternative courses of action without constant press harassment.

## Freedom of Information Act

Bureaucrats who have power to classify information tend to overclassify. This is natural because there is no penalty for over-classification, but failure to classify security information can lead to a reprimand. Further-more, the power to classify information is abused. Officials too often use their power to classify as a political weapon; the security sought is too often security of the party in power, or the personal security of officials. It is not difficult to imagine the temptation felt by officials to classify embarrassing documents. This compounds the difficulty reporters experi-ence trying to dislodge information from government agencies even when it is not classified.

After a decade of lobbying, reporters with the particular help of Con-gressman John E. Moss prevailed on Congress to enact a Freedom of Information Act of 1966. The most important part of the law establishes court review of an agency's refusal to make information available to those who ask for it, although national security information, personnel files, investigatory records, and internal documents are exempted from the law.

Actually, reporters have not made much use of the law, partly because delays in securing information through court procedure are inconsistent with a reporter's need to get information rapidly when a story is hot. On the other hand, private individuals, business firms, and scholars have made use of the law, and in some instances have bedeviled agencies with re-quests for information which would cost a fortune to supply. One oil company recently asked the Federal Power Commission to supply it with every document in the agency's possession that mentioned the word "oil." Compliance would be so expensive and arduous that the agency could not do its other work.

The law has not stopped foot-dragging by agencies in supplying infor-mation. Persons seeking information under the law may have to wait long periods for it, especially when the agency does not have enough personnel to search its files. Some applicants for information have been asked to pay the agency to hire people to search out the information. Also, applicants for information must have a reasonably definite idea what documents they want to see, which is sometimes difficult without first seeing them.

## The Dysfunctions of Secrecy

Secrecy has its price, its dysfunctions, its liabilities. Often the price is worth paying. Still, it is a good idea to look at what that price is, because in some cases, perhaps many cases, the price is too high and is greater than the price of openness. Secrecy may not be worth buying.

The most obvious cost of secrecy in a democracy is the deficit it leaves in the ability of the people (and their representatives) to be self-governing. If press, people, and Congress are kept in the dark about the Central Intelligence Agency's work and how much it costs to do that work, then, how can Congress or the people know whether the CIA is doing a good job, or whether there should be a CIA at all, and how much money ought to be spent on it? Yet, if Congress and the people know all about the CIA, then so will the enemy, and most of the agency's usefulness would be lost, for much intelligence work must be secret to be done at all. A democratic country must weigh the cost of secrecy against the benefits of secrecy. This, however, asks the impossible, for to weigh costs and benefits requires that Congress and people know the costs and benefits—which is absurd because then there would be no secret to weigh. Therefore, one of the costs of secrecy is that it leaves Congress and people without the means of weighing whether there should be secrecy in the first place.

A second dysfunction of secrecy compounds the first just mentioned— what people don't know about they don't pay attention to. Secrecy not only denies information to the people but also leaves them inattentive. The electorate will fiddle while Rome burns, to coin a phrase, if they don't know Rome is burning.

A third dysfunction of secrecy is the opposite of the one just mentioned. When people get the idea secrets are being kept from them, that makes them (especially the press) all the more eager to know the secrets. Of course, the best policy for those who have a secret is to both keep the secret and let it remain unknown that they have a secret. Nothing is more tantalizing or eagerly sought after than secrets. An agency involved in defense work may want to weigh whether it is worse to attract attention by being secretive, or worse to be open with the hope of being ignored.

A fourth dysfunction of secrecy is that once an officer has a reputation for being secretive, this makes people suspicious of everything he says or does. Whole agencies can find themselves disbelieved even when they don't want to be, and are trying to be open and forthright. An agency has to decide whether it is worse to be open and believable, or closed, secretive, and disbelieved. Ideally, it would be the best of all possible worlds to acquire a reputation for openness, while at the same time being secretive where necessary. To do this an agency must succeed in keeping it a secret that it has secrets.

A fifth dysfunction of secrecy, one sometimes alleged to be the kingpin of all arguments against secrecy, is that it hinders scientific progress. Military defense today is largely a matter of science. Modern nations are defended with technology. Everyone knows that advances in science and technology depend on relatively free circulation of scientific and technological information. Scientists operating on the frontiers of knowledge must keep in liaison with one another for the same reason contact is maintained between units on a war front. Suppression of professional journals and scientific conferences, suppresses science itself. This necessity for a free flow of scientific information is especially troublesome for a totalitarian closed society, which, to remain totalitarian must remain closed, yet to remain militarily strong must allow scientists an open door to the scientific world at home and abroad.

After paying these (and possibly other) costs of secrecy, the secrets so jealously and expensively kept are very likely to surface anyway. It is hard to keep defense secrets, or any other government secrets. This difficulty is something to keep in mind when the temptation to classify is present. A classifier should weigh the price (as outlined above) paid for secrecy against the actual possibility of keeping the secret.

One reason for the difficulty of keeping secrets in a democracy such as the United States is the highly decentralized character of the national government. Major departments and agencies tend to be about as responsive and obedient to their respective clientele groups as to any central authority. Among the many agencies of the federal government there is a ceaseless power struggle, often fueled by differences of opinion over great policy questions. Information is a weapon in this war of all against all in the bureaucracy. One of the best known rivalries in Washington in past years has been that among the army, navy, and air force for control of various weapon systems. One could easily imagine one service leaking information about the failure of another service to properly develop a certain weapon—information which would be of direct value to the enemy. Defense secrets are harbored by almost all departments and by multitudes of separate agencies; modern war involves almost every science and every subdivision of knowledge. The Agriculture Department may, for example, have secret information about the dimensions of a crop failure abroad, or knowledge of chemical or biological warfare methods useful against the agriculture of another country. Very possibly the best defense the American people have against excessive government secrecy is the eagerness with which bureaucrats leak secrets in their bureaucratic battles for power.

Bureaucrats leak secrets for various reasons. Vanity plays its part; leaking confidential information may give one a sense of importance, and if done publically, some notoriety. Some leakers are motivated by vengeance; a thirst to repay real or imagined atrocities, perhaps a denied promotion. Most administrators acquire a number of enemies over the course of time within their own agencies by virtue of the decision making they must do. Few decisions can please everybody, and most decisions leave in their wake some malcontents. Strewn throughout every agency are people delighted to leak secrets embarrassing to their superiors. Furthermore, within every agency are persons who feel sincerely indignant against one or another policy pursued by the agency or its managers, and will tell secrets to bring down that policy. Others are motivated to tell secrets by a wish to have their work recognized—a scientist perhaps, who, having masterminded a dramatic research triumph, does not wish news of it hidden beneath a cloak of official secrecy. Clearly the motives which impel disclosure of secrets are so numerous and powerful that any attempt to control information is severely jeopardized from the outset.

News reporters understand well these compulsions which motivate bureaucrats to leak information, and are usually anxious to convert leaks to scoops. Sometimes reporters do not need to rely on leaks. Their own intuition may be enough. When a reporter hits a stone wall of official silence concerning, say, a possible diplomatic move in the Mediterranean, he asks himself, "Logically, what is the most probable move to be expected?" Intuition gives him a suspicion. He looks for a shred or two of stray evidence, which by itself proves nothing, but when combined with intuition, justifies reporting his suspicion as fact. When this happens, people in the government responsible for keeping their mouths shut, begin looking distrustfully at one another. This intuitive process of a good investigative reporter is like the process followed by an idiot searching for his stray blind horse: "I shut my eyes," said the idiot, "and asked myself where I'd go if I were a blind horse; I went, and the horse was there."

## Value of Secrecy

Secrecy is often damned as incompatible with democratic institutions. However, there is something to be said for secrecy, not only in national defense matters, but in the nondefense side of government. It is very hard to negotiate treaties or other agreements in public. The process of negotiation is usually more successful if done confidentially. The value of carrying on some public activities behind closed doors was demonstrated at the Constitutional Convention of 1787. The convention might have been stopped in its tracks if every proposal were made the subject of public debate. It is worth noting that Congress, which likes to deplore secrecy in the executive branch, holds a good many of its committee meetings in secret, and has long dragged its feet about television coverage of House and Senate meetings.

Secrecy and propaganda are related—restrictions on the flow of information are usually combined with selective and slanted reporting of other information. Sometimes an agency finds itself tormented by the charge of propagandizing whenever it gives out information, and with the charge of secrecy if it does not.

Up to this point we have discussed secrecy and propaganda by agencies of government in matters relating primarily to national security. But there is a whole world of secrecy and propaganda which is part of all human life and of all nature. Secrecy, concealment, and protective coloration are basic processes of earthly existence. Like their human brothers and sisters, animals have to be careful what they "say." A cat is not going to meow while it creeps up on a robin, and a bird has to decide whether it is better to give its mating call at the risk of attracting a preditor, or to keep its mouth shut, at the risk of not finding a mate. Concealment is used by every creature in nature and by every sane person, whether in or out of office, and by every agency, bureau, department, or other unit of government. Nobody, no agency, tells all. Everybody, every agency, is selective in release of information. Although some are smarter at this than others, none of us is completely candid. We often withhold information and conceal that part of our lives which would be harmful if known. We do this so constantly and routinely that the process of concealment ceases to be premeditated, and is as natural as breathing.

The dimensions of informal bureaucratic concealment are simply astounding. Concealment is a major part of every administrator's work. Knowledge is power, and the power of every administrator is increased by his access to knowledge and by his ability to release that knowledge selectively to selected persons at selected times. Concealment (secrecy) on the one hand and selective release of information appropriately colored (propaganda) on the other are two important tools of every administrator.

## SUMMARY

Public agencies require political support to survive and grow. Public relations is, therefore, one of the most important functions of every agency and should be personally supervised by the agency head himself. In this he may have the help of a public-relations officer, but public relations should not be confined to him. The best public-relations program is a decentralized program in which everyone in the agency is asked to help win support.

It is often debated whether public agencies in a democratic country should deliberately try to influence public opinion. Generally it is conceded that a government should inform the public what it is doing, but the line between information and propaganda is difficult to draw. In fact, most public agencies go far beyond informing the public; they energetically woo the public, using all the varieties of propaganda described in 1939 by the Institute of Propaganda Analysis.

Public agencies also commonly withhold information. Some official secrecy is for purposes of national security, but most secrecy stems from the almost universal tendency of bureaucrats to use information as a weapon of bureaucratic politics. Selective release of information is practiced in both internal and external communications. However, secrets are difficult to keep. Furthermore, official secrecy has its dysfunctions, its price, and managers who weigh that price may discover secrecy is not always worth it.

By giving judicial assistance to persons seeking certain kinds of information from federal agencies, the Freedom of Information Act has been somewhat helpful to people trying to break through walls of official secrecy.

## SUGGESTED READING

Doob, Leonard W. *Public Opinion and Propaganda.* Hamden: Archon Books, 1966.

Hyman, H. H., and Sheatsley, Paul B. "Some Reasons Why Information Campaigns Fail." *Public Opinion Quarterly,* Fall, 1947, pp. 412–423.

Lee, Alfred M., and Lee, Elizabeth B., eds. *The Fine Art of Propaganda.* New York: Harcourt, Brace, 1939.

McCamy, James L. *Government Publicity.* Chicago: University & Chicago Press, 1939.

Nichols, David G. "Reveal Versus Conceal: A Basic Social Paradox." *Logos Report,* April 1975, pp. 35–38.

Packard, Vance. *The Hidden Persuaders.* New York: David McKay Company, 1957.

Rothchild, John. "Finding the Facts Bureaucrats Hide," *Washington Monthly,* January 1972, pp. 15–27.

Strouse, James C. *The Mass Media, Public Opinion, and Public Policy Analysis: Linkage Explorations.* Columbus, Ohio: Charles E. Merrill, 1975.

"Symposium on Administrative Secrecy: A Comparative Perspective." *Public Administration Review,* January-February 1975, pp. 1–42.

United States v. Nixon, 418 U.S. 683 (1974).

# How to Run Things 10

# How to Run Things 10

## LEADERSHIP

Leadership is the influence people exercise over each other. Leadership is not a monopoly of management, for the members of an organization are influenced by all sorts of other people besides managers. Even "followers" are leaders, for they too influence others, perhaps more than they imagine. Wherever there is human interaction there is leadership; everyone influences everyone else, but some are more influential than others. While everyone leads to some degree, the term "leader" usually refers to the most influential.

### What Makes a Leader? Traits versus Situation

To the question, what makes a leader, two competing theories are generally offered, the "traits theory" and the "situationist theory."

*Traits:* The traits theory monopolizes popular thinking on this subject. Stop someone on the street and ask, what makes a person a leader, and the answer will commonly consist of a list of traits: leaders are "decisive and have strong opinions," are "friendly and honest," are "intelligent and enthusiastic," are "energetic," and so on.

Belief in the traits theory is not confined to the person on the street. Scholars have tried to identify leadership traits, and commonly mention physical and nervous energy, sense of purpose, enthusiasm, friendliness, integrity, technical mastery, decisiveness, intelligence, teaching skill, and faith.

When lists of this kind are drawn up a distressing confusion appears; traits seem to overlap. Take, for example, "enthusiasm" and "teaching skill;" most skilled teachers are also enthusiastic; that is, enthusiasm is

203

generally part of good teaching. And another example: "physical and nervous energy" is mentioned in the above list separately from "intelligence," yet frequently intelligence and energy are related. Also "faith" is listed separately from "sense of purpose," yet these are related too. Hardly a single trait can be defined without reference to other traits on the list.

*Situationist Theory:*   A more serious objection to the theory that leaders exhibit certain traits is that not all leaders exhibit the same traits, and, in fact, the traits of leadership seem to be different in different situations. This observation gives rise to the "situationist" theory. According to this theory each situation calls for leaders with traits appealing to people in that situation. For example, in periods following the exposure of scandalous dishonesty by officeholders, candidates must exude a greater appearance of honesty than in other periods. Perhaps it is not entirely accidental that American presidents seem to display traits appropriate to the times; Calvin Coolidge and Warren Harding seemed to fit their time, so did Franklin Roosevelt and Dwight Eisenhower.

Unique circumstances summon forth unique traits of leadership; the traits of Adolf Hitler reflected the distressed circumstances of Germany in the 1920s and 1930s. One is not certain whether Hitler would have succeeded as a YMCA director; perhaps he didn't have the traits for that. His were traits requisite for leading a certain kind of political party in a certain country in a certain era. Whether he also had traits for governing a nation or directing a war is questionable. Nations in revolutionary circumstances often give rise to leaders possessing the traits necessary for making a revolution, but lacking traits necessary for building and leading a country after the revolution. Many politicians are conspicuous examples of the principle set forth by Laurence J. Peter (the "Peter Principle") that occupational incompetence is to be found almost everywhere because people tend to rise to their level of incompetence, where they often remain for a long time. Hitler may have been an example of that, as are some United States Senators. Someone with the traits requisite for election to the Senate, may not have the traits for being an effective senator once there.

Adherents to the traits theory of leadership often mention "friendliness" as a leadership trait, but one can easily imagine situations in which obnoxious people become leaders because of favorable traits other than friendliness that they possess. A recent motion picture illustrating this is *The Flight of the Phoenix.* An airplane carrying several passengers crash-lands on the North African desert. The plane is damaged, food and water are short, daytime heat is almost unendurable, and the radio is not working. Death seems certain. The pilot (acted by James Stewart) was the popular leader of this group. However, among the passengers was a German airplane designer and builder—a somewhat objectionable and unfriendly person. He proposed that they dismantle the old plane and make a new and smaller one that would fly them to safety. He claimed, as an aircraft designer, to know how to do this. Because his proposal seemed the only hope for survival, the group submitted to his autocratic leadership. Soon it came to light that the so-called "airplane designer" did not design and build real planes—only toy planes. He was employed by a toy manufacturer. Morale sunk, but he persuaded the desperate group that the principles governing flight of toy planes are identical to the principles governing flight of real planes; also he said the principles of aircraft design are identical. And so he continued to lead the group, even in the face of disagreements and clashes with the popular pilot who in normal circumstances might have been the leader. A new plane (called the Phoenix) was successfully built, and the movie ends when the survivors fly to safety. However, *The Flight of the Phoenix* presents a very unusual and crisis-laden situation. Most human situations are not that extreme, and possibly there is actually a certain uniformity of traits among leaders in most ordinary human situations.

## Democratic and Authoritarian Styles of Leadership

What style of leadership results in the greatest productive effort by subordinates? A great deal of intellectual effort has been given to this question, and there are various hotly contended points of view. The answer to the question depends on the answer to another question: what motivates human behavior? And the answer to that question depends on a still deeper question: what is the nature of human nature?

Scholars have attempted to analyze human motivations, and they present us with a dazzling array of theories to choose from, all the way from the fundamental concept that man is a beast to the reverse concept that man is an angel. The diversity of views about human motivations and how managers should attempt to lead (influence) is revealed by Douglas McGregor's description of two rather opposite views which he calls Theory X and Theory Y.

*Theory Y and Theory X:* Managers who adhere to Theory X tend to think the ordinary person dislikes work and will avoid it when possible. To keep such a person on the job and working it is necessary to threaten, control, coerce, and direct him. Not only does the average person dislike work, but when under pressure he does work, he wants to be directed, wants to avoid responsibility, manifests little ambition, and wants first and foremost security.

McGregor does not think this view is supported by evidence. On the contrary he feels Theory Y is more in accord with reality as revealed by social science research. Theory Y holds that work can be a source of satisfaction and that most people under the right conditions want to work.

It is true that people can be threatened and coerced into working, but when workers are committed to what they are doing they will not only like work but will welcome and even insist on it, and will want responsibility. Workers under such circumstances wish as much self-direction and self-control as possible. With the right kind of leadership, managers can create a work environment in which workers find many personal rewards over and beyond wages, rewards such as ego satisfaction and self-actualization. Under these circumstances workers seek responsibility and are ambitious. While they may value security, they do not under these circumstances value it above all else. When workers find ego satisfaction in their work and are able to self-actualize, this releases a tide of creativity, imagination, and ingenuity. The challenge for modern managerial leadership is to create conditions on the job that will allow workers to find this kind of satisfaction in their work, but unfortunately, much of modern management is authoritarian and represses these satisfactions, and is detrimental to the achievement of organizational goals.

McGregor, as we have seen, suggests that a manager's style of leadership will reflect his view of human nature. However, others have observed that the selection of a style of leadership is also governed to some degree by the social and cultural environment of an organization.

## Motives of Workers

What are the motives of workers in organizations? McGregor suggests ego satisfaction. Rensis Likert mentions appreciation, recognition, and influence. Robert Dubin, however, says most workers do not seek ego satisfaction or fulfillment of their personalities on the job so much as they seek a pay check to make satisfactions elsewhere possible. Most workers, says Dubin, only tolerate their job, and find their real satisfactions in social groups, clubs, hobbies, and other off-the-job pursuits. Chris Argyris denied money is the best motivator; workers want to be self-reliant, want to express themselves, to self-actualize. Money can never satisfy a worker; no worker will be satisfied unless he is self-actualizing. So long as this urge to self-fulfillment is repressed a worker will all the more insistently press for pay increases to compensate for dissatisfaction, but no amount of money can ever be enough, for it can never produce satisfaction. Abraham H. Maslow also stressed the need for self-actualization, but he said there is not just one motivation but a hierarchy of motivations. First, there are physiological needs for such things as food, safety, and love. After that is the need for self-fulfillment. Although self-fulfillment is less fundamental than the physiological needs, it is the one least satisfied by most employers and is therefore the one most in need of emphasis by managers who seek to influence workers to contribute more to organizational goals.

## Democratic Administration

Human relationists generally argue that morale is important to production, and that to have high morale it is necessary to satisfy the ego needs of workers and to make it possible for them to self-actualize (to fulfill their personalities) on the job. One way to satisfy ego needs is to make workers feel they are not just small cogs in a machine directed by others, but are important people who participate not only in the work but also in the decision making affecting their work.

A style of management which gives workers the feeling they are actually participating in management is called "democratic (or participative) administration." This approach to management is widely accepted (or at least mouthed) as the best method of managerial leadership in most situations. Leadership is democratic rather than authoritarian when the manager appears to listen to the recommendation of subordinates and to give those recommendations serious and prayerful thought before making a decision. Just what the term democratic administration includes is not precisely defined, but normally it includes at least some form of consultation with employees on various matters, and may go so far as to include worker elections on various questions. Democratic administration is said to have great influence on a worker's attitude toward his job; it changes him from a mere order-obeying employee to a person who has some degree of responsibility for directing the agency's work. It gives him a personal stake (ego involvement) in the success of decisions commonly arrived at; this makes him a better motivated worker. The democratic administrator involves workers with the goals of the organization by involving workers in the manufacture of those goals.

## Some Criticisms of Democratic Administration

It is sometimes said that managers should employ whatever techniques of leadership will bring forth maximum effort by subordinates. Democratic administration has been offered as the ideal technique, and has been so glowingly praised that one almost fails to hear arguments against it. So much is said for participative management and for the human relations emphasis that to question it is almost like questioning motherhood. But let us put on our battle helmets and storm the fortress, just, if for no other purpose, to test the quality of its defenses.

One problem with the theory that participative management produces high performance is that many jobs allow little opportunity at all for high performance. It is difficult for an assembly line worker to do much to improve his performance; he does the same mechanical tasks whether he loves or hates the firm. There are more of these jobs in the world than one thinks. Output in many lines of work, even some managerial work, generally depends on work flow and output demands. A bank teller, a mail clerk, a bomber crew: they all tend to do what is required of them. The effect of human relations is slight. People generally work to the utmost limits of their skill. They may quit the job if they do not receive ego satisfaction, or do not like the way they are treated, but so long as they stay they usually perform in accordance with their skills and not in accordance with their enchantment or disenchantment with management. A higher turnover rate may be the only significant negative effect of poor leadership.

Also, the level of satisfaction a worker finds in his job may have more to do with success in practicing his skill than with styles of managerial leadership. People take pride in a job well done, and that may be a greater source of ego satisfaction than a sense of participating in management.

From the point of view of management, the value of one style of leadership over another is measured by its effect on worker productivity. But in our technological world, changes in productivity are almost always the result of changes in technology. The ability of banks to handle accounts is much more affected by developments in electronic data processing than by human relations in the banking business. Democratic administration and human relations generally have only a slight effect by comparison with changes in productivity wrought by technology.

Furthermore, leadership style often has far less to do with productivity than other things managers do. Take, for example, an executive in a book publishing company who is autocratic and disliked, but who unerringly senses which books will sell and should be published, and which will not sell. His skill at analyzing the market may have much more to do with the firm's productivity than his style of leadership. The human relations school has, according to its critics, made it sound as if human relations is critical to productivity, when in fact, productivity is much more affected by technology and by other managerial skills.

Furthermore, the critics of democratic administration have some irreverent remarks to make about the supposed value of on-the-job self-actualization. Self-actualization, they say, can have a Frankenstein quality; the ego satisfactions of one employee tend to collide with the ego satisfactions of managers and of other employees. One occasionally sees this state of affairs on university campuses where democratic administration unleashes a flood of self-actualization among professors who collide with each other in participative management of the school. The campus becomes a theater of war and a snake pit of intrigue, hate, disillusionment, and bitter dissatisfaction for many of the most active self-actualizers. Not only do they often end up fighting each other, but they often end up suppressing each other.

Another question about democratic administration has to do with whether managers are really fooling anybody with their picturesque attempts to be democratic. Everybody knows there must be a limit to the willingness of managers to submit to subordinates. Owners of business firms and managers of public enterprises simply are not going to abdicate all their authority. There is a point (very quickly discovered by self-actualizing workers) beyond which a manager will not budge no matter how democratic he purports to be. Basically every organization is managed in the interests of the managers; they can not and will not use democratic administration where fundamental rights of management are at stake. Workers know in their heart that there are forbidden zones in the practice of on-the-job democracy. This makes democratic administration ring false; it does not always have the tone of genuine democracy. On the contrary, it can have the ring of phony manipulation. Managers may allow worker participation in decision making at the periphery, but never at the core. If subordinates sense this basic phoniness in the processes of democratic administration, it may cast a depressing shadow over what was intended to be an ego-satisfying experience.

One of the alleged advantages to be gained from democratic administration is that it reduces conflict within organizations; the processes of democratic administration and the whole human relations approach to management are said to grease organizational wheels with improved communications and smoother interpersonal relations. However, critics of democratic administration doubt that it has much value for reducing organizational conflicts. On the contrary, they suspect it may actually fuel conflict. Power struggles within organizations are the chief cause of internecine strife; it is hard to quell a power struggle with the balm of human relations. The fundamental cause of conflict does not go away, nor can it be smoothed over except superficially.

Furthermore, conceding the possibility that good human relations may decrease organizational conflict, who says conflict is always bad? Critics of the human relations school sometimes point out that power struggles are good, even hate and ill-feeling are good, or can be good, because these things motivate high performance. War brings out the best in us as we strive to defeat rivals. Furthermore, strife, rivalry, and hate may offer more opportunities for ego satisfaction and self-actualization than do conditions of peace and harmony. Also, people may be happiest when they are at war. Strife can be a source of endless joy to participants, although they may profess to hate it. Research has shown that the suicide rate drops in times of national crisis. The same no doubt extends to crises within lesser organizations; suddenly life takes on new meaning.

Some advocates of democratic administration concede that its greatest benefit may not be in the area of increased production, but in the area of human happiness. Even if democratic administration does not significantly increase production, the value to be gained is simply a human value. Thousands, millions, hundreds of millions of people might have happier lives if democracy were applied at the workplace, a very important value in an ever more impersonal world.

## Teaching Leadership

Since it is next to impossible to identify what makes a leader, it is therefore also next to impossible to teach anyone to be a leader; nobody can say with certainty what to teach, much less how to teach it. This does not stop the attempt. Leadership courses are popular, even though sometimes ill-conceived and/or fraudulent. A great deal of money is made by "consultants" (some with degrees in administration) who are hired by public agencies such as police departments to give education in leadership and human relations.

These gatherings are sometimes called "training groups" or "T Groups" in the professional jargon, and their alleged purpose is to "expand interpersonal consciousness, to substitute collaboration and problem solving for coersion and manipulation." There is little evidence that T Groups have any permanent effect on the leadership styles of those who attend. Of course, many who attend come home ecstatic about their experience, and often claim to have been wonderfully transformed and benefited. But after three or four stimulating days at a T Group, most managers fall back to their old authoritarian ways.

Undeniably many T Groups are fun. Managers are lifted out of their dreary routine and dropped for several days into this jolly encounter group where everyone lays bare the intimate, personal, and private side of their institutional lives for mutual savoring. All this stirs the juices of tired managers and inspires them to give glowing testimony to the value of such sessions. But once back in their old hierarchies, the refreshing, reforming experience fades and their old authoritarian hierarchical lives resume.

If by chance a T Group should succeed in converting a manager from authoritarian to democratic administration, the new convert might find himself disasterously out of tune with his organization, might even be blackballed by colleagues. If it could be shown that democratic administration results in increased production, martyrdom might seem more worthwhile. But proof of any such beneficial effect is thin.

## SOME PATHOLOGICAL BEHAVIOR BY MANAGERS

When people use the word "bureaucrat" they often mean to imply something they don't like, or perhaps a whole collection of things they don't like about government employees, for example, the apparently self-serving behavior of some civil servants. In his book *Modern Organization*, Victor A. Thompson employed the term "bureaupathology" to represent the self-serving behavior patterns of some bureaucrats, and their "excessive aloofness, ritualistic attachment to routines and procedures, and resistance to change; and ... petty insistence upon rights of authority and status" (p. 152). Insofar as these behavior patterns interfere with organizational goals, they are pathological to those goals and are, says Thompson, "bureaupathic." The following discussion draws heavily on Thompson's work, but must be considered a variation on his theme rather than an exact report.

The behavior signified by "bureaupathology" is simply an exaggeration of behavior one finds normally exhibited in any bureaucracy. For example, one finds a certain amount of social distance between superiors and subordinates in any organization, but when that social distance is exaggerated into aloofness owing to the superior's feelings of insecurity, it then becomes "bureaupathic," for it is behavior which, though functional to the superior, may be dysfunctional to the goals of the organization as a whole.

## Why Managers Cannot Manage

Some managers can manage, but they are mostly at the bottom of the hierarchy. The person in charge of a pool of ten or twelve typists can probably understand and control the work of those under her charge to a degree sufficient for all needs of the organization. Managers of most small shops or offices can adequately understand and control what is going on there. On a military base the mess sergeant can control his mess hall, the supply sergeant his supply room, the first sergeant his orderly room; the sergeant of a small radio shop can probably understand and control his shop, and so can the sergeant of an aircraft instrument shop. The chief of each of these specialized units probably knows what his subordinates are doing, and can effectively supervise their work. But what about the middle level manager who has general charge of several such specialized shops? Does he know enough about, for instance, instruments or radio or wing assembly to be sure whether those shops are being properly directed? And what about managers above middle management, the top level managers who are supposed to be in charge of an organization comprising two or three dozen such specialized operations, such as the commander of a heavy aircraft maintenance squadron? Can he possibly know enough to manage his organization? Or does he only pretend to manage, surrounding himself with the stage trappings of management?

The manager of a complex organization who cannot really manage becomes insecure. His superiors hold him responsible for "his" organization. Yet he knows it is not "his" organization, he knows he is mystified by radios, perplexed by aircraft instruments, bewildered by engines, puzzled by wing assemblies. He never learned to type and hasn't a very clear idea what constitutes efficiency in his typing pool. He doesn't really know much about supply rooms and is more or less at the mercy of his supply sergeant, nor know much about stockrooms where his people dispense ten thousand aircraft parts. He must be a real dramatist to pretend to supervise all this.

Of course, the manager of a heavy maintenance squadron may receive communications from time to time about the failures of this or that shop; pilots know when "repaired" instruments are still not working, and inspectors sifting through the wreckage of crashed planes sometimes uncover evidence of faulty repairs on wings, landing gears, tail assemblies and so forth. But all this tells a rather sketchy story. A commander's view of performance in his organization is blurred at best; the more technological and complex the organization the more blurred his vision. Managers are often forced to judge performance in "their" organizations by isolated, occasional, and inadequate reports—it is as if a tapestry connoisseur were forced to judge a tapestry by looking only at its back side.

Technology and complexity have robbed managers of considerable power to do what their title tells them to do: manage. Many modern managers are like the skin of a caterpillar left behind after the caterpillar has wriggled out; the form but not the substance of management remains. Many modern managers are not managers but are the facade of management, a counterfeit, a pretense. But being a pretense of management makes one insecure, as all pretenses do—the insecurity of knowing in your heart you cannot do what is expected of you by your superiors (who because of their own insecurity caused by their own pretense) may expect more than they should.

## How Managers Handle Insecurity

Managers (though they generally appear quite self-possessed) may as a class of people be more afflicted with feelings of insecurity than most other people, not simply because of the gap between their assumed authority and their actual authority, but because they were more insecure before they became managers. Perhaps it was those very insecurities that drove some of them to seek positions of power in the first place. It is beyond the scope of this book to probe why some people are more insecure than others; it may have to do with all sorts of childhood experiences. Be that as it may, some insecure people try to overcome it by dominating their environment—as a defense mechanism they become dominant personalities if not downright domineering. Thus, it can be argued that some people in managerial positions are there because they have tried to win security by winning power.

However, instead of finding security, power seekers often find still more insecurity; having fought their way to managerial positions they find they can not manage, they find new insecurities, new compulsions to fortify themselves and to control subordinates. If control of subordinates can not be achieved, then insecure managers try to hide their weakness, and while hiding it try to fool subordinates into believing there is power where none exists. All middle and top level officials are forced into "impression management;" that is, they are forced to stage an elaborate drama whose purpose is both to conceal weakness and to project an impression of power and control. The more insecure the manager the more he feels compelled to stage this drama.

## Fortifying the Insecure Manager

Managers troubled by the gap between their real authority and their supposed authority tend to build up a wall around themselves. Familiarity is said to breed contempt, and insecure managers fear nothing more than contempt for their authority, which they suspect is worthy of contempt. Insecure people lose confidence in themselves, and feel more and more uncomfortable as they grow more and more insecure. Some bureaupathic managers may take unusually extreme steps to hide their weakness and escape their role.

*Quantification of Their Subordinates' Performance:* One bureaupathic tendency is an exaggerated reliance on quantitative standards. This goes on in a less exaggerated form everywhere, and one sees it commonly practiced at universities by insecure administrators or by insecure personnel committees who wish to escape blame and responsibility for making touchy promotion, pay, tenure, and retention decisions. Thus, to escape blame, a system is devised for quantifying the work of professors; responsibility is then shifted to the inexorable laws of mathematics. It is not unheard of for faculty members to be rated by the *length* of their publication list. That is something quantifiable. However, it is next to impossible to quantify the *worth* of a publication and the attempt is seldom made. When the attempt is made, merit may suffer the indignity of being quantified by the number of pages—twenty pages is more meritorious than five.

Attempts are made to quantify other dimensions of a professor's performance. The number of speeches he makes in the community, the number of papers presented at conventions, and so on. Eligibility for promotions and other rewards is also so some degree in some places based on such quantifiable things as length of service and time in grade. Recently students have clamored for another quantitative measure of professorial worth: the "teacher rating" in which students at the end of a course fill out a multiple-choice evaluation form giving the professor a numerical score on his performance. Administrators sometimes welcome the students' numerical ratings as another quantifiable input which, together with other quantifiable inputs, results in decisions being made by adding and subtracting rather than by exercise of judgment. When a disappointed and angry faculty member visits a college administrator to learn the reason for his failure to be promoted, the administrator can shift blame from himself to the system, and say in effect, "Don't blame me; look at your score."

*Rules:*   Insecure administrators try to shift the blame away from themselves to "the system." Thus administrators not only try to establish a system for quantifying everything, but also to surround themselves with a barricade of rules and regulations. If regulations blanket everything, then administrators can say in effect, "Don't blame me, blame the rules." This tactic is often astoundingly successful; rules, not administrators, absorb the battering. If punishments are to be imposed, it all goes much easier for a manager who can say, "It's not me punishing you, it's the rules."

Of course, not all rulemaking is pathological. Max Weber's picture of an ideal-type bureaucracy emphasizes rules and regulations as important to every properly functioning bureaucracy. Rulemaking, however, becomes pathological when rules are designed not to serve the goals of the organization but to serve the security needs of individual administrators in ways dysfunctional to organizational goals.

*Resistance to Change:*   Casual observation suggests that administrators who feel secure in their positions seem more open to suggestions for change than insecure administrators. Resistance to change is probably a universal human characteristic, but when resistance is exaggerated to the point of interfering with organizational goals by insecure administrators, then it becomes a form of bureaupathology.

*Control of Upward Communications:*   Insecure administrators are frightened by the thought that their shortcomings will be discovered by those in the hierarchy above them. Administrators with exaggerated feelings of insecurity will try to monopolize communications with their superiors, will demand respect for the principle of "going through channels," will be resentful at news that one or another subordinate has gone "over his head," and will steal worried glances at subordinates having social conversations with higher-ups at a Christmas party. No administrator likes subordinates going over his head, but when extreme insecurity causes psychotic attempts to stop all upward communications except those coming first under his scrutiny, this becomes a form of bureaupathology.

*Protocol:*   An extremely insecure administrator may also display extreme oversensitivity to any real or imagined failure by subordinates to show respect. This leads to a pathological demand that subordinates observe every protocol in relations with the insecure administrator of whom we speak. (Communications outside official channels with the boss's boss would surely be considered an outrageous breach of protocol.) Administrators suffering self-doubt, tortured by the gap between their supposed authority and their real authority, may demand more and more outward acknowledgment of their formal authority as their real authority declines.

"Rank has its privileges" may become the guiding principle for administrators whose real authority is less impressive than their formal rank. The smaller an administrator's actual power the greater his thirst for the trappings of power. This brings us to "dramaturgy."

*Dramaturgy:* "Dramaturgy" means impression management. It is a weapon in the struggle for power in bureaucracies (and elsewhere). People defer to other people who seem to have power over them. Therefore, one's power can be increased by increasing the appearance of power. The impression of power gives birth to actual power. Impressions are important—power means the ability to influence others. All power rests on opinion. If a bank robber walks into a bank with a machine gun, his power rests entirely on the opinion of bank personnel that he has power to kill them. But suppose the machine gun is only a toy? Does that affect the power of the robber? No, not if bank personnel believe it is a real gun. Appearances are all important, not only for bank robbers but for administrators. Administration is exercise of power. Power belongs to those who are believed to have it by those subject to it—the greater the belief the greater the power. Play acting by administrators is especially important where the gap between actual authority and supposed authority is greatest. Thompson speaks of dramaturgy as a mechanism for legitimation of authority roles.

The job of modern managers is in large part identical to the job of playwrights, stage managers, and actors. A manager probably knows instinctively what stories and impressions he wants to give his audience of subordinates and superiors, and may think to himself, "Let me convey the impression that I am the person who by all measurements of worth certainly ought to be boss of this organization. Let me radiate ability, industriousness, loyalty, self-control, reliability, honesty, fairness, impartiality. Let me seem to shine in these qualities more than any of my subordinates or rivals so they will willingly acknowledge me as boss. Let me appear absolutely indispensable to the organization. Let me appear powerful, for the more powerful I appear to be, the more powerful I shall become."

Being the director of this show, the manager arranges his stage, and brings on the actors (himself as star performer).

Every performance consists of: (1) an audience; (2) a stage; and (3) a backstage. Let us consider first the audience. Audiences tend to believe what they see. This is what makes dramaturgy possible. We tend to take things at face value. This is perfectly natural; it is natural to believe what we see. If we see a bird flying in the sky we believe it is a bird flying in the sky—unless there is evidence to the contrary. The purpose of stage management is to make sure the audience does not see any evidence to the contrary. Stage management is a process of carefully selecting and withholding evidence. Planning and preparation for this presentation of evidence goes on backstage—one might say "the truth" is backstage. But audiences are not permitted to see backstage; not permitted to see the machinations going on there, the putting on and taking off of costumes, the manufacture of sets, the movement of these sets on and off stage. Nor do audiences very often interrupt the program and demand to see backstage. Managers are free to stage their drama without great danger of being caught.

What exactly do we mean by the "stage." Most of us encounter the stage when we visit the boss's office. First, the boss does not have an "open door." He places himself in an "inner office." To get to the inner office one must first go through an "outer office," guarded by a very efficient, cool, and condescending secretary seated behind a steel desk. She does not permit you to see the boss at once; this would imply he has nothing better to do than await your arrival if you have an appointment. If you do not have an appointment the wait will be longer, for he must appear to be the one indispensable, and therefore busiest, person in the organization. You must be made to wait; this helps demean you.

One of the main things dramaturgy aims at is demeaning the audience, especially subordinates. Subordinates become more subordinate and more child-like the more they are demeaned. They must be made to stand in awe of the boss whenever possible. Thus, while you are waiting you have time to soak up the stage setting of his outer office. On center stage is the aforementioned secretary, courteous but superior. Everything in the room bespeaks the potentate you expectantly wait to see. The carpeting, the drapes, the chair you sit on, the ash trays, the pictures on the wall—all arrogant decor to soften you up. The outer office is a prelude to the opera, an ominous portent of things to come.

Finally the buzzer rings. It is the signal. Now at last you are to be allowed into the inner sanctum and come face to face with the potentate himself. The inner office is more overpowering than the outer office, the carpet thicker, the furnishings more arrogant, the desk larger and more imperial, the drapes heavier and richer, the picture frames more rococo, the insignia and regalia of power is artfully strewn everywhere. In the midst of this splendor the boss (but wait, he is not the "boss," he must have a suitably intimidating title) is seated in his high backed throne-like chair. When you approach, he does not see you immediately, but continues the urgent work you are interrupting. Finally, you are noticed.

Not even college professors are above intimidating visitors with stage settings. Students are immediately put at a disadvantage upon entering a professor's office—every wall covered with shelf upon shelf of books, diplomas conspicuously hung, stacks of papers on the desk, an array of pencils, pens, and other learned paraphernalia. Who dares argue with a professor who's knowledge clearly surpasses the comprehension of ordinary mortals.

Medical practice has its dramaturgy too. When a doctor puts on his white coat, affixes a mirror to his head, drapes a stethoscope around his neck, and meets patients in an office smelling of disinfectant, who can deny the authority of his diagnosis or the efficacy of his advice?

Every profession has its stage, its stage props, its audience, its backstage. Dramaturgy is not by any means confined to managers, nor even to the professions; it is part of each person's daily life.

If play acting, play directing, and play staging are exceedingly important managerial skills, should we not recommend courses in drama to those who would be managers? And if dramaturgical skill is vital to a manager's work, should we not encourage recruitment committees who are embarked on the search for a new manager, say, for a new college president, to face up to the fact that they should be looking for someone who can act the part of college president, who can successfully stage a road show called "Believe me, I am the president of this university," who possesses dramaturgical skill, who is on top his performance, who can control his emotions and always act the scene, who can control his face, his voice, his gestures, and above all his hostilities, who knows how to set a stage, and who knows how to maneuver and deceive from backstage?

## Bureausis

Let us briefly shift our gaze from the manager to one of the manager's chief antagonists, his "bureautic" subordinates, to use another of Thompson's words. A bureautic person finds life in a bureaucracy particularly aggravating. Bureaucracy aggravates most people to some degree; hardly anyone cares for its impersonality. But those annoying characteristics of bureaucracy are much harder for some to bear than for others; some find bureaucracy almost unendurable, and they often vent their spleen on the manager. Perhaps it is useful for managers to understand what makes bureautics tick.

Thompson discusses "bureautic behavior" as dysfunctional persistence of immaturity and childish behavior patterns.

For reasons which cannot be fully explained, some people never seem to grow up; they remain children forever. Unfortunately, childishness in a 50-year-old is less charming than childishness in a child.

What are these characteristics of the bureautic that make him so uncomfortable in the bureaucracy. Basically, it is a demand to be treated in adulthood as he was treated in childhood by his parents; he demands to be treated very personally and very lovingly by everyone around him, especially by those in authority over him who are parent substitutes. A child receives love without a price; his parents love him simply because he is their child no matter how unruly he may be. Such is parental love. But some parents are wise enough to know they must occasionally pretend to withhold their love when a child misbehaves. Yet some other parents spoil their children by an unremitting show of love even when love is not earned. In the process of growing up, most children learn that even their parents will not tolerate certain behavior, and that love can be temporarily lost for bad deeds, and that love must be earned. If this lesson is not learned from parents it may be learned from playmates and relatives.

But some children never learn; they expect to be loved all the time no matter what they do; they become bureautics. They expect to be treated by superiors in the bureaucracy in the same personal and loving manner of their parents. They bitterly object to the impersonality of a bureaucracy where their first name is not always used, where they are constantly "checked on" and 'weighed." Like children they see everyone in the bureaucracy as either a friend or an enemy. People who demand a price for love are enemies. People who weigh them and check on them are enemies plotting against them.

Bureautics sometimes have a hard time of it as college students. At college they dislike most of their professors, unless it is a very small college where professors have a cozy, supportive relationship with students. But at larger colleges where professors often have classes too large to permit much student-faculty intimacy, where professors deal with students rather impersonally, where the process of testing and grading is highly objective, routine, and cold, the bureautic may come to believe the professor has it in for him, especially when exam grades are less than perfect. The bureautic student cannot imagine that his professor is not constantly thinking about *him*, not focussing his whole attention on *him*, not showing personal distaste for *him* by being impersonal and by giving a less than perfect grade.

Of course, to repeat, most of us show symptoms of bureausis; few of us want to be treated impersonally. But because of his upbringing, the bureautic simply cannot comprehend impersonality, cannot comprehend the routine impersonal functionary. He sees enemies and plots where others recognize impersonal routine for what it is—a somewhat unavoidable characteristic of large-scale bureaucratic organization where people must be dealt with on a mass, impersonal basis or not dealt with at all.

Bureautics seldom get into the hierarchy. They tend to be thought of as odd and this makes them all the worse to deal with. They feel powerless and rejected; they become progressively more sullen and hostile, and progressively more difficult to live with. They are a special problem for managers, especially for managers who are themselves bureaupathological.

## CONSERVATISM AND CHANGE

### Resistance to Change

Perhaps resistance to change is an instinct connected with survival of the species. There is evidence (parents see it every day) that babies and young children are hostile to alterations of their routine. This carries into adult-hood and old age—security is found in routine. This, incidentally, seems to be the source of one difficulty with job enlargement which supposedly makes workers happier by delivering them from repetitive routine. Many people don't want to be delivered from routine: uncharted water apparently makes us nervous and uncomfortable. Even people with challenging jobs which offer wide latitude for innovation (the job of college professor, for example) often cling to repetitive routines from which it is difficult to shake them.

Nor is originality very common—we tend to follow precedent, our own or others'. Mimicry begins at infancy when we learn to walk by literally following our parents footsteps. By emulation we acquire the million-and-one talents and attitudes which in sum total is called "culture." Culture itself may be defined as a collection of customs and habits. Each of us is an echo of society.

Social order may depend on adherence to custom. All progress must stare down the eyes of conservatism; change, whatever its merit, is usually resisted.

Organizations, too, are saturated with conservatism, with a tendency to settle down to mindless convention. Yet organizations should, and some-times must, change to accommodate changes of environment. It is not only technological change that forces organizations to modify themselves, but also changes in public wants, changes in policy, changes of elected offi-cials, and so forth. Furthermore, public agencies, like all organizations, are confronted with an endless stream of small internal variations: changes of job title, changes of assignment, changes of office procedure, changes of work method, changes of physical arrangement, changes of equipment, and so on. Many of these seemingly minor shifts, such as shifting the time for a coffee break, are taken seriously by inhabitants of the organization who spend most of their waking hours within its walls.

It is probably safe to say that every change, no matter how minute, is met with one degree or another of hostility. Sometimes resentment is greatest in the face of what management considers the least significant changes. Resistance may take many forms, some subtle, some hidden, some open, and fierce. It may surface as a resignation, or as a reduction in output, or as a request for transfer, or as a wildcat strike. Or it may surface in psychiatric forms such as chronic quarrelsomeness or sullen hostility.

But managers simply must make multitudes of little and big changes. That is what management means. Therefore, managers should make it their business not only to learn what changes are needed and to stimulate them, but also to make those changes as palatable as possible to everyone affected. The final step, that of making changes palatable, may be the most crucial step of all. Many a devoted manager after working hard to identify needed changes is shipwrecked by a clumsy attempt to navigate those changes through the narrow straits of human and organizational conservatism.

Why might changing the location of, say, a xerox machine arouse hostility? Well, obviously, some people will not like walking further to the machine. But beyond those sorts of complaints, there may be subterranean annoyances having more to do with human relations than with anything else. Perhaps the machine in its old location had become a tiny social center—moving the machine disrupts a ganglion of human interaction. Or perhaps the machine in its old location was in a neutral spot, neutral because it did not seem to imply the superiority or inferiority of anyone. The new location might not seem so neutral, might smack of being a status symbol for someone, or, on the contrary, may seem to imply a reduction of status for someone. Or perhaps the only objectionable thing about moving the xerox machine was the high-handed manner in which it was done: nobody's opinion asked, no advance warning, just an order to move it. And perhaps that order was the least important decision made that day (in his opinion) by a harried manager who didn't mean to hurt anybody's feelings, but only wanted to clear a few square feet for "more important" uses.

Managers, of course, don't have time to research every human feeling potentially affected by every change such as a change in the location of a xerox machine, or change in the location of someone's desk. But surely, in view of the absolute certainty that every change will generate at least some kind of friction, managers should count on it, sensitize themselves to it, and get in the habit of thinking how something new will be received, and how to minimize resentment against it.

## Minimizing Resistance to Change

Quite a few bright students of public administration, having had a course in management under an enlightened professor, would at once say "participative management" is the best lubricant for change. Perhaps participative management is an answer; moving the xerox machine might be better received if the manager spends a few minutes chatting with people who use the machine, asking them what they think. Even if everyone denounces the idea, and still the machine is moved—the mere act of honoring the worth of employees by asking their opinion might go far toward preventing trouble. But do managers have time to consult personally with everybody about everything And do subordinates expect it? Perhaps the worth of subordinates can be honored equally well, and with equally good results, by simply putting out a memo explaining why the machine was moved, or by mentioning the reason orally in some meeting before or after the act.

Another approach to minimizing hostility to change is, of course, for the manager to spend what time he can studying objectionable social consequences of every planned change, and doing whatever is possible to avoid those consequences. If moving Sally's desk is important, but would separate her from her buddy Joan, then why not consider moving Joan too if such is possible without other troublesome consequences. Such social engineering by managers can go far toward smoothing the way for change.

## Kindling Change

Because individuals and organizations alike tend to resist change as one shrinks from jumping in a pool of cold water, it is useful for organizations (and individuals) to make change (or, at least, contemplation of it) a deliberate and conscious part of their daily lives. Organizations can deliberately invent ways and means to direct systematic thought to what changes are needed, and how to accomplish them. If the results of such study call for jumping (figuratively) into that pool of cold water, then organizations can mobilize themselves for doing just that. While change for its own sake is no virtue, many organizations find it profitable to invest in "agents of change," that is, to establish on-going mechanisms for spotting the need for change and for bringing it about. Some useful agents of change are sensitivity training, interdepartmental committees, study commissions and task forces, consultants, and planning.

# ETHICS FOR ADMINISTRATORS

## The Public Interest

What code of ethics should guide the work of public administrators, what system of morals, what standard of right and wrong? One view commonly expressed is that public managers should manage in the "public interest," that the public interest should be their standard of ethical behavior. According to this view, whatever serves the public interest is usually right. But who can define the term "public interest?" People differ, sometimes heatedly, over this question. Is abortion in the public interest; is "affirmative action" in the public interest; is public ownership of handguns in the public interest? Every public question betrays conflict over the public interest, and when it comes to the smaller decisions every administrator makes, the public interest seems remote at times.

Practically everything is justified in the name of the public and its interest, even burglary, embezzlement, and murder. What if a president authorizes burglary of the offices of a political opponent and justifies it as his duty to the nation? What if an intelligence agency slanders the character of a public personality on grounds it is in the highest national and public interest to do so? Those who say such things are not in the public interest are simply expressing a contrary view of the public interest.

Probably no politician in the world ever believed more fervently in the "public interest" than Adolf Hitler. Did that make him a good public servant? He was proud, he was dedicated, he was (in his way) quite honest, he was in his mind a fighter for the ultimate welfare of his people and of humanity itself. He fought for public "morality" as he saw it. To him the work of extermination camps was in the public (and world) interest.

Clearly we are adrift on an uncharted sea if managerial morality is defined in terms of something so indefinable and contradictory as the public interest.

In recent years some advocates of a "new public administration" have stated that to be moral and ethical a public administrator must seek in all his actions the goal of "social equity"—still another concept of the public interest.

## An Interest Higher Than the Public's

Also there is the morality of those who believe there is a higher duty than serving the public and its interest. Some religious groups maintain that the highest morality is service to God, not to man; God's interest, not man's, should guide the public administrator. Is a public servant practicing good ethics when he does right by God in preference to doing right by the public? Or is there a difference?

There is also the philosophy voiced by Friedrich Nietzsche to whom the highest morality consisted of service to the elite of mankind. Nietzsche distinguished between "slave morality" and "master morality". He said Christian morality is a prime example of "slave morality"—an attempt by the weak to bring down the strong. The strong, meanwhile, tend to have an opposite code of ethics (a master morality) glorifying war, conquest, exploitation, and the right of might. Master morality is the morality that should be practiced by superior people, said Nietzsche; it is their duty to evolve themselves into a new species of man, a master race, and thus to advance the human race. But to do this it is necessary for the aristocracy of talent to subjugate the slow, the weak, the mediocre. Master morality is the morality of higher man, slave morality is a conspiracy against higher man—so goes the Nietzschean argument. Obviously, any bureaucrat guided by the ethics of master morality could commit almost any crime and feel good about it.

Communists have no master race doctrine as yet, but do have a "master class" doctrine. Many communists hold that every act is justified if it serves the ultimate victory of the proletarian class and serves to erase all other classes. Any means are justified to that end.

Thus we see practically everyone preaching some form of morality based on some vision of good, and we find almost every form of bestiality justified by these allegedly good purposes.

## Fiscal Ethics

Most legislation on the subject of public service ethics aims at bribery, graft, and economic conflicts of interest. A conflict of interest is presented anytime a bureaucrat holds a position in which his official powers and his private economic interests are related and potentially incestuous. Legislative bodies are often eager to expose the danger of such conflicts in the executive branch and will not hesitate to subject potential appointees to severe inspection. However, among the greatest conflicts of interest to be seen in the United States are those committed by members of Congress and other legislative bodies. It is utterly routine for legislators to vote on questions directly affecting the fate and future of economic interests in which they are heavily invested. A legislator is often supported in his candidacy for office by economic interests which do not expect him to be a shrinking flower when legislation concerning those interests is before the body. In fact, legislators openly and proudly take seats on legislative committees where they can influence legislation in behalf of the same interests (usually economic) which they themselves represent. When legislators warn bureaucrats against conflicts of interest it is like hawks lecturing chickens on the evils of aggression.

Federal employees are prohibited by presidential order to do anything that might result in, or create the appearance of, using public office for private gain. Of course, federal criminal law prohibits bribery, graft, and economic conflicts of interest. Some state and local laws on the same subject also exist.

Noneconomic concerts of interest are rarely considered a breach of ethics when, for example, an advocate of more national parks becomes head of the park service.

## Professional Ethics

Some professional groups within the bureaucracy maintain self-imposed standards of ethical behavior governing relations between and among fellow workers, and relations between themselves and the public. Here, for example, is a list of proscribed behavior set forth by the political science department of a university for guidance of its members in their relations with one another:

1. The habitual use of insult and insinuation rather than reasoned dialogue in department, college and university affairs;

2. The outright use of the cruder tools—deliberate deceit, character assassination, academic bribery and/or blackmail—in the inevitable politics of the academic community;
4. The betrayal of a colleague's trust for personal gain;
5. The implication of students in department, college and university controversies.

The document goes on to say, "A faculty member's responsibility to his colleagues as outlined above is not to be construed as a warning that personal popularity will have any bearing on promotability. Quite the contrary, the faculty of the department of political science goes on record as respecting the right of any member to be governed by any sort of personal idiosyncrasy, as long as it does not interfere with his professional effectiveness. The right of a professor to be unloved by his colleagues is regarded as a valuable safeguard against bland academic conformity and slavish sycophancy."

Often specialized groups, such as doctors or lawyers within the bureaucracy have highly developed standards of professional behavior. Breach of these professional standards may be considered a breach of ethics. The terms "ethical standard" and "professional standard" are often used interchangeably.

To some extent the public service at large is developing professional standards. Various groups within the bureaucracy are taking the lead in this. The International City Managers' Association some years ago adopted a professional code of ethics setting forth the manager's responsibility and specifying standards for dealing with the council and the public. One often sees this code framed and conspicuously hung in the offices of city managers.

The more the public service is professionalized, the more it will develop enforceable standards. Professions tend to keep tabs on their members and to acquire powers to discipline wrongdoers. No doubt the current proliferation of schools of public administration will contribute to professionalization of public administrators, and to the establishment of professional standards of conduct. Breaches of these standards may become the subject of professional self-policing.

Professional ethics sometimes have more to do with survival and prosperity of the profession than with any sense of righteousness. Very often one hears it said that good ethics is good business. Ethical behavior is often justified for its pragmatic results. Yet one sometimes wonders whether it is ethical to be ethical just for a pragmatic result.

## SUMMARY

To manage people one must lead, and it would be very nice to know exactly what leadership is so that it could be practiced with the same exactitude one practices trigonometry. Great efforts have been made to find out what leadership is, but the results have been indecisive. To the question what makes a leader, two competing theories are generally offered, the traits theory and the situationist theory. Traits which have been identified as traits of leadership are commonly quite vague and overlapping, nor do all leaders exhibit the same traits. The traits of leadership seem to be different in different situations, hence the situationist theory which holds that each situation calls forth leaders appropriate to the situation.

Several broad styles of leadership have been identified including authoritarian, laissez-faire, and democratic styles, each of which rests on a competing theory of human nature. Democratic administration (sometimes called participative management) is often alleged to result in greater productive effort by employees because it gives them a sense of participation in organizational decision making, hence an ego involvement in carrying out those decisions. However, democratic administration may not have as great an impact on production as its champions would like to believe, although there is evidence that participative management does make employees happier in their work. Despite these confusions about the nature of leadership and the beneficial results of one style of leadership over another, T Groups (training groups) are frequently used to teach participative management. Although most who attend T Group sessions come home ecstatic about their experience, there is little evidence that T Groups have a permanent effect on the leadership styles of those who attend.

Management practices of some administrators are affected by the insecurity they feel as a result of the gap between their real authority in the organization and their supposed authority. Some extremely insecure managers employ defense mechanisms which are pathological to the goals of the organization. These bureaupathological practices include extreme efforts to quantify the performance of subordinates, extreme reliance on rules and regulations to settle all issues, extreme resistance to change, extreme attempts to control all communications to those above them in the hierarchy, extreme insistance on observance of protocol by subordinates, and excessive use of dramaturgy for impression management.

Organizations, like individuals, tend to resist change, yet an organization such as a public bureaucracy should change to accommodate changes of environment, changes in policy, changes in public wants, and so on. Public administrators should try to recognize the causes of resistance to needed change, and be skilled at minimizing that resistance. To identify and facilitate needed change, some organizations have found it profitable to establish formal agents of change such as sensitivity training, interdepartmental committees, study commissions, task forces, consultants, and planning.

There is much philosophizing about the proper code of ethics which should guide public administrators in their work. One view commonly expressed is that public managers should manage in the public interest. However, the term public interest is difficult to define. Most legislation on the subject of public service ethics aims at bribery, graft, theft, and conflicts of interest. Some professional groups within the bureaucracy, such as city managers, have developed professional standards and codes of ethics. As the trend toward professionalization of the entire public service continues, it seems possible that professional and ethical standards will continue to be developed for the public service and will be enforced by self-policing mechanisms of the profession.

## SUGGESTED READING

Association of the Bar of the City of New York. *Conflict of Interest and Federal Service: Report of the Special Committee on Federal Conflict of Interest Laws.* Cambridge: Harvard University Press, 1960.

Argyris, Chris. *Integrating the Individual and the Organization.* New York: John Wiley, 1964.

Argyris, Chris. *Personality and Organization.* New York: Harper & Row, 1957.

Beard, Edmund, and Horn, Stephen. *Congressional Ethics: The View from the House.* Washington, D.C.: The Brookings Institution, 1975.

Dubin, Robert. "Persons and Organization." In *Human Relations in Administration,* edited by Robert Dubin. Englewood Cliffs, New Jersey: Prentice-Hall, 1961.

Garson, David G., and Smith, Michael P. *Organizational Democracy: Participation and Self-Management.* Beverly Hills, California: Sage, 1976.

Geis, Gilbert, ed. *White-Collar Criminal: The Offender in Business and the Professions.* New York: Atherton Press, 1968.

Gilman, G. "An Inquiry Into the Nature and Use of Authority." In *Organization Theory in Industrial Practice,* edited by M. Haire. New York: Wiley, 1962.

Goffman, Irving. *The Presentation of Self in Everyday Life.* Garden City: Doubleday and Co., Inc., 1959.

Graham, George A. "Ethical Guidelines for Public Administrators: Observations on Rules of the Game." *Public Administration Review,* January-February 1974, pp. 90–92.

Gulick, Luther, and Urwick, L., eds. *Papers on the Science of Administration.* New York: Institute of Public Administration, 1937.

Hart, James G., and Larson, Lars L. *Leadership Frontiers.* Kent, Ohio: Kent State University Press, 1976.

Levinson, Harry. *The Great Jackass Fallacy.* Cambridge: Harvard University Press, 1973.

Levine, Ned, and Cooper, Cary L. "T-Groups-20 Years on: A Prophecy." *Human Relations,* January 1976, pp. 1–23.

Likert, Rensis. *The Human Organization: Its Management and Value.* New York: McGraw-Hill, 1967.

Maslow, Abraham. *Toward a Psychology of Being.* Princeton: Van Nostrand Reinhold Company, 1962.

Machiavelli, Niccolo. *The Prince.* New York: F. S. Crofts & Co., 1947.

Marini, Frank, ed. *Toward a New Public Administration: The Minnowbrook Perspective.* San Francisco: Chandler, 1971.

Mayo, Elton. *The Social Problems of an Industrial Civilization.* Cambridge: Harvard University Graduate School of Business Administration, 1945.

McGregor, Douglas. *Leadership and Motivation.* Cambridge: MIT Press, 1966.

McGregor, Douglas. *The Human Side of Enterprise.* New York: McGraw-Hill, 1960.

McGregor, Eugene B., Jr. "Social Equity and the Public Service." *Public Administration Review,* January-February 1974, pp. 18–29.

Nietzsche, Friedrich. *On the Geneology of Morals* and *Ecce Homo.* New York: Vintage Books, 1969.

Parkinson, C. Northcote. *Parkinson's Law.* Boston: Houghton Mifflin, 1975.

Peter, Laurence J., and Hull, Raymond. *The Peter Principle.* New York: William Morrow and Co., 1969.

Roethlisberger, F. J., and Dickenson, W. J. *Management and the Worker.* Cambridge: Harvard University Press, 1949.

Rohr, John A. "The Study of Ethics in the PA Curriculum." *Public Administration Review,* July-August 1976, pp. 398–406.

Sherwood, Frank. "Professional Ethics." *Public Management,* June 1975, pp. 13–14.

Stogdill, Ralph M. *Handbook of Leadership: A Survey of Theory and Research.* New York: The Free Press, 1974.

Thompson, Victor A. *Modern Organization.* New York: Alfred A. Knopf, 1961.

Wakefield, Susan. "Ethics and the Public Service: A Case for Individual Responsibility." *Public Administration Review,* November-December, 1976, pp. 661–666.

# Judgment Day 11

# Judgment Day  11

## PERFORMANCE EVALUATION OF INDIVIDUALS

Theologians say we will be judged in the next world by one who is all-knowing and all-wise. But for the punishments and rewards of this world there is no all-knowing or all-wise employer. Nevertheless, evaluations must be made no matter how clumsily and erroneously. No employer is going to give promotions, assignments, and continued employment to people without making *some* kind of judgment, whether based on a scientific measuring device or on bias and misinformation.

Those who favor merit as a governing principle in personnel actions are driven to find some way to measure it. But there are many pitfalls to shun in measuring quality of performance, the fundamental one being the danger of a low degree of relevance between the evaluation device and the thing to be evaluated. It is hard to find an evaluation system that does exactly what it is supposed to do, but a search must be made for one if merit is to be a governing principle.

### Purposes of Evaluation

Evaluation systems have several purposes such as helping employers make decisions about promotions, pay raises, and assignments. Also, if his evaluation system is valid it tells an employer whether various other personnel practices in his organization are valid—for example, the validity of his recruitment exams.

Employees themselves can profit by evaluation of their performance: it tells them what they're doing right and spurs them to keep on doing it, and, of course, it tells them where they might improve. It is important for an employee to know what his strong suits are; most people like to maximize their strengths. Evaluations have another important value to em-

231

ployees. It helps them to know what is expected of them, what constitutes good performance in the employer's eyes, and what the criteria of judgment are. Naturally, any employer who wants his employees to benefit from ratings will not lock the results in his safe and keep them secret from the employee. On the other hand, it is not necessarily a good idea to publish the results in a newspaper or pin them up on a bulletin board.

## Employee Participation in Evaluation

Should employees participate in evaluating themselves? Some authorities think evaluations ought to be like "client centered" therapy in the practice of psychiatry. The psychiatrist sits back and lets the patient talk, puts a question here and there, but confines himself to lending a sympathetic ear while the patient reasons out his own problem. Employees may know more about their own weaknesses than anyone suspects, and if a supervisor carries on a conversation with his subordinate, putting questions here and there to prompt the conversation down certain avenues, the supervisor may be spared having to tell his employee anything. Furthermore, an "employee centered evaluation" may have more impact on the employee than any other kind of rating—what he (the employee) learns from the session are his own discoveries, not the preachings of a boss. This system is comparable to the socratic method in education in which the teacher teaches (as Socrates did) not by telling students the truth, but by leading students to discover truths for themselves. The trouble with the socratic method as a teaching device is that it takes forever to laboriously draw students to the discovery of a couple truths. Neither supervisors nor teachers generally have that much time; therefore, they resort to lecturing on the truth, and can spew forth more truths in six minutes than Socrates could in sixty hours. The only difference is that students may remember the lectured truths only minutes, while Socrates' students carried their handful of truths to the grave with them. Bosses may prefer getting one point over by employee participation, than getting twenty points over by calling the employee in, sitting him down, and telling him the plain truth— and letting him go out grumbling, insulted, and vengeful.

## Methods of Evaluation

The best rating form for some kinds of work may consist of nothing more than production records. It is fairly easy to look at the output of a typist and compare with the known output of other typists. Production records do not always reveal quality, though they do reveal quantity and are excellent where output can be validly quantified. Production records are not so helpful where the product is a service like teaching. It is not entirely valid to measure the worth of a teacher by the number of students he has or by the number of hours he teaches.

Another device commonly used is the "rating schedule" which consists of a list (often a long list) of factors (promptness for example), and the rater is called upon to give a numerical value to each factor—perhaps a value of one to someone seldom prompt, and a value of ten to someone unfailingly prompt. By the time the rater is half way through the rating form he is exhausted, exasperated, and willing to do anything to get done with it— mark them all five or mark them all ten or skip around mindlessly from one number to another to make it look thoughtful. Various devices have been invented to ease the rater's burden such as graphic rating scales which arrange things on the page more clearly.

Still another method of evaluation is reminiscent of the "little black book" some employers are said to keep listing the sins of others which will one day be repaid in kind. This system has been elevated to academic respectability and called the "critical incident method;" the employer keeps records over the course of time on each employee, jotting down specific incidents that illustrate an employee's good or bad performance. Then, periodically, the supervisor relates this information to the employee.

One method of evaluation amounts to coaching. But coaching depends on frequent and intimate relations between supervisor and employee and takes a good deal of time. It is also dependent on the rapport between them which is not common between supervisors and employees.

In some variations of performance rating, the rating is not done by the employer, but by a panel of fellow employees or a panel of supervisors or by some other panel arrangement. A panel may be more accurate, and it certainly allows employers to escape the blame of resentful employees who receive bad news via their rating. The panel, not the employer, is blamed. Employees may have greater faith in the objectivity of a panel and be slower to blame it than to blame their boss. The committee system does actually appear to lessen somewhat the danger of bias in ratings.

### What is to be Evaluated?

Other problems pertaining to employee evaluation systems have to do with what is measured rather than how or by whom. If the object of a performance rating is to evaluate an employee's performance in a position, then obviously it could be a mistake to use that evaluation as the sole or primary basis for judging how an employee would do in another position. That would be like evaluating Albert Einstein's performance as a math- metician to determine whether he should be made president of a univer- sity—just because he is dazzling in one position doesn't mean he would be dazzling or even adequate in another. It is not uncommon in universities to make administrators out of leading scholars on the strength of their scholarship. However, insofar as talent in one position may indicate talent in another position, the evaluation must be used as a partial (and only partial) predictor of success in the other position. For example, success at a low level administrative job may to some degree suggest success in a high level administrative job. But one has to be careful here. The world is repleat with examples of people who were whizzes at managing a narrow concern who became notorious failures at managing large concerns. Adolf Hitler may be an example of that. He is said to have been a really superb manager of the National Socialist Party in its growth years. But as Chancellor of the Reich he is thought by some observers to have been a terrible failure. Also there are examples of individuals who do well at great responsibilities, but fail in small ones—larger responsibilities often bring a new sense of responsibility, awakening talent not previously revealed by performance during lesser jobs.

What should an evaluation of job performance evaluate? Suppose the supervisor is asked to say whether employee "X" is dependable. The supervisor then gives Mr. "X" a low score on dependability because recently "X" had been put in charge of the annual Christmas party and failed to take his responsibilities seriously—the party was a mess because of all the things left undone. Furthermore, "X" is frequently late to meetings. Also he frequently says he's going to do things he never does; for example, not long ago he was telling everybody he planned to resign, but didn't do it, and before that he was telling everybody he planned to take a course in computer programming at the local community college, and never did it, and three months ago he said he was going to sell his car and buy a new one, and hasn't yet. He appears to be a very dubious fellow. But, employee "X" is a janitor, and if his supervisor had focussed solely and exclusively on the work Mr. "X" has done as janitor, there would be no excuse whatsoever for saying he is undependable. If a job performance evaluation is supposed to be an evaluation of *job* performance, then the focus should be, say some authorities, exclusively on how he performed his duties, not how he performed in other areas of life. The Christmas party, lateness to meetings, plans to sell his car and take a computer course at the college are beyond the scope of his janitorial duties. If an evaluation of job performance is going to be what it says it is, then employers should confine the evaluation to actual performance, and try to forget behavior that does not affect the work actually done.

Many evaluation forms place heavy emphasis on traits such as dependability, ingenuity, integrity, initiative, tact, and maturity. But suppose an employee lacks all these traits, yet still does good work? The traits approach to evaluation is an evaluation of traits, not of job performance. Of course, there may be a relationship in many cases between success on the job and possession of these supposedly laudable traits. But still, the evaluator should focus on what was actually done on the job, no matter what traits are exhibited.

## Telling an Employee His Rating

Another problem with performance ratings is the problem of how to tell people they aren't doing well in some aspect of their work. Nobody is perfect, all have shortcomings—including the boss whose shortcoming may be an inability to communicate the failures of subordinates to them tactfully. This question must be asked: do formal job performance evaluations do more harm than good when revealed to employees? Are they counterproductive? Is there, for example, any point in telling an employee every year for 40 years that he is doing the same old things wrong and the same old things right, and risk making him mad and disagreeable and difficult every time you do it? Is the value of informing an employee of his shortcomings (which he probably knows already) so great that it outweighs the value of good employee-employer relations? Employees normally have great anxiety about their ratings, as a student has anxiety about grades. The relationship between a boss and a subordinate can be a very delicate and subtle thing, and it may be much better to let the supervisor and the subordinate work out their relationship without the clumsy intrusion of formal job evaluations.

## Bias in Evaluation

One of the greatest problems of job performance evaluation has to do with bias in the evaluation. Probably no person walking this earth is beyond bias when judging others, especially when judging those close at hand. No matter how unbiased a supervisor tries to be, no matter how scientific the evaluation form, bias will creep in, even if the evaluation is done by a committee, for committees can also be biased (and can get away with it behind a cloak of anonymity). The ever present danger of bias and the constant suspicion of it further calls into question the value of formal job performance evaluations.

## Grading Employees

Finally, it is probably a mistake to try to sum up the job performance of an employee by totaling scores on an evaluation form and giving the employee an overall grade—say a grade of B or C. No employee performs all tasks with equal ability; all are better at some than at other tasks, as a teacher may be good in seminars but poor in lectures. It is misleading to "sum up" anybody. It is more accurate to let each category of a rating form stand by itself.

Also, it is poor policy to use the same rating form for all employees. The form should be fitted to the job. Why a question about, for example, "maturity," if maturity has nothing to do with job performance?

## PERFORMANCE EVALUATION OF ORGANIZATIONS

### Efficiency Distinguished From Effectiveness

In much of the literature of public administration "efficiency" and "effectiveness" are given different meanings. Efficiency is doing a job at the lowest cost; effectiveness is reaching objectives by doing the job. By these definitions, it is possible to be efficient without being effective. One may efficiently type a manuscript, but the manuscript may not effectively achieve the goals intended. One may efficiently file papers, but the filing system might not effectively accomplish the goal intended. One may efficiently bomb the enemy, but bombing may not effectively weaken the enemy.

### Judging Effectiveness

Identifying the goal of a public agency, and measuring its (the agency's) effectiveness are both very difficult things to do. In this area the public sector differs somewhat from the private sector where goals are sometimes clearer. The goal of a business firm in classic capitalist theory is to make a profit; effectiveness is measured by that goal; the effectiveness of all employees and of all programs can be measured by their contribution to that overarching profit-making purpose. However, goals in the private sector can become unclear, and measuring effectiveness can become more difficult when profit ceases to be the central and sole object of the firm. It is not unheard of for a proprietor to stay in a certain business or to conduct his business in a certain way employing certain people for reasons apart from "maximum return on investment." For example, a proprietor may decline to move his business to a better location because for sentimental reasons he chooses to do business where his father and grandfather had done business before him. If that is his goal then the effectiveness of his enterprise may be measured by reference to it.

Of course, effectiveness may be measured by any yardstick anyone wishes to apply. Thus, a financial expert might declare a proprietor ineffective because he chose not to move to a more profitable location. But effectiveness, like pornography, is in the eye of the beholder. One can hardly conceive any single act that is effective from everybody's point of view.

Effectiveness is always measured by the goals of whoever presumes to judge. The standards of effectiveness *enforced* in an organization are always those of the power holders in that organization. However, since all organizations are to some degree pluralistic (beset with competing centers of power), there are likewise conflicting standards of effectiveness enforced in every organization.

It is particularly difficult to measure the goals of public enterprises (universities, for example) because so often their goals are numerous, unsettled, undecided, diverse, and at times aimless. Of course, a manager of a public enterprise can arbitrarily declare a goal for his agency and proceed to measure its effectiveness, and the effectiveness of everybody in it, by that goal. To some degree that is what "management by objectives" (MBO) is all about—it is really "management by the manager's objectives" (MBTMO).

But the manager is not the only person with goals in an organization, for, to repeat, organizations are in varying degrees pluralistic. Every member and group of members within an organization has private goals and tries to steer the organization toward those private goals. Even managers have private goals. The announced goals of organizations are often a deceptive facade behind which numerous private goals are pursued. Many writers, such as Chester Barnard, believe it is an important duty of every manager to do what he can to make the private goals of employees mesh with official goals of the organization.

## Responsiveness as a Goal

One overarching goal of every public agency in a democracy is, one might think, to be responsive. If an agency pursues goals identical to the goals of the people it serves, it is responsive and (in that sense) effective. However, there are a few problems with the term "responsive." If the effectiveness of an agency is measured by whether it pursues goals identical to the goals of the people it serves, who is to say what people an agency serves or what their goals are? Pluralists might argue that an agency like a public university serves no single public, but many diverse publics, a mass of overlapping groups and interests. Thus, the effectiveness of a public agency is seen differently and measured differently by different groups. Perhaps in the eyes of some university students, a university is effective if the degree it offers is valued by employers. On the other hand, to some faculty members, a university may be effective if it attracts and holds bright students. To the Chamber of Commerce a university might be considered effective if it boosts business. And so on. The very question, "What is effective education?" may be answered differently by different groups.

## Performance Testing

As if identifying the "proper" goals of public agencies were not hard enough, measuring whether an agency does, or noes not, serve any given goal is equally perverse. Are you going to test for "results?" If so, what about an agency that can't show any results because the goals sought cannot be achieved except over a long time-span—a disarmament agency, a race relations agency? And what about an agency whose results are vague and cannot be quantified—a museum, a university, or almost any service agency? Stress on "results" unfairly rewards agencies that happen to be doing highly visible and quantifiable work like paving streets and going to Mars.

## Measuring Efficiency

Efficiency, to repeat, is here defined as doing a job at the lowest cost. But it is difficult to measure cost, and difficult to know whether performance is "good" in light of what it costs. A few common methods for measuring efficiency are the "costs per unit" method, "best practice" method, and the "results" approach.

*Cost per Unit:* Cost per unit is a culturally valued and very popular measure of efficiency. However, anyone using cost per unit should keep his eyes open for some of its tricky problems. First, cost per unit means nothing until compared with the cost per unit of the same or similar product produced at a different time or place. And right there is a central danger point in using this measure of efficiency—what was produced at a different place and/or time must have been produced under different circumstances to a greater or lesser degree. It is sometimes exceedingly difficult to find products produced under precisely the same circumstances. Take trash collection for example. One might try to determine the efficiency of trash collection in a certain district by comparing its cost per ton with cost per ton in another district. And after making the cost per ton comparison one finds that trash collection in one district is fearfully more expensive than in the other. But does that mean the expensive district is less efficient? Perhaps not; in fact, the more expensive district could be more efficient—given the circumstances of collection. After all, districts differ. Some are hilly, some are "exclusive" with mansions distantly spaced, some are inhabited by heavy trash producers. Cost per unit comparisons can be grossly misleading unless the conditions of production are almost identical.

Volume also affects cost per unit. Governmental units differ greatly in size. Frequently a town is so small it cannot fully utilize the equipment it has, say, a trash truck that stands idle much of the time because there is not much trash to collect. Governments, unlike many private concerns, do not have a choice where to do business. They must serve a set clientele on a set piece of geography; some governments are more favorably situated than others when it comes to cost per unit of service.

Also, those who make cost per unit comparisons must be alert to price changes and price levels. Wages in one place may differ from wages in another, and prices may be higher today than a year ago. Also cost per unit calculations should not overlook the possibility that the products being compared are not exactly identical. Comparing the cost per unit of water in two towns may overlook water purity. Town A's water may cost more, but may also be purer. Similarly, in comparing cost per unit of gas, the heat content of the gas being compared should be checked.

Those who make cost per unit calculations should also make sure the methods of calculating the cost of the products being compared are identical. In comparing the cost per unit of water in two towns, did both towns include interest on the money borrowed to construct the water processing plant, was depreciation of facilities calculated in both towns, was overhead correctly calculated in both towns (does city A have lower overhead costs for water production because its utilities department is not charged for using a room in city hall while city B's is)? Many of these potential pitfalls in cost per unit comparison are typical cost accounting problems. The central problem is to decide which costs should be counted as a cost of the product, and not to overlook any.

Cost per unit calculations are not altogether hopeless, nor are they useless. One simply has to be careful about comparisons. Among the safest comparisons to make are those between two different methods of doing the same job under identical or nearly identical circumstances, for example, using two-man trash collection crews one week, three-man crews the next, to compare productivity of the crews.

*Best Practice Method:* Because quantitative comparisons (such as cost per unit) are often unreliable, there are some nonquantitative socially approved measures of efficiency. These consist of admonitions from the mouths and pens of those who claim to know what is "best practice." Over the past several generations many occupational groups have formed professional associations: budget officers, personnel officers, planning officials, police officers, fire officials, and numerous others. Many of these professional organizations sponsor research to determine which methods constitute best practice for the work of their members. Results of these studies are published and kept up to date. "Best practice" however, can vary, and depends on whose point of view is considered.

*Results:* Another approach to efficiency is to look at the results of an effort, say the results of police work, and, if good, then declare the procedure efficient; thus, if the crime rate is low, police might claim this to be evidence they are on the ball. This measure of efficiency, however, is strewn with booby traps for the unwary. The crime rate in a town may look very good (from a law and order point of view) and the police might not have had a thing to do with it. Some small communities have no police at all, and no crime. To laud the police of a rural village for "maintaining" a lower crime rate than prevails in New York City may be quite unscientific; the two communities are in no way comparable. Nor obviously, would it be scientific to call the New York police more efficient than the police of a rural village because in New York they apprehend more criminals per capita and solve more crimes. The village may lack crimes to solve and criminals to apprehend no matter how clever the police.

## SUMMARY

Attempts are made to evaluate both individuals and organizations—both exceedingly difficult. Supervisors are going to make evaluations of subordinates whether they do it secretly or openly, or whether they do it well or poorly. Since evaluations are of necessity going to be made, then, everyone has a stake in seeing that they are done the best way possible, especially in seeing to it that the so-called performance evaluation actually does what it is supposed to do.

Measuring the performance of organizations is perhaps more difficult than measuring that of individuals. Efficiency is defined as doing a job at the lowest cost; effectiveness is defined as reaching objectives by doing the job. Effectiveness is hard to measure except in relation to goals, and the goals of public agencies are often numerous, elusive and unfathomable. Responsiveness as a goal is particularly enigmatic and hard to measure because of the uncertainty what the word means—to whom should an agency be responsive? As for efficiency, most measures of it, such as cost per unit, are very tricky to handle.

## SUGGESTED READING

Barnard, Chester I. *The Functions of the Executive.* Cambridge, Mass.: Harvard University Press, 1938.

Barrett, Richard S. *Performance Rating.* Chicago: Science Research Associates, 1966.

Cummings, L. L. and Schwab, Donald P. *Performance in Organizations: Determinants and Appraisal.* Glenview, Ill.: Scott, Foresman, 1973.

Fried, Robert C. *Performance in American Bureaucracy.* Boston: Little, Brown, 1976.

Lopez, Felix M., Jr. *Evaluating Employee Performance.* Chicago: Public Personnel Association, 1968.

Rowland, Virgil. *Managerial Performance Standards.* New York: American Management Association, 1960.

Symposium on Productivity in Government." *Public Administration Review,* November-December 1972, pp. 739–850.

"Symposium on Program Evaluation." *Public Administration Review,* July-August 1974, pp. 299–340.

*

# High Rollers and Moneygrubbers 12

# High Rollers and Moneygrubbers 12

## THE BUDGET PROCESS

The federal budget is bigger than the Los Angeles phone book. Some years ago there were contests among members of Congress to see who could tear the document in half. No one tries anymore. The annual budget tearing seemed to many people the only interesting thing about a budget; the very word "budget" was sleep-inducing, chloroform in print. College students would brace themselves for an ordeal of boredom whenever the subject of budgeting came up. Budgeting seemed destitute of emotion. This attitude was usually justified because budgeting was often presented as a series of mechanical steps—the agency head does this, the department head does that, the bureau does something else, and so on. Those procedures are, of course, important, but in describing them the politics, the passion, the power struggles seething behind them were too often neglected. Just when the study of public budgeting had sunk to its most barren and insipid state, Aaron Wildavsky came to the rescue with his book, *The Politics of the Budgetary Process*. This classic work, as its title implies, probes beneath the mechanics of budgeting.

### What is a Budget?

A budget is not an appropriations bill, nor is an appropriations bill a budget, though in common parlance one often hears the expression, "My budget was cut," meaning a reduced appropriation. The word "budget" (as distinguished from "budgeting" and "budget process") refers strictly to a proposal for expenditures drafted in advance of actual appropriations. While an appropriations bill is not a budget, it is part of the "budgetary process" that includes all struggles and decisions touching the outflow of public money, whether before or after appropriations.

To a very large degree, when you talk about the budget process, you're talking about the whole political process because all political activity is a contest over who gets what. The budget process largely determines who gets what; the dollar sign is a symbol of power. The power of any agency to do anything depends chiefly on money—without money there would be no employees, no resources. Budgeting is the terrain over which many power struggles are fought.

Even the seemingly dull mechanics of the budget process signify a great deal about the power struggle; the mechanics give clues where power lies; those who have power will include themselves in the machinery of decision making. Power may be divided among several competitors, each clinging to a piece of the decision-making machinery like a dog with a bone. Budgeting is at bottom, to repeat, a political process, and anyone who attempts reforms which do not comply with political reality has an uphill battle. Changes in the budgetary process result from changes in the power structure. It is naive to propose changes in the budget process without at the same time suggesting a practical plan for changing the political power structure underlying that process. Many beautiful thoughts have been spun about how budgeting "should be done" without adequate concern whether the idea could possibly work in political reality.

## Combatants in the Budgetary Process

If budgeting is at bottom a struggle for resources with which to build power, who are the combatants in the struggle? Most of the fighting is done by countless institutions both public and private. A great part of what we call "pressure politics" is the effort of groups to influence the flow of public money. To that end Congress and every major and minor center of power capable of influencing that flow is lobbied by numerous groups and individuals who have an interest in it. This war of all against all is somewhat chaotic in a pluralistic democracy such as ours, but battles for power and money go on in all governmental systems, even in the most totalitarian dictatorships. Albert Speer's *Inside the Third Reich* describes the backstabbing politics that went on behind the monolithic facade of Hitler's government. The formal budgetary process at the federal level is scattered among various centers of power within Congress and the executive branch; it is similarly dispersed within state and local governments.

## The Fiscal Year

The word "fiscal" comes to us from the Latin *fiscus* meaning purse. Anything fiscal pertains to public financial matters. The word "year" does not necessarily mean calendar year, but is any twelve month period used for accounting purposes, a period with reference to which appropriations are made and expenditures authorized. Most state and local governments use a fiscal year running from July 1st to June 30th. The federal government also used that period until the beginning of the 1977 fiscal year when the year was changed to run from October 1st to September 30th to give Congress more time to enact its appropriation bills. The fiscal year gets a jump on the calendar year; thus, the fateful year 1984 will arrive three months early for federal fiscal matters, six months early for most other governmental units.

## The Office of Management and Budget

Before 1921 we had a happy-go-lucky system in which each agency of the federal government went directly to Congress to plead its case for money. Congress in that era received no single coherent document from the executive branch stating what the whole government was asking for, received no overarching picture of proposed federal expenditures. In 1921 Congress enacted the Budget and Accounting Act which directed the President to prepare an annual budget recommendation to Congress incorporating the requests of all agencies. It set up a Bureau of the Budget to help the President gather the necessary data in time for him to submit a budget to Congress early in January accompanied by this budget message.

In its first years the Bureau of the Budget took a conservative view of its functions, but in the course of time the bureau acquired great influence owing to the enormity of its job and the inability of the President to do much more than set broad guidelines. By executive order in 1970, an Office of Management and Budget was set up in place of the Bureau of the Budget. The inclusion of "management" together with "budget" in the name of the new agency testifies to the fact that a budget agency is usually driven by the nature of its job to look into how well each agency is using its resources (hence, how well it is managing itself). Budget agencies are forced to become organization and management experts, and can point out to the agencies how their operations can be made efficient and economical.

It is the President's job through the Office of Management and Budget to recommend how much money each executive branch agency should receive from Congress. The agencies are expected to support the President's budget and are not supposed to strike separate deals with Congress. However, this is difficult to prevent because there is usually a cozy relationship between agency heads and the key people in Congress with whom they deal. A constant flow of communication and contact goes on between them. Also, most government agencies serve the same clientele as do their oversight committees of Congress (both the Agriculture Department and the agriculture committees, for example, respond to organized agriculture). This three-way relationship draws executive agencies and congressional committees together. Of course, the President is not without power to make his ill-will felt against the heads of agencies who deliberately and overtly flout his budget, but the President also has sense enough to realize that many of his "subordinates" have close contacts with powerful interest groups and with Congress, and that in truth they are not as totally subordinate to him as the organization chart might suggest. A president cannot fire a secretary of agriculture for light causes—not so long as that secretary enjoys the support of organized agriculture.

Therefore, although the Office of Management and Budget is supposed to make a budget and hand it to Congress through the President, many agencies can circumvent that process and discreetly push their own budgets before Congress. The Federal Bureau of Investigation under J. Edgar Hoover was a notable example of just such autonomy.

## The Budget Calendar

A budget is a plan for future spending, and this planning is started about two years before the beginning of the fiscal year in question (three years before the end of that fiscal year). First, the President gives his guidelines. He may say, "submit a balanced budget to Congress," or he may say, "a balanced budget isn't necessary, but don't let it go in the red over 20 billion." Whatever his instructions, they are usually quite broad, though occasionally he might take detailed interest in one or two particular agencies. With the President's instructions in mind, the Office of Management and Budget calls agencies to project estimates of their financial needs for the fiscal year being planned. This call sets in motion a dialog between and among the OMB and the various departments and agencies and other interested parties. This process goes on through spring, meanwhile OMB gets projections of estimated revenues prepared by the Treasury Department, and projections of the economic outlook prepared by the Council of Economic Advisers and other agencies. Budget requests submitted by agencies are reviewed in detail by OMB throughout the fall and early winter, and are presented to the President in the form of a completed budget document in time for him to transmit the budget to Congress in January.

## Congress

Congress receives the President's budget and, using it as a guide, proceeds to appropriate money. Most of the budget simply continues programs already established, although in some areas the budget may seek to curtail or abandon programs, or in other areas to expand or begin new programs. Congress may or may not adhere to the President's recommendations. However, because of the enormity of the budget, and the inability of Congress to duplicate the work of OMB, most agencies get substantially what the President recommends. Most presidents have considerable influence in Congress, even presidents of a party opposed to that controlling Congress. Furthermore, when making the budget the President and OMB generally take into consideration most of the same political forces which Congress takes into consideration when enacting an appropriations bill. Thus, in many instances, Congress will not need to alter the President's budget in order to satisfy major interest groups.

## Authorizations and Budget Authority

Congress operates in two stages, first, it "authorizes" programs, then it gives "budget authority" by passing an appropriations bill. If Congress wants to start a program of, say, dental care for veterans, it first authorizes an agency to carry out the program for a certain period of time, or perhaps indefinitely. This is done by means of a bill generated primarily in a subject matter committee. The bill must pass through all the hurdles of congressional consideration. Then, in still another bill which must also navigate dangerous legislative waters, Congress gives budget authority, normally for only one year even though the program itself may have been authorized for several years or indefinitely. However, in a few cases, Congress gives budget authority under which funds become available annually without further congressional action: interest on the national debt and contributions to trust funds are examples of this.

## House and Senate Roles

Traditionally Congress follows a certain set procedure for appropriating money. Appropriations bills are traditionally considered first in the House of Representatives and then in the Senate. The main job of establishing the amount of money to be received by each agency falls to the House. The role of the Senate in the appropriations process is often that of an appeals body; the Senate quite frequently reserves its energies for those segments of the bill most objected to by agencies or other interested parties. There are several reasons for this division of labor between the House and Senate. The smallness of the Senate and the largeness of the House has something to do with it. A great deal of manpower is required to study the financial needs of agencies and there are many more representatives than senators. Most of this work is done by the appropriations committees of the two houses; the Senate Appropriations Committee has a membership of 26, the House Appropriations Committee, 55.

Another reason for the primacy of the House of Representatives in appropriations has to do with the history of the two houses. Inasmuch as the Senate was not (until 1917) an elected body, the fathers' of the Constitution thought it right and just to give exclusive authority to the House of Representatives to initiate revenue (not appropriations, but revenue) measures. However, it became traditional for the House of Representatives to take initial responsibility in both types of bills.

## Committees

Within the House and Senate appropriations bills are handled by appropriations committees which are divided into numerous subcommittees which in turn are further divided into individual members, each of whom becomes expert in some narrow subject matter with which the appropriations bill is concerned. The subcommittees of the two appropriations committees (House and Senate) are identically named and have the same subject matter responsibilities. The subcommittees of both committees are:

Agriculture and Related Agencies
Defense
District of Columbia
Foreign Operations
HUD and Independent Agencies
Interior
Labor, Health, Education and Welfare
Legislative
Military Construction
Public Works
State, Justice, Commerce, Judiciary
Transportation
Treasury, U.S. Postal Service, General Government

Remember that there is a difference between an "authorization" to carry out a program, and "budget authority" to carry out a program. Appropriations bills concern only "budget authority." "Authorizations," on the other hand, are handled by numerous other subject matter committees of the Congress. For example, the armed services committees of the two houses will study bills to authorize establishment of, say, a new armed forces school, but only the appropriations committees will consider an appropriation to provide money to finance the new school.

Consideration of the President's budget is done in a highly piecemeal fashion. Requests of separate agencies are often handled by separate subcommittees of the appropriations committees; various segments of an agency's request may be handled by different individuals on a subcommittee. Thus, every agency within the federal bureaucracy must be concerned with a particular subject matter committee in each house and with particular subcommittees of appropriations committees of each house.

Subject matter committees (sometimes called "standing committees") are "committees of oversight" and consider it their responsibility to keep an eye on the agencies within their sphere. There is generally a very intimate relationship between oversight committees and the agencies they oversee. As mentioned earlier, both the agency and the committee respond to identical organized clientele groups, and both are themselves in a sense overseen by those groups. It is not always certain whether the subject matter committee oversees the agency or whether the agency oversees the subject matter committee. Just who is overseeing whom is one of the enduring uncertainties of American pluralistic democracy. Although appropriations committees (unlike subject matter committees) are sometimes not considered to be "oversight" committees, they are, in fact, very much addicted to oversight of administration by virtue of their hand in appropriations. Very frequently, the same aforementioned intimate relationship exists between subcommittees of the appropriations committees and the agencies under their purview.

Subcommittees of the House Appropriations Committee call upon agency heads to appear and defend their budget requests. Occasionally this is eyewash; many or most agency heads have already been in regular informal communication with the pertinent subcommittees. Sometimes agency heads will go so far as to give friendly members of the subcommittee a list of "perceptive" questions to ask. This makes the members look smart and diligent, and helps agency spokesmen make their points. Sometimes when the President's budget has slighted an agency, subcommittee members supporting the agency will ask "questions" calculated to give the agency spokesman an opportunity to escape his obligation to support the President's budget. An admiral who really wants six aircraft carriers instead of the two recommended in the executive budget can be asked, "How many new carriers did you recommend to the President for inclusion in the budget?" and "Why did you recommend six carriers?"

When the House Appropriations Committee finishes with the bill, it goes to the floor of the House, and thence to the Senate. Disagreements between House and Senate appropriations bills are resolved by a conference committee made up of members of both House and Senate committees. The compromise bill is then usually passed by both houses and sent to the President.

## Budget Committees

The Congressional Budget Act of 1974 made several significant changes in congressional appropriations procedure. It established a new legislative agency, the Congressional Budget Office, to serve both houses. It also established a committee on the budget in each house. The new law requires that a "current services budget"—one that projects estimated outlays for the fiscal year ahead based on current program levels—be submitted to Congress by November 10th each year. By the following April 1st, each committee of Congress is supposed to submit budget estimates to the Senate and House budget committees, and by the same date the Congressional Budget Office gives back to the budget committees a fiscal policy report. By May 15th Congress is supposed to adopt a concurrent resolution stating governmentwide budget targets for Congress; and by September 15th a second concurrent resolution containing budget ceilings for congressional budget action. Whether these new mechanisms and procedures are going to collide with the still existing old mechanisms and procedures will ultimately become clear.

While the purpose of this new machinery may be to curb the tendency of each committee of Congress to spend without regard to how others are spending, any attempt to curb spending will naturally upset those who are being curbed. Centralization of power over spending means centralizing the power structure within Congress. Members of Congress who fear loss of power under this new plan will certainly resist it. Power is the name of the political game; no one in government wants to lose it, especially members of Congress whose whole professional existence is a fight to get it.

## Incremental Budgeting

Practically all governmental budgeting is "incremental," another of our words stemming from Latin *(incrementum)* which means in English about what it meant in Latin: something added. Most public budgeting is incremental because the budget makers normally make budgets by simply looking at what an agency got last year and adding a little to it this year. That may not be a very creative approach to budgeting, but, on the other hand, it cannot be said to be wholly mindless either. It is true that "incremental" budgeting operates on the often feeble assumption that the agency's appropriation last year was justified. It might be wiser to make every agency justify its entire budget as well as its excuse for existence, not merely this year's increment. But "zero based budgeting" makes political waves by threatening bureaucratic empires as well as the clientele of those empires; rarely is anyone strong enough to seriously practice it. The closest thing to life without end on earth is the life of a government agency, and zero based budgeting is certainly an inviting idea to those who want to bring mortality back into government. But the budget process is a political process, and most politicians are comfortable with incremental budgeting because it leaves almost everybody a little happy, and almost no one fighting mad. From the politician's point of view, incremental budgeting is the heart of rationality.

However, the idea persists that an agency's budget should rest on something more discerning than last year's figures which were based on the previous year's figures, which were in turn based on the previous year's figures, and so on. There is an ever growing belief in rationality, not just the politician's rationality, but a rationality more profound and intellectual. In recent years successive waves of this new "higher" rationality have swept across the landscape.


## Performance Budgeting

One thing that needs to be done, if budgeting is to be made rational, is to make the budget document itself understandable. One of the worst things that can becloud, befog, and mystify a budget is the practice of listing everything to be bought in endless lists of items (two typewriters, ten reams of paper, and so on for countless pages) without arranging these costs by program. The so-called line item budget may clearly tell a city councilman how many typewriters the city should buy, but it does not tell what the typewriter is going to be used for. Legislators at all levels of government, and the general public, need to know what they are being asked to buy—not alone in terms of items—but also in terms of programs. Funds, of course, are always limited; there is not enough money to give everybody everything. So, a legislative body must choose among programs: does it want parks more than it wants police protection, does it want culture more than it wants welfare? Naturally, in a small village, line item budgeting is permissible because council members more or less know the purpose and program to be served by each item. But in larger jurisdictions long lists of items, even when arranged by agency, obfuscate the budget because agencies carry on many different programs, and because a number of programs are carried on jointly by several agencies.

In the late 1940s, the Hoover Commission drew attention to the confusing character of the federal budget which in 1949 contained well over a thousand pages of small print, little of which gave any clear idea what work was to be accomplished. The commission recommended arranging the content of the budget to show what functions, activities, and projects are to be performed by the proposed expenditures. This type of budget came to be known as a "performance budget" or "program budget." Soon thereafter the federal budget was redesigned along performance or program lines, but unfortunately the much ballyhood change did not clarify the budget as much as had been hoped.

What went wrong? Looking at the Defense Department budget of 1950, which was supposed to be a performance budget, we see that it subdivided proposed expenditures into eight categories—military personnel, operations and maintenance, procurement, military construction, research, development, testing, and evaluation. That was a nice set of categories, but a "category" is not necessarily a "program." These categories did not tell Congress what various kinds of defense strategies it was buying. Take the category military personnel. What are these personnel going to be doing concerning different forms of defense: how many of them are for strategic retaliatory forces, how many for research and development, and so forth?

## Planning Programming Budgeting System (PPBS)

In the 1960s a somewhat different system of budgeting was brought on stage to make budgeting more rational by further clarifying choices for decision makers. Budgeting, it should be kept in mind, is decision making; a dollar sign on a budget is a decision sign. To make rational decisions the budget maker must, as we have noted, be able to see and understand the choices open to him. How can decision making be rational if the decision maker doesn't know which alternative methods of reaching a goal exist, and what the costs and benefits of each is?

The planning, programming, budgeting system was introduced to help clarify those choices. The method was "cost benefit analysis," sometimes called "cost effectiveness analysis" or "cost utility analysis." Whatever called, its purpose is to compare costs and benefits of several choices in the light of goals: shall we buy apples or shall be buy oranges? What is the cost of apples; what is the cost of oranges? What are the benefits of apples; what are the benefits of oranges? Which (judging by "analysis") is the best choice?

But before the analysis is made, it is necessary to have a goal in mind; that is, one must "plan." How else can one measure whether apples or oranges are more beneficial unless one has an objective? Planning comes first, then programming. One plans an objective, say to get vitamin C. If only two sources were to exist in the world, apples and oranges, then there would be only two possible programs, the apple program and the orange program. A cost benefit analysis determines which program gives the most benefit for the dollar. One then considers how much of that benefit one can afford in light of other demands on the money supply. That's budgeting. That's reasonable budgeting say PPBS advocates. That's making choices on the basis of statistical analysis of costs and benefits after planning and programming.

*PPBS in the Department of Defense:* The Defense Department under

Robert F. McNamara was first to adopt PPBS in the federal government. We just noted how "program" budgeting was designed as an imporovement over line item budgeting, and how, in the case of defense, the alleged improvement was not really much improvement at all because the program budget categories were not a great deal more meaningful than the old line items. PPBS came, then, as a successor to program budgeting. PPBS, as we have seen, emphasizes budgeting by objectives. "Personnel" (one of the old performance budget categories) is not really an objective; strategic retaliation is, however. The McNamara budget was arranged under nine such objectives. The weapons systems budgeted under each of those nine headings were determined by "cost benefit analysis." Computers were fed all available data about all known methods of staging "strategic retaliation" (one of the nine purposes of expenditure in the DOD budget). As many variables as anyone could think of were handed the computer, firepower, speed, and so on. Statistical analysis of choices was used at every stage of budget making.

McNamara's ideas about budgeting, by the way, stemmed partly from his familiarity with a book written by Charles J. Hitch and Roland N. McKean, *The Economics of Defense in a Nuclear Age.*

*Johnson's Order:* President Lyndon B. Johnson was impressed with McNamara's approach to budgeting. One morning in 1965 Johnson called a meeting of his cabinet and ordered PPBS put into effect promptly throughout the federal government. He said it was time we started to control the budget instead of the budget controlling us. That was the beginning of one of the classic fiascos of federal administration. PPBS was never successfully implemented at the federal level of government, or at any other level of government because (as Johnson would have perceived if he had taken longer to think it over) budgeting in a pluralistic democracy is at heart a political process. Cost benefit analysis too often ignores the political benefits of a choice. It may be that oranges are a better buy than apples, but the apple lobby may have more clout than the orange lobby. An "analyst" can prove twenty ways that oranges are the best buy, and back it up with cost benefit analysis and computer readouts twenty feet high. But the apple lobby isn't impressed.

*Benefits:* Eventually the PPBS craze faded. There was more wrong with PPBS than its seeming disregard for the single most important reality of budgeting. It had another weakness almost as great. Keep in mind that PPBS depends on the ability of analysts to quantify costs and benefits of one option and to compare them with the costs and benefits of other options. But unfortunately, no one has yet found a way to measure the benefits of a great many government programs. What are the benefits of education? How do you quantify it? Although it may be possible for the Defense Department to quantify the benefits of a stated quantity of firepower directed at a stated target, it is not so easy to quantify the benefits of something like a mental health clinic, a day care center, a park, a rehabilitation of alcoholics program, or any other so-called "soft" program of government.

One can surely understand the dream of PPBS, and perhaps even sympathize with its goal: the goal of providing some basis other than politics for making budget choices. But even if depoliticizing the budget process were possible, the quantification of many choices remains impossible. Is a scenic highway better than a dull highway? How do you quantify that? Is heart research more beneficial than liver research? Is a public administration program in a university more beneficial than a teacher education program?

Furthermore, what do you call a "benefit?" Is pride a benefit? If the choice is between, say, a Cadillac and a lesser car, or, say, between a moon landing and some less spectacular space feat, is pride a "benefit" to be weighed? And if so, how is it weighed?

*Program:* There are other problems such as what constitutes a program? If a PPBS analyst is going to put his computer to work figuring out the cost of a new rocket for space exploration, for instance, what costs is he going to let the computer count? Is our analyst going to add some of the cost of previous space programs as an element of cost of the new rocket? To use another example, how do you figure the cost of operating a park? Do you include the cost of fire and police protection at the park? If so, then where do you put those police and fire costs in your budget— under the public safety program, or under the recreation program? Just what exactly is a "program" and how do you separate one program from another in order to apply cost benefit analysis to it?

*An Army of Analysts:* Even if politics could be erased from the earth, even if benefits could be identified and quantified, even if one program could be surgically separated from another for analysis, who would do all this analyzing? There are not enough analysts in the world to thoroughly research the costs and benefits—all the costs and all the benefits—of everything done by Reno, Nevada, let alone everything done by the United States Government. Furthermore, when can you say that a particular program has been "analyzed?" We are told by philosophers that everything is related to everything else; that every cause is itself caused. When you start analyzing the cost of something, you have to consider the costs of programs which make the program under study possible, as one might calculate the cost of previous space adventures as a partial cost of present space adventures. Also one must consider the cost of the results of the program being analyzed. Part of the cost of A is its negative effect on B, part of the cost of B is its effect on C, and so on. How many variables is a cost benefit analyst going to feed into the computer, how many can he even identify? PPBS is complicated by the inability to identify and weigh all variables. How does one assess everything affecting cost?

*Cost Benefit Analysis of PPBS:* President Johnson's order in 1965 directing that the entire federal budget be drafted henceforth according to the style and procedures of PPBS was not enthusiastically received everywhere in the federal bureaucracy, nor was it complied with everywhere. The President can order something done, but he can not stop bureaucrats from dragging their feet. Many officials instantly saw the folly of trying to rationalize the nonrational, trying to quantify the nonquantifiable. They forsaw a massive disruption of customary budgeting procedures which could not in their opinion be justified by the insignificant benefits to be gained over existing practices. Opponents of PPBS, in other words, did a quick "cost benefit analysis" of PPBS itself and found it not worth the cost when applied to budget decisions which are basically political, or which relate to programs whose benefits are difficult to identify and quantify—in other words, not worth the cost when applied to a major part of most budgets.

Nor did many agencies have enough trained analysts to even contemplate analyzing every benefit and every cost, nor did many administrators have time for it. Top officials are under constant pressure to respond quickly to periodic crises; this occupies most of their time. They tend to put long-range problems on the back burner, and PPBS by its nature must focus on operations sufficiently distant and remote to permit time to accomplish the analysis required by PPBS. Generally there is an insufficient data base on hand to analyze a current crisis to the full extent contemplated by PPBS.

One of the worst charges hurled against advocates of PPBS was that they really wanted to substitute their own rule for the rule of politicians. Some members of Congress saw in PPBS a conspiracy by the executive branch to remove more decision-making authority from legislators. Others, both inside and outside of Congress, thought they saw in PPBS a dangerous force for centralization—an attempt to bring the whole federal government and all its diverse programs and agencies under the czardom of one single oligarchy of planners in the Office of Management and Budget.

Furthermore, a perverse idea circulated around the bureaucracy that president Johnson didn't really understand PPBS, wouldn't have ordered it if he had, and that the Bureau of the Budget (predecessor to OMB) was trying to enforce PPBS partly to satisfy the President and partly to satisfy a "tribe of PPBS zealots" within the Bureau of the Budget. Many top officials apparently felt they were being put to all this disruption of their usual budget practices, not for their own benefit, but for the benefit of the Bureau of the Budget and its handful of PPBS fanatics. A great deal of PPBS activity, thus, was executed halfheartedly. A survey made in 1968 concluded that budgeting in the federal government was done just about the same as it was before President Johnson's order three year's previously. Changes in format and style of the budget document did not often reflect changes in substance. Few decisions were made differently because of PPBS.

*What is to be Said For PPBS:* PPBS was and is, let us not fail to note, embraced by many people who sincerely wanted to "rationalize" budgeting. However, one cannot resist the temptation to wonder whether some of this effort to rationalize and quantify the budget process may in some instances be a kind of dramaturgy employed by insecure top level managers to cast an occult spell over their farflung and unruly agency by pronouncing the abracadabra of PPBS, wrapping themselves in the aura of computer science, and demanding submission to "reason," that is, to themselves.

On the other hand, simply because a certain approach to budgeting is imperfect may not justify abandoning it entirely. No approach to budgeting is perfect from every point of view. PPBS may be most useful simply as an exercise. There may be value in forcing administrators to take time and effort to make long-range plans, to think about the future, to think out alternative programs for reaching that future, to run as many cost benefit studies as possible, and at least consider following the path of greatest benefit for the least cost where costs and benefits can be figured. All this is good for the same reason it is good for us as private individuals to take at least a little time to ponder our future and how best to get there. Planning, programming, and budgeting is important; cost benefit analysis is important, even if it doesn't work perfectly and even if we don't have time or ability to calculate all the costs and all the benefits. The process of trying to think things out rationally is the enduring value of PPBS.

## Management by Objectives (MBO)

PPBS was a new "system" of budgeting which annoyed and confused people accustomed to the old ways, and imposed endless, ceaseless, staggering paper work on agencies. Management by objectives is not exactly a new system, nor does it persecute managers with a paper hell, at least not the MBO of Richard Nixon's director of the Office of Management and Budget, Roy L. Ash, and Ash's deputy Frederic V. Malek. But they wanted to save one plank from the wreckage of PPBS. They wanted to save the idea that agencies should at least try to set their objectives down in black and white, and then budget toward those goals. Ash and Malek required each federal agency to submit a statement of its objectives annually. The object of this was to give the President (and the President's Office of Management and Budget) a chance to correct those objectives when they swerved off the road of presidential objectives. The purpose of MBO was to make it possible for the President to delegate responsibility to the departments and agencies without losing control. This, likewise, can be the purpose of MBO at all levels of management—to give each manager at each level of the hierarchy a mechanism for finding out what objectives their subordinates have in mind so that a slap on the wrist can be administered where necessary. A further purpose of MBO, naturally, is to give managers an excuse for taking time to think about their agency's objectives and about ways and means of reaching those objectives.

Some observers argue that MBO and its predecessor PPBS are most effectively used at the lower levels of bureaucracy where goals are more clearly defined and fewer in number. While the goals of a university may be vague, numerous, and mysterious, the goal of the payroll office within a university is fairly definite. Once goals and objectives are defined, then the full array of quantitative methods and computer science can be brought to bear to consider alternative methods of reaching those goals, and managers can actually manage by objectives.

The cult of management by objectives was brought from the private sector to government by Roy Ash and Fred Malek, both successful businessmen. Management by objectives is most at home where objectives can be most readily identified. Traditionally, the supreme objective of a private firm is to maximize profit. However, the objectives of many public agencies are not easily defined, and therefore it is harder to practice MBO in a government agency than in a private business. Government managers can, of course, demand pursuit of certain goals, or try to demand it. But the turnover rate of top officials in government is high, and it is difficult to manage by objectives when a new set of managers intrudes every couple years to change the objectives. Objectives shift as political leadership and political conditions shift. This is a classic problem of all government planning, especially of planning in a parliamentary democracy.

## The Federal Budget

Anyone who wants a copy of the federal budget can buy it from the United States Government Printing Office. Keep in mind we are talking about the "budget," not the "appropriations bill." *The Budget* is a 400-page paperback. Also there is a similar sized volume called *Special Analyses*, and a booklet called *The United States Budget in Brief*, and a bulky *Appendix*.

*The Budget* opens with the President's budget message followed by an explanation of the message and a description of economic assumptions underlying it. This is followed by a discussion of revenues. Then comes a rather lengthy description in prose (not deathless) of budget outlays describing the functions being served: (1) national defense; (2) international affairs; (3) general science, space, and technology; (4) natural resources, environment, and energy; (5) agriculture; (6) commerce and transportation; (7) community and regional development; (8) education, manpower, and social services; (9) health; (10) income security; (11) veterans benefits and services; (12) law enforcement and justice; (13) general government; (14) revenue sharing and general purpose fiscal assistance; (15) interest; and (16) undistributed offsetting receipts.

Looking at "law enforcement and justice," as an example, one can see that it consists of a brief description of proposed outlays for various sub-functions such as federal law enforcement and prosecution, civil rights, federal judicial activities, federal correctional and rehabilitative activities, and law enforcement assistance. A table shows recommended outlays for each. All sixteen functions are similarly handled. The last half of *The Budget* is simply a list of dollar amounts for each federal agency.

Now looking at the volume called *Special Analyses*, it contains about seventeen studies highlighting various program areas such as education, manpower, health, income security, civil rights, crime reduction, federal aid to state and local governments, research and development, environmental protection. The volume also discusses how government operations affect the economy.

*The United States Budget in Brief* does exactly as its title implies—in 60 pages of prose, charts, and figures it provides a concise, less technical overview of the budget.

At the other extreme, the huge *Appendix* contains masses of detailed information. To quote the *Appendix*, "it includes for each agency the proposed text of appropriation language, budget schedules for each account, explanations of the work to be performed and the funds needed, proposed general provisions applicable to the appropriations of entire agencies or groups of agencies, and schedules of permanent positions."

Thus we see that the various federal budget documents yield something of interest to adherents of nearly every budgeting philosophy. The budget documents present the budget from numerous perspectives, useful to those who seek different kinds of information, and provide Congress with programmatic overviews, and with agency by agency details.

## SPENDING

### Appropriations

Usually Congress appropriates money on an annual basis; that is, it authorizes agencies to spend ("obligate") a certain amount of money during the fiscal year in question. Once that fiscal year has ended, no further obligations may be made on an account even if there is money left over. That, to repeat, is the general practice. Most appropriations are what one calls "one-year appropriations." However, Congress may, if it likes, appropriate for periods longer than one year. Some appropriations are "multiple-year appropriations" and some are "no-year appropriations." A no-year appropriation makes the money available for obligation until the objectives of the appropriation have been met—appropriations for construction, research, and for most trust funds may be no-year appropriations. Normally, an appropriation is for a specific amount ("definite authority"), however, in some cases Congress cannot determine exactly how much to appropriate (interest on the national debt, for example) and therefore makes an "indefinite appropriation" contingent on specified circumstances.

## Apportionment

Some agency heads, either by design or want of character improvidently use up their annual appropriations before the year is ended. Some pursue a deliberate policy of going broke in mid-year to give an excuse for twisting the legislative arm for "supplemental appropriations." To control extravagance, the President, through his Director of the Office of Management and Budget, apportions appropriated funds to agencies by time periods, usually quarterly, or apportions by function. No funds may be obligated in excess of those apportioned. Another protection against a sudden and untimely exhaustion of appropriated funds is establishment of "reserves" to cushion the borders of budget authority.

## Impoundments

The United States Constitution gives Congress power to appropriate, but does not explicitly require agencies to spend the appropriated money. More than one president has declined to spend appropriated funds, and this practice became especially obnoxious to the Democratic Congress during the presidency of Republican Richard Nixon. Concerned about what he considered "reckless" spending by Congress, Nixon impounded billions of dollars, curtailing or nullifying several programs passed by Congress. Many members of Congress resented this nullification of congressional power, among them some who shared the President's low opinion of the curtailed programs.

Numerous law suits were brought by people and organizations having a reasonable expectation of receiving money by release of the impounded funds. These suits generated an array of fascinating constitutional arguments touching the basic powers of Congress and the President. It was pointed out on behalf of the President, that impoundment is nothing new. President Thomas Jefferson declined to spend $50,000 which Congress had appropriated to buy fifteen gunboats to patrol the Mississippi. Jefferson said the gunboats were not needed because of a peaceful turn of events on the river. However, Jefferson ultimately did spend it for gunboats. Franklin Roosevelt was the first president to refuse to spend money for the purpose appropriated; succeeding presidents continued the practice on a modest scale. Nixon's impoundments were the first on a massive scale. In 1972 he asked for two billion dollars for the food stamp program; when Congress gave him 200 million more than he asked for he simply told OMB to set the "allowable spending" level at two billion. By 1973, impoundments of this type had mounted to a total of nearly 18 billion dollars.

Lawyers for Nixon argued that an appropriation bill is not a command to spend but is permission to spend. The President, they argued, is charged by the Constitution to execute the laws; impoundment is simply an exercise of presidential discretion how best to execute the laws. Furthermore, said the President's lawyers, a president often looks to the intent of Congress in determining how best to execute the laws, and Congress often seems to intend contradictory things; while on the one hand Congress intends to establish "countless expensive programs," on the other hand Congress also wishes to see "price and wage stability." When Congress is in conflict with itself, and fails, for example, to say whether the battle against inflation has higher or lower priority than the battle against proverty, the President is justified in choosing between them. Furthermore, on behalf of the President it was argued that Congress itself had in its budget act of 1950 allowed the President to establish "reserves" whenever savings would be made possible "through changes in requirements, greater efficiency of operations, or other developments."

However, lawyers opposing presidential impoundment power argued that when Congress passes an appropriation bill, that bill is a law, and the clear intent of the law is that the exact sums appropriated should be spent; to execute the law means to spend the money. Lawyers opposing impoundment also argued that if the President had legal power to impound, he would acquire an item veto which the Constitution does not allow. A president may not veto items of appropriation bills, but must veto the entire appropriations bill if he wishes to veto any part of it. Furthermore, if presidents were allowed to use this backhanded form of item veto, it would deny Congress an opportunity to override that veto. The results of litigation over impoundment leaned against presidential power to impound funds.

In 1974 the Congressional Budget and Impoundment Control Act was passed requiring the President to ask Congress for a recision of budget authority if for any reason he elects not to spend appropriated funds. If Congress fails to pass a recision bill within 45 days of a continuous session, the budget authority remains available for obligation. If the President only wants to defer spending temporarily, he may do so if, after asking Congress, neither house passes a resolution disapproving the deferral. If the

President impounds funds in violation of the act, he may be sued by affected parties. Also the Comptroller General (chief auditor of the federal government) is authorized to bring civil actions to obtain compliance with the act.

## Purchasing

Every expenditure is a form of purchasing, and the whole object of budgeting is, in a sense, to decide what shall be purchased. Purchasing is the moment of attainment toward which the budgetary process aims; everything leads to it. Those who buy for governments can by their errors defeat the object of collecting, budgeting, and appropriating revenues. The most common error in government purchasing (an error most of us as private individuals also constantly inflict on ourselves) is paying more than we should. Individuals cannot often buy in quantity, but most governments usually can if they take the trouble. This demands some degree of centralization in purchasing. If every office and unit is allowed to do its own purchasing, then obviously fewer benefits of bulk purchasing can be reaped. Governments and individuals also commonly fail to search out vendors who will sell at the lowest price; both buy too often on impulse. If a government sets up a purchasing department, hires a purchasing agent, and starts going about its purchasing in a professional manner, one of the first things to be done by that department is to systematize the process of finding the best buy on a given commodity. Competition among vendors can be stimulated by inviting sealed bids, and buying from the lowest bidder. Of course, the bidding system doesn't work where only one vendor handles a certain commodity, or where the commodity specifications are such that only one vendor can supply those specifications. But even where there is only one vendor, a purchasing agent can supply the cool, hard-headed approach to buying so often lacking when the bug to buy bites. A purchasing agent can also save time, trouble, and expense by inspecting and testing purchased commodities immediately when they arrive to see whether the vendor has supplied the quantity and quality ordered.

Centralized and professional purchasing by governments can also forestall the spectacle of one agency dumping surplus at a fraction its purchase price, while at the same time another agency is buying the same commodity at full price. Preventing this requires centralized supply management with a centralized inventory system. It also requires vigilance to prevent overbuying.

Purchasing officers need to be carefully watched. A great deal depends on retaining the services of an honest, competent purchasing officer; some vendors are not above making them generous gifts.

## The General Services Administration

The General Services Administration is the centralized purchasing and property management agency of the federal government. However, since the federal government is so massive, many federal purchasing functions are subdelegated to departments, and a few agencies such as the defense department have the option of excluding themselves from GSA jurisdiction.

GSA operates through ten regional offices. Thus centralized purchasing and property management is not (for the most part) centralized nationally, but regionally. GSA performs a cluster of duties related to federal property. For example, it provides centralized management of federal property and records; it constructs and operates buildings, procures and distributes supplies, and provides centralized management for property disposal, transportation, communications, stockpiling of strategic materials, and operation of government-wide automatic data processing resources. The Federal Supply Service of GSA procures many of the things government agencies want to buy. These purchases run the gamut from small commonly used items such as pencils to highly sophisticated civilian aircraft. The Federal Supply Service writes specifications for the things it purchases and sees to the quality of goods supplied by vendors.

## AUDITING AND ACCOUNTING

Once money is appropriated, a system of reviews and audits keeps agencies from spending the appropriated money for purposes not intended by Congress. This is done partly by the Comptroller General who is the chief detective employed by Congress to audit, examine, and evaluate government programs to see to it that spending by agencies squares with the purposes set forth in the appropriations bill, and with various procedures for obligating and spending money. Also, the Office of Management and Budget has a lively interest in seeing to it that appropriated funds are used to pursue the goals intended by the President's budget. OMB requires reports from agencies concerning their expenditure of funds and their progress toward program objectives.

## The General Accounting Office

The General Accounting Office (GAO) is part of the bureaucracy outside "the bureaucracy"—one of several agencies not within the executive branch, but which works directly for Congress. (The Government Printing Office and the Library of Congress are two other such agencies.) GAOs job, and that of the Comptroller General who heads GAO, is to police almost every other agency and department of the federal government to determine whether they are spending appropriated funds in the manner and for the purposes intended by Congress. GAO helps Congress control the receipt, disbursement, and application of public funds. The Comptroller General determines the legality or propriety of payment of such funds. These decisions are legally binding on the executive branch of government (and on the GAO itself), but are not binding on either Congress or the courts.

The power to audit is obviously a great power. Expenditures of public funds are illegal if they do not conform to the intent of Congress. But what is the intent of Congress? Often Congress itself has only a vague idea of its own intent, and it is not uncommon for Congress to deliberately pass vague bills when legislators differ over the specifics of a bill, but agree on its general purpose.

GAO takes a generous view of its power. To GAO "auditing the use of public funds" includes examining into efficiency of operations and program management, and determining whether government programs are achieving the purposes intended by Congress and whether alternative approaches have been examined which might accomplish these objectives more effectively and economically. In short, GAO evaluates the management of agencies and judges their efficiency in achieving program results. GAO has become a vast team of "organization and management" specialists and takes upon itself to make recommendations for greater economy and efficiency in government operations, and reports significant matters to Congress for use in carrying out the congressional oversight function. About a quarter of its work is done at the behest of individual members of Congress.

Power of the General Accounting Office is augmented by the job security of its chief executive. The Comptroller General and his deputy are appointed by the President with advice and consent of the Senate for a term of fifteen years and are subject to removal only by joint resolution of both houses of Congress for specified causes, or by impeachment. It is very hard to get rid of a Comptroller General.

There are some exceptions to the general snooping powers of GAO. The Federal Reserve System is beyond its authority, and so are the Central Intelligence Agency and various other intelligence services.

To audit the vast operations of the federal government, GAO has to insist that all agencies keep their books in a style readily understandable to GAO and its auditors. GAO could hardly make head nor tail out of things if all the agencies used their own exotic system of bookkeeping. Thus, GAO has power to prescribe the method of accounting used by executive branch departments and agencies. GAO works with the agencies to help them design accounting systems which are acceptable to GAO and at the same time serve the peculiar needs of the agencies.

Clearly GAO and OMB have many areas of common concern. Both are interested in auditing the performance of executive agencies, both see themselves as "organization and management" people, both are interested in the proper and legal use of money, both are interested in sensible bookkeeping methods. The areas of potential cooperation between GAO and OMB are great. And to this duo is added a newcomer: the Congressional Budget Office.

## Auditing

Although the word "accounting" is featured in the name of the General Accounting Office, GAOs fundamental purpose is "auditing," not accounting. An accountant keeps a record of transactions, while an auditor looks to see whether the accountant's record is correct and legal, and whether the transactions themselves are legal. Naturally auditors are also experts at accounting, for otherwise they could not understand the accounts being audited. As we have seen, GAO considers its auditing function to require investigation into whether the policies, practices, and management of government agencies conform to the intent of the law.

A distinction is made between "preaudit" and "postaudit." A preaudit is made before a transaction occurs; a postaudit afterwards. Postaudits are generally conducted on behalf of the legislature by persons outside the executive branch to check on whether spending and other agency actions square with legislative intent. A preaudit, on the other hand, is generally a procedure used by high level managers to keep lower level managers on the straight and narrow. Managers are interested in what their subordinates are about to do. Since the executive branch and the legislative branch may differ in their purposes, it is not unusual for a preaudit conducted by managers to conflict with the preaudits or postaudits conducted by agents of the legislature. Congress is not satisfied to leave preauditing entirely to the executive branch, and has given GAO authority to preaudit as well as postaudit. Of course, this does not prevent the executive branch from conducting its own preaudits.

## Accounting

One of the persistent controversies between GAO and the executive branch is which of them should have power to design the accounting system used by agencies. Accounting is often thought to be primarily a managerial tool—a system of bookkeeping that shows information the agency needs for its own purposes. An agency may not want to keep its books in the manner preferred by the postauditor. GAO has its needs, agencies have their needs. Whose needs should prevail? Congress has given power to GAO to force its will on the agencies, but GAO ordinarily works with agencies to arrive at some degree of compromise.

Because of the gigantic volume of federal business, GAO cannot with its limited staff begin to keep constant surveillance of all transactions, although several years ago it attempted to do so. Today GAOs auditing is primarily through the process of overseeing each agency's mechanism for internal self-audit; agencies audit their own transactions under GAO supervision. Of course, where GAO suspects irregularities it is free to audit individual transactions, and may also direct its special attention where suggested by members of Congress or congressional committees.

Federal accounting is now done primarily on an "accrual" basis (the way you keep your checkbook). When you write a check, it may not be cashed for a month, but you assume the money is gone from your account the instant you write the check. "Cash accounting," on the other hand, focusses on actual cash outlays, and is good for telling how much cash you have in your account, but is misleading if you've committed yourself to paying money that has not actually been paid. Accrual accounting is necessary for the cost accounting upon which modern budget making increasingly relies; it tells how much was spent for various things during a given time period just as your checkbook tells you how much you paid for groceries in April (if you paid for them all by check), whether the checks were cashed in April or not. Of course, the cost accountant will also use accrual principles to calculate consumption of supplies, materials, and equipment already on hand.

## SUMMARY

Many combatants participate in the "budget process," a process that includes making a budget, appropriating money, spending money, and auditing. The political dimension of budgeting may exceed all other dimensions. Struggle for power over the flow of public money involves many private pressure groups and public agencies including the executive and legislative branches of government, and their respective satellites such as the Office of Management and Budget (OMB), the General Accounting Office (GAO), the appropriations committees, the subject matter committees, and the Congressional Budget Office.

Since the Second World War successive waves of budgeting philosophy have swept the land. Prior to these reforms, budgets were chiefly "line item" and largely "incremental." (They still are largely incremental.) But in 1947, to give decision makers a clearer idea what programs they are buying, it was proposed by the Commission on Organization of the Executive Branch of Government, and by others, that budget recommendations be shown by program. In the 1960s "planning, programming, budgeting system" (PPBS) was introduced with the intent of further "rationalizing" the budget process by: (1) planning goals; (2) identifying alternative programs for reaching those goals; (3) running cost-benefit analyses of each alternative; and (4) budgeting the program that gives the most benefit for the cost. However, PPBS encountered problems because of the difficulty of identifying and measuring the benefits of programs. But, whatever its shortcomings, PPBS did encourage bureaucrats to think about the future, and to think about costs and benefits.

During the Nixon administration, practice of PPBS declined, and OMB stressed "management by objectives," an attempt to tie budget making and spending to the President's objectives. Federal budget documents in recent years have presented the budget from various points of view reflecting various philosophies of budget making.

Once the budget is made and the appropriations bill passed, the budget process continues into the spending stage. Recently severe limitations have been placed on the President's power to defer spending and impound appropriated funds. Purchasing is a very important phase of the budget process, for it (purchasing) can defeat all preceding steps in the process if not done wisely. Centralized purchasing departments, such as the federal General Services Administration (GSA), can greatly facilitate intelligent purchasing. To see that spending conforms to the intent of Congress, Congress has set up a General Accounting Office (GAO) with power to audit spending.

## SUGGESTED READING

Brady, Rodney H. "MBO Goes to Work in the Public Sector." *Harvard Business Review*, March-April 1973, pp. 65–74.

Commission on Organization of the Executive Branch of the Government. *Budgeting and Accounting.* Washington, D.C.: U.S. Government Printing Office, 1947.

DeWoolfson, Bruce H., Jr. "Public Sector MBO and PPB: Cross Fertilization in Management Systems." *Public Administration Review*, July-August 1975, pp. 387–395.

Dorfman, Robert, ed. *Measuring Benefits of Government Investment.* Washington D.C.: Brookings Institution, 1965.

Hitch, Charles J., and McKean, Roland N. *The Economics of Defense in a Nuclear Age.* Cambridge, Mass.: Harvard University Press, 1960.

Holzer, Marc, ed. *Productivity in Public Organizations.* Port Washington, New York: Kennikat Press, 1976.

Lee, Robert D., Jr., and Johnson, Ronald W. *Public Budgeting System.* Baltimore: University Park Press, 1973.

Levinson, Harry. "Management by Whose Objectives?" *Harvard Business Review*, July-August 1970, pp. 125–134.

Livingstone, John Leslie, and Gunn, Sanford C., eds. *Accounting for Social Goals: Budgeting and the Analysis of Non-market Projects.* New York: Harper and Row, 1974.

Schick, Allen. "A Death in the Bureaucracy: The Demise of Federal PPB." *Public Administration Review*, March-April, 1973, pp. 146–156.

Speer, Albert. *Inside the Third Reich.* New York: Macmillan, 1970.

"Symposium: Management by Objectives in the Public Sector." *Public Administration Review*, January and February, 1976, pp. 1–45.

"Symposium on Planning-Programming-Budgeting Systems." *Public Administration Review*, December 1966, pp. 243–309.

"Symposium on PPBS Reexamined." *Public Administration Review*, March-April 1969, pp. 111–202.

Wildavsky, Aaron. "The Political Economy of Efficiency: Cost Benefit Analysis, Systems Analysis, and Program Budgeting." *Public Administration Review*, December 1966, pp. 292–309.

Wildavsky, Aaron. *The Politics of the Budgetary Process.* Boston: Little, Brown and Company, 1964.

Wildavsky, Aaron. *Budgeting: A Comparative Theory of Budgetary Processes.* Boston: Little, Brown, 1975.

\*

# Pink Spiders in Policy Making 13

# Pink Spiders in Policy Making 13

## POLICY DECISION MAKING

A policy is a big decision governing how a cluster of little decisions will be made. What is "big" and what is "little" is entirely in the eye of the beholder.

All decision making, no matter what it concerns, or who makes it, is done by the same basic stages. First, (1) there is a want; then (2) a demand to satisfy the want; then (3) a clash of alternative ideas for achieving satisfaction; then (4) a decision what to do; then (5) an implementation of the decision; then (6) an evaluation of the decision. One might use the analogy of the basic need for food to illustrate the process: first (1) hunger; then (2) a demand for food; then (3) a debate how best to get food; then (4) a decision how best to get food; then (5) action to get food; and finally (6) evaluation of the food.

All decision making is accomplished by the same fundamental process. Tortured attempts may be made to distinguish one kind of decision making from another—that of Congress from that of the President, for example. But at core, there is no distinction between decision making by individuals and decision making by groups; nor between small groups and large groups, nor between public agencies and private agencies. Of course, the number and type of forces at work in each step along the way of decision making are different from one situation to another. Forces which drive a family to rake the lawn are different from forces which drive a nation to war. But the same elemental stages of decision making are present in both.

### Policy Making by Administrators

In the lore of early twentieth-century scholarship in public administration, policy making was not the business of public administration. To the great

273

minds of that era legislatures made policy, administrators executed policy, and judges decided legal controversies. Those were the days when up was up and down was down and everything clear and simple. Separation of powers meant separation of powers. Today, those who say administrators do not make policy run the risk of being laughed out of the public administration society. Clearly administrators make policy, sometimes directly in the process of deciding how to implement programs; sometimes indirectly by influencing other policy makers such as legislative bodies; and they make policy by adjudicating controversies. In Chapter 1, The Managerial Revolution, we discussed why public administrators are making more policy today than ever before—we pointed to the weaknesses of modern legislative bodies, and the peculiar strengths of executive agencies. We discussed the ability of bureaucracies to navigate waters of technological complexity, and the floundering inability of legislators to handle some complex issues.

## Can Policy Making Be Rational?

*Can a "Want" Be Rational?:* All policy making begins with a want, sometimes with a collection of wants, often with competing and hostile wants emanating from different quarters. Can such basic wanting be called rationality? Yes, perhaps, if one believes all nature is rational, part of God's "plan." Otherwise, one hardly sees much cerebral activity in it. The cerebral activity comes afterwards and points the way to fulfillment.

*Rational Weighing of Nonrational Wants:* But how rational is the rational component of policy making? Can a decision be rational if it fails to calculate the nonrational? Most would agree that it is rational for a pedestrian to consider the feelings of a barking dog when he decides which side of the street to walk down. And would agree that it is rational for the same pedestrian to take into consideration the apparently mindless forces of nature—lightening, the possibility of rain—in determining whether to take a walk. But if it is rational to allow nonrational forces to influence decisions, then obviously, nonrationality can be a gigantic part of every supposedly rational decision. The weighing and considering is perhaps rational, but not necessarily the raw material.

*Infinity of Relevant Data:* Before any decision can be totally rational, would it not have to be based on all the facts? If so, this immediately condemns all decisions to some degree of nonrationality, for it is manifestly impossible to get *all* the facts bearing on anything. Even a decision whether to eat a peanut butter sandwich must rest on grossly incomplete information: one cannot know for sure exactly what one is eating, nor can one ever hope to calculate *all* the costs and benefits of all possible alternative courses of action—whether, for example, going hungry might be more beneficial than eating, or whether eating something else at some other time might be more beneficial. Nor can one know for sure what ramifications will result from eating it, or making it. Inability to calculate all the ramifications of a decision condemns every decision to partial nonrationality. A decision to eat a fried egg instead, might (who knows?) result in a marriage with someone who fries the egg, the effects of such a marriage to be felt for all-time.

Guesses about the costs and benefits of a proposed decision can be made, but total rationality requires total information. Knowledge required to make a totally rational decision upon even so small a matter as whether to open the window or shut the door would fill all the world's libraries and overwhelm all the world's computers. It would involve total analysis of every other possible course of action, time of action, manner of action, and place of action. And when one thinks of the legion of facts, the legion of variables, affecting large public policy decisions such as whether to grant a pardon to draft evaders, or whether to build a fleet of bombers, or whether to pursue detente with Russia, or whether to socialize medical care, the amount of information required for a totally rational decision is beyond human imagination, utterly impossible to acquire. Because everything in the universe affects everything else, a totally rational decision about anything (whether to cross the street, whether to go to war, whether to swat a fly, whether to extend medicare for the elderly) would require nothing less than absolute omniscience: but only God is all-knowing. Knowledge may be as infinite as space and time.

*Time:* No one has forever to make decisions. Life is short, time for decisions even shorter, sometimes only a split second. Pressure for action constantly harasses decision making. Indeed, it is demand itself that initiates all decision making, some demands furious and raging such as those caused by an international crisis, other demands may be cool-headed but still pressing. Administrators are constantly working under deadlines. Furthermore, much of their time may be taken up with a dozen other problems all insisting on attention like a dozen children beseiging their father to play different games. Even if a decision maker could acquire infinite knowledge bearing on each of his problems, he would not have time to do so. Thus, every decision is condemned to nonrationality by lack of time to acquire facts, as well as by lack of time to consider and ponder and analyze the facts.

Even when the administrator has time to dawdle over a decision, he may want to impress people with his no-nonsense ability to get things done. There are rewards for promptness. Of course, there can be disaster in it too—when, for example, a new up-and-coming city manager impetuously decides one night to fire his "incompetent" police chief without fully realizing how lethal the chief's political connections are. The manager, not the chief, may go.

*Money:* Even when there are lots of facts available, and lots of time to ponder them, it takes money to gather, systematize, and analyze data— money to buy the machines and hire the people to do the work. A nation that lacks money to maintain a world-wide intelligence network is simply going to make more nonrational decisions in international affairs. Business firms lacking money to do market research are simply going to end up making more nonrational decisions about what, when, where, and how to sell.

*Rejection of Rationality:* There is pressure on public officials, both elected and appointed, to be popular, to propose popular policies, to make popular decisions, and to find popular answers to problems. But it is not always popular to be right.

The personal fate of many public policy-making officials and the fate of their agency depend on success in cultivating the special interests upon whose support they depend. To an elected district attorney it may be more important to get a conviction than to convict the right person. To the department of labor it may be more important to keep unions happy than to make "rational" decisions. To the Veterans Administration it may be more important to keep the friendly support of the American Legion than to be totally balanced and sober. To the Department of Agriculture it may be more important to win the support of corn farmers than to be completely intelligent about price supports on corn. Many agencies of government are the captives of their client groups; regulatory agencies seem especially subservient. All elements of government are in some degree captive, and therefore in some degree hostile to rationality.

All in all one would have to say there is a persistent tone of hostility against rational decision making in the public bureaucracy. Even universities, where rationality is supposed to be in charge, have little interest in rationality when it comes to their own empire building budget—facts are suppressed, statistics distorted, figures exaggerated by university administrators with the same joyful abandon as by any other red blooded bureaucrat.

Rationality within the bureaucracy is further burdened by ruthless bureaucratic politics. In universities, for example, the rationality of decision making is impaired by the competing and sometimes hostile subdivisions of the university. When a university tries to make policy decisions it often fails miserably in its performance.

Bureaucracies tend to be much less coordinated than they appear to outsiders. Their policy decisions often mirror the uncoordinated interests of subagencies, each marching to its separate drummer. Some agencies are more disintegrated than others. The Department of Agriculture has fewer independent-minded subagencies than does the Department of the Interior. Agriculture listens basically to a single client—agribusiness. Interior listens to many clients, each with its claws on a piece of the department. Universities are similarly disintegrated, partly because some departments such as medicine, engineering, law, and education have their special power bases in the community, but also because in university tradition each department, whether it has a community power base or not, is itself a power center. Departments, such as political science or biology, have egos, departmental power drives. This is characteristic of all bureaucracies, public and private. The decisions of bureaucracies are nonrational to the extent that they must reject rationality to satisfy the power drives of their individual subdivisions. This is why it is a mistake to look at the federal bureaucracy and see it as a monolithic whole under the President's thumb. It is not under the President's thumb, it never has been under the thumb of any modern president: each piece has a will-to-power of its own. President after president has agonized over his inability to control the federal bureaucracy, and over his inability to make it produce rational decisions unaffected by the clash of special interests. The rationality of bureaucratic decisions is severely limited by the internal disintegration of bureaucracies.

*Communications Failures:* Insofar as organizational decision making depends on an uninterrupted flow of accurate information through organizational channels, any disease of the communications system becomes a disease of the decision-making process by infecting the flow of facts upon which rationality depends. Earlier in this book there was a discussion of impediments to organizational communications. Without repeating everything here, suffice it to say that these impediments and distortions are enormous and enormously damage rationality in decision making. For example, a manager who surrounds himself with cowering "yes" men will soon lose touch with reality and will unavoidably make blundering decisions based on distorted information. The most conspicuous example of this in recent history was Adolf Hitler.

*Personal Failures of Decision Makers:* To all the forces of nonrationality described above must be added certain personal characteristics of decision makers. Probably every passion by which they are driven is hostile to clarity of perception. The divorce rate testifies to the effect of passion upon rationality. Is not everything we do influenced by passion in some degree: getting up, eating, going to work, and so on through the day and through life? Passion leads us to color facts, passion assigns weight to facts, passion blinds us to some facts and opens our eyes wide to others. How we see things depends on how we feel about them: perception is selective.

Truth itself is sometimes said to consist of whatever one's passion declares to be the truth. When an inmate of the state hospital says pink spiders are crawling on his flesh, or that Napoleon has just entered the room, who can say these things are not true in the patient's eye? Philosophers debate whether any such thing as objective truth exists, any such thing as objective fact, any such thing as rationality. To a child who is committed to the idea that werewolves roam London at night, rationality seems to consist of seeing evidence confirming this truth and rejecting everything to the contrary. Under these circumstances, is it really rational to affirm the existence of rationality?

Surely the passions which (wholly or in part) rule our lives must be counted among the obstacles to a balanced view of facts in any given situation, and hostile to a balanced search for facts.

Some individuals in some situations are less passionate and, perhaps, more "rational" than others. But here there is danger. Acquisition and consideration of facts takes energy; not everyone is equally energetic. Some decision makers may be quite phlegmatic and "rational" but not sufficiently stimulated to dig out the facts or analyze them. And who is most energetic? Very often the zealots!

Various other habits of mind affect the rationality of decisions. For example, some decision makers are more "scientific" than others in their approach to problems; by upbringing and education some are more willing to defer judgment until the facts are in, and try to see all sides. Education in public administration (indeed, all education) should perhaps stress the scientific method, and should try to instill a scientific attitude as part of the professional equipment of graduates. Professors can help by setting an example of balanced consideration of facts, can exhibit more analysis and less preaching—more asking and less answering. And of course, the techniques of data collection and analysis should be taught.

## Computers

Probably nothing has contributed more to rationality in policy making than electronic data processing equipment. But having said that one must hasten to add that a computer cannot be more rational than its human master: "garbage in, garbage out" is the slogan. The great service to rationality offered by computers is not the rationality of the computer, but the ability of these machines to store incredible supplies of data, and add and subtract and carry on every conceivable mathematical and statistical process at lightening speed, and to rapidly process, and reproduce at the touch of a key, vast quantities of information. In short, what computers have done for rationality is to greatly extend the ability of decision makers to put their hands on facts bearing on a problem. With computers, a decision maker can instantaneously summon information which might otherwise take days, months, years, centuries to acquire. Rationality is thus fostered by extending the data base upon which decisions are made, and by avoiding certain kinds of human error in processing.

Computers can not be of much help in goal setting, for goals have much to do with nonquantifiable wants. But they can be very helpful in mobilizing information bearing on alternative methods of accomplishing goals, where goals are clear and well defined.

## Incrementalism, Heurism, and Mixed Scanning

Rationality, if it exists at all, is a tiny flame in the interstellar space of darkness. Why even talk about "rationality?" Its meaning is very imprecise. Why not simply look at what we actually do when we make decisions?

To what extent do we look at the facts when decisions are made? This may depend on how important the decision is, upon whether we are making new policy or simply modifying old policy. Most of the time we are simply trying to improve existing policies. We make small adjustments here and there periodically. As Charles Lindblom put it, we "muddle through," we tinker with what we have. Our tinkerings are heuretic, that is, they are inventions of the moment to serve the needs of the moment. Of course, some decisions are more "fundamental" and less "incremental" than others: we are more likely to scan the facts pertinent to fundamental decisions which establish major new departures than the facts pertaining to incremental decisions which adjust existing policies. In other words, we practice "mixed scanning" (Amitai Etzioni's term).

Yehezkel Dror accuses incrementalists of fostering a state of mind that reinforces the inertia already present in most organizations. An incrementalist state of mind, says Dror, lets us fall into the habit of "muddling through." We should, he suggests, be constantly in an analytical frame of mind.

## RETURN TO POLITICAL SCIENCE

Public administration as a modern academic study grew up in the house of political science. At teenage she became a juvenile delinquent and ran away from home. Her parents notified the police, but the truant is still at large, behaving as though she never had a home, claiming, like Tania, to be absolutely unique and sovereign and independent and immaculate. Lustily public administration is discovering the world as if no one ever discovered anything before. Forgetting its past, public administration stumbled across political science and with a scream of delight proclaimed it a ninth wonder and labeled it "policy studies." Journals with boards of editors, and associations with secretary-treasurers have emerged to adore the "new" field, and universities prepare to set up schools, hire deans, and launch degree programs in the subject.

It was love at first sight—this meeting of public administration and policy studies. The one has sexy legs and a provocative voice, the other wavy hair and a sensitive mouth. Something strange and wild drew them together. Sitting on a park bench, public administration gazed into the blue eyes of policy studies and said, "Nobody understands me." Policy studies drew closer and said, "Nobody understands me either." These two confused, lost, and bewildered souls have found fulfillment in each other. Public administration has promised to change her name to "policy studies" after the wedding.

## WHO MAKES PUBLIC POLICY?

Asking who makes public policy is like asking who built your car. The answer could be longer than anyone would want to read or hear. To say public policy is made by "policy-making officials" would be too simple and superficial. Public policy is, of course, made by "officials"—but it is also made (and primarily made) by those who generate policy demands and bring those demands to bear on officials. Officials respond (some more than others) to influential forces from wherever they may exist—outside or inside the government. Policy-making officials, whether they be legislators, executives or judges, respond to client groups, to elected officials, to legislators, to mass communicators, to political parties, to professional specialists, to religious leaders, to lobbyists, to community leaders, to bureaucrats, to everybody who has influence, and to the people who stand behind them, and to the people who in turn stand behind them, and so on ad infinitum.

As has often been claimed, we live in a pluralist society, a society of divided and fragmented power. Government has no monopoly on power. It and its officers are but one source of influence among many. But, in addition to being an influence on policy making, government is simultaneously the mechanism by which public policies are "enacted" (made "legitimate" and enforceable by executives and judges). The machinery of government is, first, a terrain of battle, and second, a tool for application, implementation, and enforcement.

To explain who makes public policy is to give a course in political science: it involves an explanation of the machinery of government (including the entire legislative, executive, and judicial apparatus) and an explanation how the forces of a pluralistic society apply their strength through that machinery to produce policy and to apply it. Public administrators rightly consider themselves very influential in this process—very influential in public policy making. Some of the reasons for this influence were mentioned in an earlier chapter on the managerial revolution.

Every course in political science is a course in public policy making. Within the "discipline" of public administration there is now much recognition that public policy making is perhaps the most important function of high level administrators. But the PA discipline does not want to call "policy making" "political science." This is partly the hesitancy of a runaway to come back home, and partly the belief that home was too narrow, too provincial, too confining, not sufficiently interdisciplinary. For to public administrators the bright new future requires that they be experts not just in old hat political science, but in numerous departments of knowledge, especially those areas that help them make "effective" public policy and help them anlyze the degree of a policy's effectiveness. Thus, "policy studies" is a new bottle into which one hopes new wine will be poured.

## SUMMARY

How much room is there for rationality in decision making when one considers that every decision arises from a nonrational want of some sort? How can one arrive at a decision about how to satisfy that want when most of the logical process involves consideration of the impact of other nonrational forces upon one's ability to satisfy one's own nonrational want,—on top of that it is simply impossible to acquire all the data impacting on a question, since knowledge like space and time seems infinite? Furthermore, there is insufficient time to gather infinite knowledge, or to analyze it, and very often decisions must be made so speedily that no one begins to have time to consider or analyze even the salient facts. Anyway, who wants to be rational? Most public policy making is done by people with axes to grind, oxes to gore, clients to be served, and power to be won. And even if a policy maker should want to be rational, there may be communications failures that inhibit the accurate flow of facts upon which decisions rest, and there may be personal failures in decision makers themselves which cripple their ability to rationally gather and weigh facts. Finally, no one seems very fluent in defining what a "fact" is or what "rationality" means.

Most policy making consists of modifying existing policies. This incrementalism is not usually accompanied by an analytical spirit or by a very exhaustive survey of facts. More analysis, however, normally occurs when fundamental new policies are under consideration.

## SUGGESTED READING

Dror, Yehezkel. *Public Policymaking Reexamined.* San Francisco: Chandler, 1968.

Dye, Thomas R. *Understanding Public Policy.* Englewood Cliffs, N.J.: Prentice-Hall, 1975.

Friedman, Robert S.; Klein, Bernard W.; and Romani, John H. "Administrative Agencies and the Publics They Serve," *Public Administration Review,* September 1966, pp. 192–204.

Jones, Charles O. *An Introduction to the Study of Public Policy.* Belmont, Calif.: Wadsworth, 1977.

Lowi, Theodore. "Decision Making vs. Policy Making: Toward and Antidote for Technocracy." *Public Administration Review,* May-June 1970, pp. 314–325.

Lindblom, Charles E. *The Policy Making Process.* Englewood Cliffs, N.J.: Prentice-Hall, 1968.

McCamy, James L. "Analysis of the Process of Decision-Making." *Public Administration Review,* Winter 1947, pp. 41–48.

Morehouse, Thomas A. "Program Evaluation: Social Research Versus Public Policy." *Public Administration Review,* November-December 1972, pp. 868–874.

Simon, Herbert A. *Administration Behavior.* New York: Macmillan, 1957.

# Controlling the Beast 14

# Controlling the Beast 14

## ABUSES OF POWER

Opportunities for abuse of power by public officials are numerous and come in many sizes and shades ranging from lawful to unlawful. First, there is a collection of abuses which do not necessarily involve wrongful intent: gross inefficiency, neglect of duty, failure to show initiative, and unfair treatment of employees to suggest only a few. Second, there is a collection of abuses sometimes within the law, but tinged with conscious intent to do wrong: unethical behavior, disregard for legislative intent, conflicts of interest, and so forth. Thirdly, there is a collection of flatly illegal abuses including some which are criminal such as theft and graft, and others which are civil wrongs such as acting beyond one's authority and violating due process of law.

## CHECKS ON EXECUTIVE POWER

The fundamental check on all government power in the United States, including that of the bureaucracy, is the division and separation of power. Having won a battlefield war against a "tyrannical" British King, the authors of the United States Constitution did not want to reestablish a new tyrannical central government. Yet they wanted a government strong enough to do the things that needed to be done, and so they tried to fashion a strong but limited government by fragmenting power and setting power against power. Power was made to check itself; was divided between the states and the federal government by a constitution that neither could amend without the consent of the other; and was divided within the central government among the legislative, executive, and judicial branches. Thus, the primary checks on executive power within the central government are the judicial and legislative branches. The picture is much the same within state governments and within numerous local governments.

However, we, and the world, are in the midst of a managerial revolution the dimensions of which were discussed in an earlier chapter. Executive power in the realms of legislation and adjudication has grown. Once separated powers are becoming less separated; ever more they are becoming unified into the hands of executives. Separation of powers is declining as a defense against tyrannical power, though it is not by any means completely dead in the United States. Legislatures and courts still do stand as checks against abuse of power.

## Legislative Checks

*Enabling Legislation:* The Constitution of the United States says nothing whatsoever about the structure of the executive branch of government, except that there shall be a president and that he shall be vested with "the executive power." The Constitution assumes there will be an army and navy for it makes the President commander-in-chief, and assumes there will be departments for it gives the President power with consent of the Senate to appoint department heads, and assumes there will be ambassadors for it also gives the President power to appoint them in the same manner. Beyond this there is no hint in the Constitution what the executive branch is supposed to look like. In his oath of office the President promises nothing more than to execute the office and defend the Constitution. Most President's orders beyond that come from Congress, and the entire structure of the executive branch which now employs some three million civil servants is established and shaped directly or indirectly by Congress. What Congress orders, it can also rescind, what Congress creates it can also amend or abolish—any program, any agency—and this, needless to say, is a powerful legislative check on the executive. However, there is a gap between theory and practice here, for Congress in recent generations has slipped more and more under the influence of the executive which it is supposed to check. The executive branch more and more tells itself, through Congress, what to do. And Congress has abandoned vast areas of lawmaking directly to the executive branch, as the shelf-sagging volumes of the *Code of Federal Regulations* testify. Decline of legislative power weakens all legislative checks on the executive.

*Power of the Purse:* The Treasury Department is not mentioned in the Constitution of the United States, nor does the Constitution give the President or anyone in the executive branch power to spend money. Only Congress has power to "pay the debts and provide for the common defense and general welfare of the United States," which it does through appropriation bills authorizing the President to spend. Thus, no one in the executive branch can spend any money for any purpose whatsoever without the prior consent of Congress. This power of the purse is jealously guarded by Congress. Obviously, it is a source of great leverage over every nook and cranny of the executive branch. Congress prefers to keep agencies on a very short fiscal leash by making annual appropriations.

However, congressional power of the purse is not as great in practice as it is in theory. Cynics might even say the President "appropriates" money, not Congress, owing in part to his influence over members of Congress, in part to his control of budget making, in part to his ability to thwart the "will" of Congress, and in part to his ability to play "shell games" with money already appropriated. Some of the shells in the shell game are these: (1) his "tranfer" authority gives the President power to shift millions from one program to another; (2) his power to dispose of "obsolete" excess stocks gives him power to equip operations not funded by Congress; (3) his control of billions of dollars of "secret funds" hidden in the appropriations bills for various confidential operations that even Congress doesn't know about; (4) his control of billions of dollars of unspent money in the pipeline appropriated under full-funding clauses—money which need not be returned to the treasury at the end of the fiscal year; and (5) the commitments made by Congress to pay cost overruns when necessary for "national defense."

*Oversight:*  Executive agencies are the creatures of Congress, and the indispensable mechanisms by which its laws are administered. Thus, Congress oversees and investigates these agencies. However, the boundary line between "oversight" on the one hand, and actual participation in administration on the other is somewhat vague. Congressional oversight is marred by its meddling into administration, and by its temptation to practice a kind of codirectorship of the agencies they oversee. The effectiveness of oversight is also marred by the political vendettas which sometimes masquerade as "oversight," and by the seeming preference of Congress for capricious sifting through detail rather than focussing on significant major policy issues.

Congress is not equipped to do more than a hit-or-miss job of oversight. To do a good job Congress would need some way to regularly and systematically—not sporadically and haphazardly—review every agency; it would need some way to detect when agencies waver from the intent of Congress, and to detect when their performance declines; and above all, Congress would need some way to determine whether it is being told the truth by executive agencies. The General Accounting Office is some help to Congress, but fundamentally there is only one agency in the federal government equipped and motivated to practice systematic oversight and that is the Office of Management and Budget—in the Executive Office of the President.

*Congressional Casework:*  An important part of every legislator's work is errand running for constituents hung up with, or seeking the favor of, one or another executive agency. Through this contact Congress throws its weight around the bureaucracy, and acquires intelligence about miscellaneous trouble spots that need attention.

*Confirmation of Appointments:* The United States Constitution gives power to the Senate to participate in the appointment of judges and executive officers. Congress has vested the appointment of most inferior officers in the President or in the heads of departments, but retains the power confirm presidential nominees of all judges, ambassadors, and various other superior officers. Although Congress customarily concurs with most presidential nominees, the power of confirmation represents a great potential lever over the executive branch, and gives the Senate some influence over the manner in which laws are enforced. Every official of the political high command owes his post at least partially to the good grace of the Senate, although very few presidential nominees fail to win confirmation.

*Government Accounting Office (GAO):* The Government Accounting Office controls the bureaucracy primarily by auditing its expenditures of money. GAO determines whether an expenditure is legal, whether it squares with the intent of the law authorizing it. Since the intent of Congress is not always clear, the GAO has considerable latitude of judgment.

*Impeachment:* Although the Constitution of the United States provides that the President, Vice-President, and all civil officers of the United States may be removed from office by impeachment for treason, bribery, or other high crimes or misdemeanors, this power is rarely used or even threatened. Nine of the twelve impeachments that have reached the Senate for trial have concerned judges, not executive officers. But, of course, the threat of impeachment remains an important shotgun behind the door. Most impeachments, certainly those of President Andrew Johnson and Supreme Court Justice Samual Chase, were disgraceful political episodes having little to do with treason, bribery, or any high crime or misdemeanor. Congress cannot be overruled, no matter how great its miscarriage of justice, and is free to interpret the constitutional grounds for impeachment any way it wants without fear of contradiction.

## Separation of Powers

In a government "of laws and not of men" it is, of course, important to keep bureaucrats within and under the law.

Not every action beyond the law is a crime: many illegalities are not criminal. Failure to pay a just debt is illegal, but not a crime; we have no debtor's prisons. Hiring, promoting, disciplining, or firing civil servants without adherence to civil service laws is illegal, but usually not criminal. It is illegal for building inspectors to enforce rules not in the building code, but seldom a crime. Few acts can be criminal without *intent* to do wrong. Even killing is no crime where there is no intent to kill, although extreme want of care (extreme negligence) can be criminal. Bureaucrats and private citizens alike commit all sorts of illegalities unintentionally. A private citizen's unintentional failure to pay taxes is no crime, but that failure is nevertheless illegal, and the government may sue. Likewise, a tax collector may unintentionally demand more taxes than the law allows, but he has not committed a crime, though he has acted illegally.

Laws which make certain acts illegal, but not criminal, are called civil laws. Criminal laws, on the other hand, make certain acts both illegal and punishable. Any wrong for which the law provides punishment is a criminal wrong; most wrongs for which no punishment is provided are civil wrongs. Thus we have civil laws, civil wrongs, and civil cases; and we have criminal laws, criminal wrongs, and criminal cases. Most of the wrongs committed by bureaucrats which come to courts are civil, not criminal.

## Ultra Vires

Very frequently the illegalities of bureaucrats are cases of ultra vires, which in Latin means acting in excess of one's authority. A tax collector who attempts to collect taxes beyond those enacted by the legislature is acting ultra vires—beyond his authority. A dogcatcher whose authority extends only to catching dogs is acting ultra vires when he catches cats.

There might be less official wandering beyond authority if the boundary lines of authority were as clear and simple as the boundary lines on a tennis court. But most grants of authority are of necessity communicated by the printed word, and there are few words in any language so precise as the lines on a tennis court. All statutes are tinged with vagueness, and the basic law of the land is one of the vaguest of all writings. To this are added the inevitable obscurities which afflict all expression of complex ideas. And to those are added deliberate obscurities written into some legislation by lawmakers intent on leaving the details of legislation to be worked out by administrators through quasi legislation or quasi adjudication, or by the adjudicatory processes of courts. And to those are added further obscurities often characterizing legislation written by lawmakers who cannot agree except upon the lowest common denominator of ambiguity. Legislation may go forth from Congress no clearer than the bark of a dog, conveying one or another hazy concept inviting litigation or subordinate legislation by administrators. Owing to its vagueness, the United States Constitution itself is a treacherous siren call steering bureaucrats into traps of ultra vires behavior.

The Supreme Court wavers in its tolerance for statutory vagueness. It has little patience where first amendment freedoms are concerned; any law affecting freedom of speech, press, religion, or assembly must be crystal clear, must leave almost no room for discretion by administrators or for confusion. The court views these freedoms as essential to any system of ordered liberty, and looks sharply at all legislation affecting those rights and will not tolerate any confusion in the meaning of such laws. A somewhat similar view is taken by the court with regard to criminal laws. If something is going to be made criminal, courts demand a clear law that leaves little doubt what acts are punishable. Judges do not like to send people to jail for committing a wrong which they could not have known was wrong by reading the statute.

With those important exceptions, courts seem resigned to statutory ambiguity. Several generations ago courts were stiffnecked about vagueness in delegations of quasi-legislative and quasi-judicial power to administrators. Some courts held (and still do on occasion) that legislative bodies may not under the doctrine of separation of powers and under the doctrine that delegated power may not be subdelegated, give any part of their legislative authority to administrative agencies. Congress gets its legislative authority from the people and cannot subdelegate it without the people's consent (in other words, without a constitutional amendment), for the constitution says, "All legislative powers herein granted shall be vested in a Congress. . . ." Thus, it would be illegal and unconstitutional for Congress to allow executive agencies to legislate.

However, Congress has been letting, indeed commanding, executive agencies to legislate for almost 200 years now. Such rulemaking has increased rapidly since the 1930s, and today is greater than legislation Congress itself produces, not only in volume but possibly also in importance.

Still, in constitutional theory, none of this is really legislation, and for years the United States Supreme Court and all other courts of the land have had to feign blindness to this monumental growth of legislation in the executive branch. Courts still doggedly maintain the fiction that rule making by bureaucrats is not true lawmaking, but only "quasi legislation." The same, by the way, is said about the court-like activities of executive agencies which, for the sake of appearance, are called "quasi adjudication." But, as William Shakespeare says, "A rose, by any other name would smell as sweet." It might be well here to note that while administrative rule making is recognized only as "quasi" legislation, the rule itself is recognized by courts as "law." Likewise, administrative adjudication may only be "quasi" adjudication, but its decisions are often recognized as comparable to decisions of courts of original jurisdiction, appealable straight to appellate courts.

At various times courts have held that the power of agencies to make rules must be circumscribed or "channeled" by clear "standards" delimiting the use of that power. If a legislative body does not clearly define, limit, and channel its delegation of rule making power, then it is guilty of delegating actual legislative power itself, not just quasi-legislative power. Therefore, when a party comes to court claiming the rules of an agency are unconstitutional because they are based on a statute which is vague and sets no clear standard for the agency to follow in making rules, the court must look at the standard and its clarity to determine the constitutionality of the rules made under it.

The high water mark of judicial insistance on "standards" came in 1935 when the United States Supreme Court in *Schechter Poultry Corporation* v. *United States* struck down sections of the National Industrial Recovery Act of 1933 which gave the President power to make rules (codes) by executive order for governance of various industries. Nothing in the law gave the President much guidance as to what those codes should include, but simply said he could promulgate any code acceptable to industry-wide trade associations. After the Schechter Case the court gradually changed its membership and its general attitude about delegations of legislative power. Today the United States Supreme Court seems able to live with almost any congressional grant of undefined rule making authority such as that granted to the Federal Communications Commission to regulate the air waves in the "public convenience, interest or necessity." In 1963 the Supreme Court upheld a congressional delegation of authority which permitted the Secretary of the Interior to apportion Colorado River water in time of shortage without any standards at all.

Obviously, when the borderlines of executive authority are shrouded in fog it is not difficult or unusual for administrators to stray quite innocently over the line. But opportunities for deliberate ultra vires action are inviting to those so inclined.

## Fairness

Perhaps the most important "law" in the field of administrative law is to be found in the due process clauses of the Fifth and Fourteenth Amendments to the United States Constitution. The Fifth Amendment is directed at the federal government, the Fourteenth Amendment is directed at the states and all their instrumentalities including local governments. The two amendments forbid governments to take "life, liberty, or property without due process of law." The term "due process of law" has been repeatedly defined by courts, and these definitions can be boiled down to the word "fair." Due process means "fair." Thus, governments are forbidden to take life, liberty, or property unfairly. But governments are not forbidden to take life under this amendment, nor are government forbidden to take liberty, or forbidden to take property. Indeed, governments do little else but take liberty or property; most laws do to some degree take liberty, and many take property—tax laws for example. The Constitution only commands governments to be fair in taking life, liberty, or property—it does not forbid the taking.

The due process clauses greatly affect every public administrator because they put upon administrators a constitutional command that they be fair in every official act. Not only must the substance of the law they execute be fair, but also the manner in which they execute it. The process by which they make rules, the process by which they execute rules and statutes, and the process by which they adjudicate controversies between themselves and other parties—all must be fair. Deviations from due process are beyond the law.

But here too the boundary line between fairness and unfairness is murky, the line between constitutionality and unconstitutionality is dim. Courts have tried to spell out what constitutes fairness in rule making, in law enforcement, and in adjudication, and there are some rules of thumb administrators can follow to be more or less on the safe side. But still, no matter how often courts have tried to define fairness, it is easy for administrators to slip over the line. Our system of common law adds to the uncertainty, because we can only know what *was* legal, not what *is* legal.

## Fairness in Rule Making

Courts have not developed many standards of fairness for rule making, any more than for lawmaking by legislatures. Courts hesitate to go beyond enforcing a legislative body's own rules of procedure. Partly this hesitancy is for political reasons, partly it stems from the tendency of courts to be more concerned with the interests of individual parties than the interests of the general public, and partly it stems from the impracticality of applying the same standards of due process to a legislative proceeding that are applied to adjudicatory proceedings. Legislation does affect rights of countless people in the general public, but legislation could never be accomplished if every party affected by it were given a right to, say, an oral hearing in the legislature before the law was enacted. For this reason administrators are not as bedevilled with concerns about procedural correctness when they are engaged in quasi legislation as when they are engaged in quasi adjudication. The main problem is to know which is which—adjudication and legislation can look suspiciously similar at times.

There are, of course, some procedural limitations upon quasi legislation. Congress and many state legislatures have enacted "administrative procedure acts" which, although they concern mainly quasi adjudication and judicial review, also generally touch briefly on rule-making procedure as well. Statutory requirements for fairness in rule making often require some sort of public notice before rule making, often also require that an opportunity be given interested parties to submit their views in writing about proposed rules, and often require that rules be published and that their effectiveness be deferred until published. In some particular subject matter areas, statutes may require administrators to hold public hearings, and/or to solicit the advice of interested parties before promulgation of new rules.

## Fairness in Enforcement

When we say an administrative agency represents a union of powers (rather than a separation of powers) we mean that it possesses (1) legislative; (2) executive; and (3) adjudicatory functions. Looking at the executive function through a magnifying glass it becomes almost indistinguishable from the other two powers, legislative and judicial. Civil-law controls over executive power consist largely of controls over adjudicatory power. Whenever any administrator deprives a party of his, her, or its rights, it usually may be done only after a right to full and fair adjudicatory hearing has been afforded. The occasional annoyances perpetrated by some bureaucrats by their offensive demeanor, by their slowness, their inefficiency, and so on, are not ordinarily subject to a judicial check. These lend themselves more to legislative or internal administrative checks.

Police are in a somewhat unique category among administrators because their behavior is to some degree governed by the constitutional guarantees of a fair trial set forth in the Bill of Rights of the United States Constitution. Although most of these procedural guarantees concern only trials, courts have held that the fairness of a trial may depend partly upon the fairness of certain procedures before trial such as, for example, the fairness of police in obtaining confessions. Therefore, police are governed by the procedural guarantees of the Bill of Rights insofar as their activity is considered to be an extension of a criminal trial. (The Fourth Amendment, however, guarantees the right of the people to be secure in their persons, houses, papers, and effects against unreasonable searches and seizures whether or not the search and siezure is for use in a criminal trial.)

## Fairness in Administrative Adjudication

Administrators are ordinarily required by due process of law to go through, or offer to go through certain procedures before they take any official act that negatively affects the legal rights or duties of individuals. Since both quasi legislation and quasi adjudication affect people's rights and duties, and since procedural rights are more numerous in adjudication, the question must always be asked whether the action constitutes legislation or adjudication. Briefly, there are two measures commonly used to distinguish one from the other, neither of which is adequate. The "past-future" theory holds that an act constitutes legislation if it concerns future behavior, and constitutes adjudication if it concerns past behavior. The "general-specific" theory holds that legislation addresses itself to a general category or class of parties without naming any particular party; but in adjudication, by contrast, the parties are named, or if not named are so few as to be readily identifiable.

Any named or readily identifiable party has a right to a fair adjudicatory procedure before any official action is taken affecting his legal rights or duties. But not every right is a *legal* right, nor every duty a legal duty. A child may feel he has a right to an ice cream cone every time he goes to the shopping center, but that is not necessarily a legal right. Legal rights are those we have by virtue of statutory or common law. And the law distinguishes between "rights" and "privileges." A medical doctor may have no legal right to be given a license to practice medicine, but after the license is granted he then has a right to that license and a right to a fair adjudicatory procedure before it is taken away.

Once it is determined that a named or identifiable party is involved, that a legal right or duty is involved, and that adjudication rather than legislation is involved, then all that remains is to apply fair adjudicatory procedure. And what is that? First, the potentially affected parties should be given timely notice that something is about to be done which affects their rights or duties. The notice should include enough basic information to enable parties to prepare their case. Then, besides notice, there is a right to an oral hearing, a right to counsel, a right to present evidence, a right to rebut evidence, a right to cross-examine witnesses and accusers, and a right to have the decision based only upon known evidence in the record. These rights are the basic ingredients of a fair hearing.

Most administrative adjudication, however, is informal and does not exhibit this entire array of procedural rights. Only a tiny fraction of all disputes are carried to the point of a complete formal hearing. Although every party has a right to insist on a formal hearing, most issues are settled informally over the telephone or by conversation with contact people in the agency. But even the most formal of formal administrative adjudication tends to be less formal than that of courts of record: rules of evidence are normally much relaxed and parties need not ordinarily be represented by counsel.

## Judicial Review

Civil disputes between citizen and state have increased in number and complexity because the functions of government have increased in number and complexity. Courts would be swamped if administrative agencies did not themselves adjudicate most of these disputes in the first instance, swamped not only by the volume of litigation but by its often rather specialized nature. Many judges, for example, dread the sight of a tax case because of the intricacy of tax law, and would just as soon see the revenue department adjudicate the issues before it comes to court. As a matter of fact American courts have made it a policy not to hear a civil dispute involving the government until the relevant agency itself has initially heard and decided it. This is called the "primary jurisdiction doctrine." Nor, as a general thing, does anyone with a civil dispute with a government agency have standing to sue in court until he has exhausted all his remedies within the agency. These two doctrines, "primary jurisdiction" and "exhaustion of remedies" have done much to increase the volume of administrative adjudication, and much to spare the courts.

Most issues of law adjudicated by administrative agencies may be appealed to courts, but courts try to make a distinction between issues of law and issues of fact, and do not review fact findings by administrative agencies when those findings of fact rest upon substantial evidence as most of them do. This keeps judges (who, after all, are experts in law, not in every other technical specialty) focussed on law issues and spares them to some degree the entanglements of fact issues foreign to their expertise. Of course, it is difficult to disentangle fact from law, but where possible the appellate courts will try to do so. This means, however, there is virtually no appeal from the purely fact findings of administrative agencies—little more than from the purely fact findings of courts of original jurisdiction. Insofar as appellate courts treat facts, they do so as a by-product of treating law questions: was the finding of fact legally (fairly) arrived at, is it based on substantial evidence, and so on. Appellate courts review the adjudicatory findings of administrative agencies almost exactly as they review the decisions of lower courts of record. For all practical purposes, each administrative agency in the United States is a court of original jurisdiction for many civil disputes involving itself.

## Tort Liability

Governments not only commit illegalities, they also sometimes hurt people in the process. Injured parties want courts to do more than put a stop to the illegality; they also commonly want damages. But, under the doctrine of sovereign immunity, no one may sue a government without its consent for injuries caused in performance of its governmental functions. However, governments may and often do enact tort liability laws voluntarily making themselves liable for certain torts. (A "tort" is a civil wrong or injury.)

Tort liability acts, however, usually do not open the government to suit for damages when government agents have exercised due care in performance of their duty. A fireman may cause damage to unburned property by spraying water to put out a fire, but the government cannot normally be sued for such damage if the fireman exercised due care in attempting to extinguish the blaze. Nor do governments customarily consent to be sued for injuries caused by performance of a discretionary duty. A judge, for example, is hired to use his discretion (judgment) in deciding cases, just as a professor is hired to use his discretion in deciding grades; an error of judgment cannot ordinarily be the basis of a damage suit, nor can a failure to act or to judge. Tort liability acts are usually accompanied by a long list of exceptions such as those mentioned above, leaving governments in most instances liable mainly for using property (such as automobiles) negligently, or maintaining property (such as sidewalks) in a dangerous and defective condition.

A distinction is made between "governmental" functions and "proprietary" functions. The doctrine of sovereign immunity applies only to governmental functions, that is, to injuries caused by governments exercising their traditionally governmental functions. But when governments engage in business-type functions not "traditionally" governmental—running auditoriums, utility companies, and so forth—then any victim of a tort committed in the process may sue for damages whether or not there is a tort liability act.

Sometimes governments voluntarily pay for some of their torts even when they cannot be sued. Occasionally governments insure themselves and their employees against some suits, thus indirectly paying via the insurance company. Governments also sometimes pass private laws reimbursing persons injured by government acts, even when there is no want of due care.

The doctrine of sovereign immunity has come under severe attack not only because it is difficult to distinguish between proprietary and governmental functions, but also because many people feel governments should pay for their legal wrongs no less than private individuals.

While governments may have sovereign immunity, individual officers of government do not, and in English common law they were no less subject to a damage suit for their torts committed in the course of their official duties than for torts committed while not on duty. This to some extent has curbed irresponsible, malicious, and autocratic exercise of government power, but it also tended to make officers too careful, and fearful to act where there is possibility of error. The case of *Miller* v. *Horton* is often cited as a classic example of the trouble public officers could get into in the course of doing their duty; a board of health was sued for killing a horse it thought was afflicted with glanders. By law the board had authority to kill horses afflicted with glanders, but in this case the killing resulted from an erroneous diagnosis, and a court ordered the members of the board to pay for the horse out of their own pockets. Courts today have modified their stand on officer liability, and as a general thing no longer hold officers liable for torts caused in exercise of their discretionary duties. Furthermore, in those areas where officers are liable for torts committed in the course of their official duties, governments quite commonly protect their employees through insurance, or stand ready to indemnify them.

## Ombudsman

Perhaps the most wrongful and hurtful things bureaucrats do are not illegal—failure of a social security office, for example, to send out checks on time or to keep accurate records on individuals. A mechanism of growing popularity for checking this category of wrong is the "ombudsman." As used in Scandanavia the ombudsman's job is to investigate and publicize wrongdoing in the government which is not necessarily illegal wrongdoing. He has no power whatsoever, except to investigate and publicize—to draw attention to the alleged wrong. Various American governments, agencies, and institutions have employed ombudsmen with similar investigative and reporting functions, but their success has been questionable. American culture is not identical to Swedish, Danish, or Norwegian culture, and it is difficult to transfer institutions between cultures. Perhaps in the United States it is harder to conceive of an ombudsman so pristine and immaculate that he would refrain from using his powers of investigation for partisan hatchet jobs. Furthermore, American legislators (federal, state, and local) want to be "ombudsmen." They earn a lot of political currency by doing "legislative case work" and running trouble-shooting errands for constituents. They don't want an ombudsman siphoning it off. Also, we have various other ombudsman-like institutions: grand juries, investigating committees, and, of course, the press. In the armed forces there are inspector generals and chaplains.

## SUMMARY

Since the history of government on this planet is primarily a history of tyranny, it is fitting to conclude a book on public administration with a chapter on controlling administrators. Although American public administrators are theoretically "under the law," there are countless abuses of power—some technically legal, others obviously illegal.

The authors of the United States Constitution apparently believed the best check on power was to divide it—set power against power. Thus, power spends itself in a ceaseless political civil war. However, we, and the world, are in the midst of a managerial revolution; the once separated powers are reuniting within the executive branch. Checks on managerial power grow more anemic. However, separation of powers is not by any means dead in the United States; legislative controls exist but seem infected by a fifth column of executive influence. Neither the power of the purse nor legislative oversight rises to the full vigor of former eras.

Nor do the courts seem able to cope with rising executive power. They hardly ever strike down delegations of legislative power to the executive; executive lawmaking is allowed to masquerade as "quasi legislation." Furthermore, with judicial praise and approval great chunks of adjudicatory power have been ceded to the executive. Every administrative agency is now for all practical purposes a court of original jurisdiction. All this successfully passes under the gaze of judges who declare it to be nothing but "quasi adjudication" and therefore no threat to the integrity of separation of powers.

Still, the courts of record are possibly the most effective check we have on executive power. Courts try to keep administrators within and under the law, and measure administrative acts against various statutory and constitutional standards of legality, not the least of which is the standard of fairness set forth in the due process clauses of the Constitution. Tort liability acts add fairness to the system by opening governments to damage suits where the doctrine of sovereign immunity might otherwise foreclose such remedies.

But perhaps the most wrongful things administrators do are not legal wrongs, but are various degrees of nonfeasance beyond reach of the courts. And for these wrongs it is hoped that a sufficient remedy can be found in grand juries, investigating committees, the press, inspector generals, professional standards of ethics, and even chaplains and ombudsmen.

## SUGGESTED READING

Davis, Kenneth C. *Discretionary Justice: A Preliminary Inquiry.* Urbana: University of Illinois Press, 1971.

Gellhorn, Ernest. *Administrative Law and Process in a Nutshell.* St. Paul: West Publishing Co., 1972.

Harris, Joseph P. *Congressional Control of Administration.* Garden City, N.Y.: Doubleday Anchor, 1965.

Lorch, Robert S. *Democratic Process and Administrative Law.* Detroit: Wayne State University Press, 1969.

Miller v. Horton, 152 Mass. 520 (1891).

Ogul, Morris S. *Congress Oversees the Bureaucracy: Studies in Legislative Supervision.* Pittsburgh: University of Pittsburgh Press, 1976.

Schecter Poultry Corporation v. United States, 295 U.S. 495 (1935).

Stigler, George J. *The Citizen and the State: Essays on Regulation.* Chicago: University of Chicago Press, 1975.

United States v. Nixon, 418 U.S. 683 (1974).

# Index

†